D0353678

A Woven Silence

MEMORY, HISTORY & REMEMBRANCE

FELICITY HAYES-McCOY

The Collins Press

First published in 2015 by
The Collins Press
West Link Park
Doughcloyne
Wilton
Cork

A CIP record for this book is available from the British Library.

Paperback ISBN: 978-1-84889-252-1
PDF eBook ISBN: 978-1-84889-503-4
EPUB eBook ISBN: 978-1-84889-504-1
Kindle ISBN: 978-1-84889-505-8

Typesetting by Carrigboy Typesetting Services
Typeset in Minon Pro
Printed in Poland by Białostockie Zakłady Graficzne SA

Contents

Acknowledgments

THIS BOOK WOULD NOT HAVE BEEN WRITTEN had it not been for the hundreds of letters I received from my late mother, and the long hours we spent in conversation. While it is by no means a history, I owe an immense debt of gratitude to the historians, biographers, folklorists, poets, playwrights and political commentators whose works I have absorbed and returned to over a lifetime of reading and writing; and to the colleagues and friends, including the late Peter Fozzard of the BBC, who, over decades, have contributed to what remains an ongoing exploration of the nature of art and memory. Any errors I have made and conclusions I have drawn are, of course, my own.

My thanks are due to many individuals. In Galway, they include Librarian John Cox and Archivist Barry Houlihan at NUI Galway's James Hardiman Library, where the G. A. Hayes-McCoy papers are held. In Dublin, Raghnall Ó Floinn, Director of the National Museum of Ireland, provided information relating to my late father's responsibilities there, and Dr Pauline O'Connell, formerly of St Ultan's Hospital and what is now the Coombe Women & Infants University Hospital, spoke and wrote to me about medical and social conditions during the early years of the Irish State. I owe particular thanks to Lucy Keavney of The Countess Markievicz School who gave me permission to use her tweets from the 2015 Hanna Sheehy Skeffington School. In Corca Dhuibhne I received constant help from Bernard MacBrádaigh and his colleagues in Dingle Library. I am also grateful to my Kerry neighbours, particularly the women who contextualised my knowledge and experience both of the place of women in rural Ireland and of the Irish language. In Enniscorthy, Katch Kavanagh was generous with her memories of Marion Stokes, and Maria Nolan of the Focal Literary Festival facilitated my initial talk in the town and subsequent visits there. I am also grateful to Jarlath Glynn, Enniscorthy's Librarian, Gráinne Doran, Wexford's County Archivist, and, of course, to the woman at Enniscorthy Castle who raised her hand and asked the question that originally sparked this work.

In the months when I was working on this book in the UK, I began each day with a pencil, paper and a cup of tea in the More London branch of Pret A Manger. I'd like to thank all the friendly staff there for the cheerfulness and interest with which they kick-started my mornings.

My thanks are also due to my husband, my brothers, my brother-in-law Seán O'Leary, and to numerous individuals who sent me memories and material, including Cormac Lawler and his mother Geraldine Lawler (née Cunniffe). Finally, I am grateful to all at The Collins Press and, as ever, to my agent Gaia Banks at Sheil Land Associates.

Readers unfamiliar with the Irish language will find assistance in pronouncing the Irish words in this book on my Facebook author page.

Experience suggests that this book may produce further discussion of the issues it explores. I would be delighted if readers would like to share in my conversations on Twitter @fhayesmccoy or to contact me by email at fhayesmccoy@btinternet.com

1
The Kaleidoscope Turns

THIS BOOK TELLS MANY STORIES. Some contradict each other. Some may not be true. All depend on angles of perception and on memory. Awareness depends on where you stand when you look at things, and many layers of emotional inclination and unconscious prejudice intervene when you're looking back. Individual, family and communal memory shape our sense of who we are and where we belong. So do imagination, aspiration and chance. So does the absence of memory.

I remember a night in Sinnotts pub on Dublin's King St in the 1970s. It was drinking-up time, the door was bolted and Eugene was gathering glasses, washing up and asking if we had no homes to go to. At the end of the bar the actor Alan Devlin was getting obstreperous. Eventually Eugene, who had had a long night, told him to get out. There was a moment when it looked as if Alan was going to be difficult but a friend threw an arm round his shoulders and eased him out the door, and someone bolted it behind them. Moments later, someone else unbolted it again and Devlin sidled through the crowd and back onto his barstool. He was wearing a brown paper bag over his head. Eugene turned round, saw him and roared at him. 'Right, that's it, feck off out of it, Devlin; you're barred.' Alan removed the bag from his head to reveal a look of wonderment. 'How', he asked, 'did you know who I was?'

More than half my life has been spent as an Irish emigrant. I went across the water to England in my early twenties, married and built a career there. Yet as long as my mother continued to live in the family home in Dublin I never thought of myself as having emigrated. Throughout nearly forty years of living and working in London, despite the fact that I have had little or no contact with the Irish Diaspora there, my sense of identity has remained entirely Irish. Now, thanks to budget airlines and broadband, I divide life and work between an inner-city flat in London and a stone house at the end of Ireland's Dingle Peninsula. But for the majority of my life my physical roots were in one country while my cultural and ancestral roots were in another. Even when Twickenham or Ealing or Finchley was home, I had an untroubled sense that home was some place else. Who I am appears to hinge on my being Irish.

My experience is not unique, either to me or to Irish people; often identification with 'the old country' can persist through generations, though in many cases a return to it at such a remove would be disorientating and disillusioning. A sense of identity is a complex thing. It is shaped by subtle interfaces between individuals, family and community as much as by location, education, customs and traditions. It relies on the passing on of memories from one generation to another and the constant rearranging and reinterpreting of related and unrelated fragments of information, in repeated attempts to produce narratives that make sense. Wired into human consciousness is an instinctive need to pass on the stories that, by providing links to our ancestors, provide us with informed, healthy and enhanced perceptions of ourselves.

The story of this book began two years ago with a random question. I was in Enniscorthy, County Wexford, the home of my maternal grandmother's people for generations and a place I remember well from my childhood. I had been invited to speak at a literary festival, in a wide, elegant room on the first floor of the grey Norman castle that dominates the town. We were talking about shared memory when a woman in the audience raised her hand and asked a question. 'How do you know that what you remember is the truth?' She was one of five siblings, she said, 'and we all shared the same experiences. We lived in the same house with the same people. But not one of us remembers anything in the same way.' The book I'd been talking about, called *The House on an Irish Hillside*, is a memoir, so I had been involved in many discussions about memory since I had written it. But this woman's question provoked a particular response. Heads went up and body language changed. From my seat on the platform I could see people all round the room exchanging glances. Some smiled. Others looked uncomfortable. Up to that ripple of recognition I had been holding my audience. From that point on, the event belonged to them.

That evening, in the house that my brother had built for our aunt in our grandmother's orchard, I went online and, having checked my emails, idly clicked on a search engine. In the afternoon, when the talk was over, several people for whom I had signed copies of my book had said they remembered my family. And one man had talked about a woman whose name I hadn't heard for years: Marion Stokes. She was my grandmother's cousin, twenty years old when my mother was a child of six. Now, typing Marion's name into Google, I remembered another occasion in Enniscorthy Castle, when I was nine or ten years old. In my mind I climbed the winding stair to that same elegant room on the first floor. The steps are cold and worn, and the only light comes in through narrow windows. I'm touching the curved wall with one hand, and with the other I'm hanging on to Marion's skirt. She was formidable and elderly, square and calm in her tweed coats and skirts, neat shirt-blouses and sensible shoes. Staring at my computer screen, I remembered her black leather handbag which always contained a white cotton handkerchief, and the fearsome bottle of Mercurochrome she used as an antiseptic to treat childhood cuts. Inconsequentially, I remembered her instructions for using egg yolks as a hair conditioner: you massaged them into wet hair and rinsed them out, making sure that the water was lukewarm. (Hot water, apparently, would scramble the eggs.) Nothing useful was appearing on my computer screen, so I added the word 'Enniscorthy' to Marion's name. As I did so, I remembered her neat, spiky handwriting on postcards, and the book of pages, hand-stitched and bound in a brown paper cover, in which she had drawn up an outline of her family history. Carefully written in black ink, each page lists several generations of names, trades and relationships, the fields they farmed, the marriages they made and the graveyards in which they were buried. The book was sent to my mother by a relative a year after Marion's death, and given by my mother to me on a visit to London. I had hardly looked at it at the time and now, sitting at my laptop, I wondered vaguely where I had put it. Then a link appeared on the screen in front of me; I clicked on it, and a central aspect of my sense of identity changed.

I had found what was then the sole reference to Marion on the Internet. It was written by the Irish writer Colm Tóibín in *The New York Review of Books*. 'She was the least likely ex-terrorist you could imagine, polite and sedate and distantly smiling.' Tóibín is an Enniscorthy man. His family and my grandmother's were neighbours and, though I hardly knew him then and hadn't seen him since, he and I had been at university together in Dublin in the 1970s. Now, staring at my computer, I tried to get my head around what he had written about my grandmother's cousin Marion. Then memories, dates and half-forgotten references began to shift in my mind like images in a kaleidoscope, shaping and reshaping both the present and the past.

All my life I've known that when Marion was hardly out of her teens she was a member of Cumann na mBan (pronounced something like 'kum-en nah mon'), a women's organisation set up in 1913 as the country was about to embark on the struggle which ultimately established it as a republic. I knew, too, that the fearsome bottle of Mercurochrome in her black leather handbag was a legacy of her many years as a nurse. So, though I knew that Cumann na mBan members had a role in the 1916 Rising that ushered in the final phase in Ireland's resistance to eight centuries of English rule, I suppose that, if I thought about it at all, I had imagined that Marion's time in the organisation had been spent going to lectures on first aid. Now my eyes widened as I scrolled on through Tóibín's paragraphs. '... *with two other women ... she raised the Irish flag over one of the main buildings of the town of Enniscorthy in the 1916 Rebellion.*'

That afternoon, the woman who had arranged my event at the castle had talked about 1916, the turning point in modern Irish history which began the process that culminated in the setting-up of the state into which I was born. Obviously a stalwart committee member, she led me up the winding stair, chatting over her shoulder. 'The garrison here in Enniscorthy was the last to surrender', she told me. 'They took over the Athenaeum as their headquarters and raised the tricolour over the roof.' I had passed the Athenaeum building myself that day on my way to the castle. A plaque on the wall read '*In proud memory of the Irish Volunteers, Fianna Éireann and Cumann na mBan who took part in the Rising of Easter Week, 1916.*' The Athenaeum is a handsome nineteenth-century building, once the town hall and a theatre; however, as I walked past, its boarded-up windows and peeling paint had looked unimpressive. Apparently there was a plan to restore and redevelop the structure and interior in time for the upcoming 1916 centenary. It looked to me as if, in a country struggling with debt and recession, that was a fairly big ask.

Now, staring at Toibín's words on the screen, I found myself feeling slightly stupid. I had learned history at school. I knew that Cumann na mBan had taken an active part in the Easter Rising against British rule in Ireland. Why hadn't I known Marion's story? I tried another search engine and found nothing new. Then I shrugged and abandoned the laptop. I was tired; it had been a long day and I fancied a glass of wine in the garden, watching the flutter of birds' wings in my granny's apple trees. So I stepped out into the evening sunshine, wanting a break before thinking about the workload lined up for the following day. Soon the garden, the glint of sun on my wine glass, and the chiming of the town's cathedral bell worked their magic. That night I slept well. By next day life and work had taken over again and my mind had moved on.

The festival in Enniscorthy took place in midsummer. My English husband, Wilf, and I had driven across the country to it, and I had other signings to do on our way back. We drove home between green and golden fields where farmers were cutting and baling silage, and stopped in little towns where bookshop managers were already gearing up to cope with the back-to-school rush. On the way I found myself pondering that question about memory and truth. Since the publication of *The House on an Irish Hillside,* readers had got in touch with memories of their own sparked by my story or by other readers' comments on the book's Facebook page. People would come up to me at readings, eager to share their family stories; sometimes they would bring letters, faded certificates or photos, the sort of dog-eared treasures that most families have at the back of a drawer. Often they'd say they had no idea who the laughing couple on the beach or the serious little girl posed in a painted Victorian arbour actually were. 'I suppose when you look at the bathing costumes it might have been taken in the thirties, so it could be my husband's mother's family – they lived by the sea.' Or 'I found it in my grandmother's prayer book. It might be my great-aunt who died as a child.' Often there would be contradictions, producing laughter and, sometimes, anxiety. 'I'm sure my mother said it was her cousin's but my sister says not.' It was fascinating to see the photos and hear the stories, but sometimes I wondered why they had brought them to me, a stranger sitting at a table in a bookshop. All I could do was nod and listen and agree that it's important to write names on old photos and to tag and caption shots in digital albums. And then everyone would nod back and the fragile treasures would carefully be tucked away. I don't think anyone imagined that I would provide answers: they just wanted to share their connections with the past. It was as if they saw their lives as part of a bigger picture in which the threads of their family's history had been woven together for generations. The half-remembered stories and unidentified faces belonged to that picture and, even if the threads were frayed and ravelled, it was important that they be preserved.

I understood that, because the instinct to preserve evidence from the past is bred into me. My father was a historian. I grew up studying history and folklore, and the dynamic between those two disciplines is what made me a writer. The study of history is largely about written records. You gather all you can find, collate, compare and set about establishing facts based on recorded evidence. Folklore puts more emphasis on oral memory. It deals with songs, stories, rituals and place names, testimony passed down through generations, sometimes even across millennia, before written records began. In one sense the two disciplines are incompatible. Because, while historians traditionally rely largely on the testimony of educated, male officialdom, folklorists investigate the world of conversation and imagination, and they collect largely from field and fireside, hearth and home. In another sense folklore and history are complementary, capable of coming together to produce a more balanced whole.

Later that month, back in London, I found myself drawn back to Colm Tóibín's reference to Marion. I had tried again to find her name on the Internet and each search brought me back to the same, single reference. By then I was more relaxed, and between projects, though my mind was still circling around memory and truth. One afternoon, with a mug of tea at my elbow, I reread Tóibín's piece. Once again the kaleidoscope shifted, and this time the swirling shards produced a new picture. According to what I read on the screen, each evening in Easter week in 1966, Marion had visited Tóibín's family home in Enniscorthy. There, polite, sedate and distantly smiling in her tweed suit, her neat shirt-blouse and sensible shoes, she had sat down to watch a drama series about a Rising that, fifty years earlier, she had taken part in herself. I was marvelling, as Tóibín had, at the strangeness of that idea, when I was hit by the significance of the date. I was twelve years old in 1966. I remember that week-long drama series, which was called *Insurrection*. Its scriptwriter, Hugh Leonard, described it as 'a, near-as-dammit, full-scale reconstruction of the Rising'. Everyone talked about it. While

Marion was watching it in Enniscorthy with the Tóibíns I was watching it in Dublin with my parents. I remember that year's commemorations, the parades, the documentaries, *Insurrection* with its prime-time slot, the books specially written for the half-centenary. For a whole week the national radio station's schedule seemed to consist of wall-to-wall documentaries and reminiscences. Marion had taken an active part in the Rising we were all commemorating. Why hadn't we talked about that?

2
The Sliding Stones

IT WAS NOT AS IF I WAS UNAWARE THAT Marion Stokes had been a member of Cumann na mBan. But along with that information, absorbed in my childhood, came an unspoken sense that questions about it would not be welcomed. At the time, that didn't bother me. Marion lived to be eighty-seven and died in 1983, so I could have had an adult relationship with her. But, as it happened, I didn't. I left Ireland for London in the late 1970s, a year after I left university. My mother often came to visit me and once, on a walk by the River Thames, she mentioned that though Marion had grown up in Enniscorthy and died there, she had spent time nursing in England. I remember asking why she left Ireland and my mother shaking her head and saying that she didn't know. Marion, she said, 'didn't like to talk about the past'. I could well believe it. The Marion I knew in my childhood was not someone who would let her hair down, put her feet up and engage in girly chats. She carried an air of authority and you didn't wriggle when she reached for the Mercurochrome. My mother said she had always been like that and I suppose that, when she told me so, I assumed it went with a lifetime of responsibility, starched aprons and hard work.

Hard work seems to have been a characteristic of the women in my mother's family. My grandmother was born and raised in Enniscorthy but when she met my grandfather she was working in a Dublin shop. Her sister Margaret, known to my mother and aunts as Aunt Magger, worked as an accountant for the Co-op in Enniscorthy. I don't know when or why my grandmother moved to Dublin from Enniscorthy but I know that her first home after she married was a rented house on Dublin's north side. My mother and her two sisters were born there. Then, when my mother was eleven or twelve years old, the family moved back to Enniscorthy, where they were living when my grandfather died. After his death Aunt Magger came to live with them; the regular wage packet from the Co-op must have helped to pay the household bills and complete my mother and aunts' education. I remember an exhortation of my grandmother's, often used by my mother in my own childhood: 'We have to keep the best side out.' I have always admired the courage implicit in that philosophy, though I have never ceased to question its wisdom.

On some childhood visit of my own to Enniscorthy, long after Aunt Magger died, I was shushed by my mother for calling Slaney Street, which leads from the town centre to the riverside, 'a steep, narrow little lane'. My grandmother agreed with her: Slaney Street might be narrow but it certainly wasn't a lane, and people down from Dublin should keep their mouths shut when they didn't know what they were talking about. Calling it 'steep', however, was apparently fair enough. It certainly couldn't be contradicted because the town overlooks a river valley. Enniscorthy grew up around a Norman stronghold overlooking the River Slaney. For as long as I can remember it has felt modestly prosperous and assured, equally proud of its imposing grey castle and its soaring Roman Catholic Pugin cathedral, which was built below my grandmother's house in the mid-nineteenth century. All Enniscorthy women, according to my mother, have great legs, the result of a lifetime spent walking up and down the town's hills. When I was small we spoke of going down the hill to the cathedral, the cinema, the castle and the chip shop; over the hill to visit my mother's relations; and up the hill to the Fair Ground above the Duffry Gate. Vinegar Hill, which overlooks the town from the opposite side of the river, is a constant physical reminder of the area's past. The last battle of Ireland's unsuccessful rebellion against British rule in 1798, inspired by the republican ideals of the French Revolution, was fought there, and in the streets of the town. I can't remember a time when I didn't know the legends of the 1798 Rebellion or the words of 'Boolavogue' and 'The Boys of Wexford', two ballads that memorialise it. And when climbing the hill to my grandmother's house from the train station as a child I always wanted to stop for breath under the statue of the 1798 pikeman, which depicts a defiant young man and a gesticulating priest furled in a bronze flag and gazing towards Vinegar Hill. Maybe those songs and stories account in part for my childhood lack of curiosity about Marion's part in the Rising in 1916. When a brawny pikeman is your image of a freedom fighter, you are unlikely to wonder if your granny's female cousin might perhaps have been one, too.

Most of my teenage years were spent locked in silent conflict with my mother about everything and anything, but I had long conversations with her as an adult. In the years after my father died, on her frequent visits to me in London, we would spend hours walking and chatting by the river or sitting in a coffee-shop window. Window seats mattered to her: she was a people-watcher with a quiet sense of humour, a creative imagination and a shrewd eye for character. In those years, when she was in her seventies, she and I took several holidays together and many of the family stories she related come back to me now coloured by the sound of waves slapping against the prow of a Rhine boat or the scent of salt and wildflowers on a high cliff on one of the Scilly Isles. I wish now that I had asked her more questions about Marion. But I doubt that I'd have got more answers.

When I first conceived of this book I did what I always do: I wandered the streets thinking about it, talked endlessly to my husband, Wilf, about it and, eventually, made some notes and fixed a meeting with my agent. Her office is down the way from the Charles Dickens Museum in London's Bloomsbury, and the museum's coffee shop does an amazing lemon drizzle poppy-seed cake. We sat at a table in the garden and I waved my hands, drew circles on pieces of paper, and tried to describe a book which, at that stage, hadn't really crystallised. My agent's mind is orderly and sharp but she also has the invaluable ability to sit back and let things happen. In the course of that meeting and others, I drank a lot of coffee, licked a lot of lemon drizzle off my fingers, and identified the different strands that made up the ideas I wanted to explore. For me, the process of putting together a pitch for publishers is always complicated by the fear that it may short-circuit the other process, the actual writing of the book. By imposing a structure on ideas yet to be explored, you are in danger of leaping from conception to conclusion without passing through discovery in between. But experience teaches you to seal off one part of your mind until you are ready to start the real writing. Meanwhile, with the other part, you go through a different process which you hope will provide a structure clear enough to communicate, firm enough to act as a template, and supple enough to be bent without breaking.

Since the publication of *The House on an Irish Hillside* I had been focused on memory. Now I wanted to explore its absence. The impetus was the absence of Marion's story in my own memory. The time frame was to be the century from the 1916 Rising. The story would be an Irish one but, as I knew from the hundreds of Facebook comments, conversations, emails, letters and messages I had had about *The House on an Irish Hillside*, memory and its absence are universal themes. In the course of those conversations with my agent we talked about the *Who Do You Think You Are?* phenomenon, which began as a BBC television series and is now the tip of an iceberg of popular interest in genealogy. It has been suggested that this growth of interest has arisen from an increasing use of previously unavailable technology – that we are out there searching for our ancestors simply because it has never been easier to find them. But other factors, such as the perennial challenge of a quest and the perceived romance of the past, are also part of the picture, just as they were before the advent of the Internet, and while intellectual curiosity is a stimulus, emotion appears always to have been a fundamental motivator in individual research into family roots. Some of the most moving moments in *Who Do You Think You Are?* occur when a trail runs cold. Just when the subject of an episode discovers a great-aunt who flew biplanes or an ancestor who was Nelson's gardener, the web of connectivity can break, leaving both the audience and the participant with no idea why the flyer converted to Buddhism or the gardener died in prison. Those broken threads produce more than just a sense of drama; frequently they provoke a sense of guilt. The idea that a family story has been lost forever can bring with it a sense of neglected responsibility – how have we allowed those who belong to us to be forgotten? But the truth is that, over time, threads get broken. There is a difference, however, between the natural effects of time and the unnatural results of censorship. And censorship is a central factor in the loss of Marion's story.

The Ireland I was born into was still largely dominated by the political, cultural and economic policies of Éamon de Valera, revered as the last surviving leader of the 1916 Rising, and my generation grew up with no sense of how much the country that we lived in differed from the country that Marion and her comrades had been willing to die for more than thirty years before. Yet it was very different, and the reasons for that are complex, not least because, when the Rising was being planned, there were evolving and contradictory visions of what it could and should achieve. Part of the reason for my generation's ignorance of that complexity was active reshaping of the legend of how the state was founded, and one aspect of this was government control of the acquisition of, and access to, witness statements made by men and women who took part in the struggle for Ireland's independence.

In the 1940s a group of historians initiated the establishment of the Bureau of Military History, which was ultimately set up and funded by the government of the day. Its purpose was to gather statements from activists who had witnessed the events of the 1916 Rising and the years that followed, and from their families. An advisory group, which included my father, was tasked with considering methodology and offering advice to the civil servants and army personnel who handled the collection process. From the outset the historians were concerned that the academic reputation of the members of the advisory group might be used to legitimise an exercise in state suppression or control. So they may have been foolish to believe the government assurances that that would not be the case. In the event, and despite their repeated objections, the collection was made without regard for many of the historians' concerns about methodology. And, as the process continued, political concerns about the nature of the material emerging in the statements became increasingly evident. Inevitably, some of what was being said by the witnesses did not tally with the various sanitised legends favoured by the revolutionaries-turned-politicians who by then were running the country.

In 1958, after the collection process had ended, the advisory group recommended that the material be given to the National Library, where it could be accessed by the public. Instead, the entire collection was classified as part of the State Papers and sealed until the last person mentioned in the statements was dead. The men and women who contributed statements had not been told what would happen to the stories they wanted to leave on record; each of them had been offered the opportunity to mark their individual contributions as confidential and, although some took the option, the vast majority chose not to. I never heard my father speak about what happened, and that doesn't surprise me: the anger, frustration and humiliation he and his colleagues felt was not something he would have wanted to share with his children. Shortly after his death in 1975, when I was still a student, I came across some of the blank forms used by the Bureau of Military History and asked my mother what they were. She said that my father had been involved in the collection of statements from people who had been part of the fight for independence and that, because the information was sensitive, it had all been locked away. Given her own involvement in my father's work, she must have been aware of what had actually happened. Clearly, she didn't like to talk about it.

Those witness statements remained classified until 2003. There was much press coverage of their release and a statement made by the government of the day expressed pleasure at the marking of an event 'of the utmost significance to the birth of our modern democracy'. No mention was made of the struggle between the historians who had initiated the collection and the politicians and government officials who had hijacked it. The absence of that memory leaves the present generation with a remarkable body of stories which, while it remains a fascinating archive and a touching inheritance for the families whose relatives contributed to it, is difficult to evaluate. Not everyone who might have contributed to the collection while it was being made was prepared to cooperate. Some were suspicious of it. Others may just have preferred to forget the past. In shaping this book I have wondered why Marion herself contributed no statement. Perhaps she didn't want to or just didn't get around to it. Perhaps she was aware of my father's growing concerns about how the material was being gathered and what would happen to it. One way or the other, the omission is sad. She had the instincts of a historian and her memories would have been valuable. In the 1960s she was one of a dedicated group of Enniscorthy people, which included Colm Tóibín's father, who worked to establish a local museum in the castle. My own first experience of its stone walls and curving turret staircase was on some visit when she had asked my father for some advice about display, and her spiky handwriting on the museum's lists and labels can still be seen in the county archive.

The men and women who planned and fought in the 1916 Rising spent much of their time focused on who they thought they were. They argued, held debates and attended meetings. They wrote books and plays and poems, political pamphlets and polemics, struggling to define and express a sense of identity; and in hindsight their conclusions could easily be boiled down to the negative statement that being Irish means you are not English. That trite dismissal of the social, political and cultural issues faced by Marion's generation was, to a large extent, all that Ireland's education system offered to my own generation, and our children hardly fared better. What it conceals is a story of complex, often contradictory, aspirations which – good, bad, indifferent, and even ludicrous – are part of our inheritance. Had that story been handed down to us uncensored, Ireland might well be a different country today.

When my mother left school, she moved back to Dublin from Enniscorthy. Like my grandmother, she worked in a shop, and when she and my father married they rented their first home on Dublin's south side. I am the youngest of five siblings, a small family by Irish standards of the 1940s and 1950s, and one which would have been larger had my mother not had several miscarriages. My brothers' and sisters' birth dates were roughly within a year of each other, after which there was a gap of five years before I was born. In the year that my mother was pregnant with me the family moved to a new house with an extra bedroom, so that my father's mother, who was widowed and getting frail, could come to live with us. My older siblings formed a unit with a shared past in the house where the family had lived before my arrival. They also shared a closeness that came with closeness in age. So, while I have fond memories of being the youngest in a united family, there is a sense in which I was an only child. My eldest brother had left home by the time I reached my teens and the age gap between me and my sisters was such that, at one time or another, each of them taught me at school. This sense of belonging to a slightly different world from my siblings' was increased by the fact that my adolescence coincided with a period of accelerating openness in a country that previously had been locked in isolationism. Although the differences were not extreme, we grew up experiencing variously overlapping stages of the nation's political, economic and social containment and subsequent release. Looking back now, it feels that, in many ways, the ten-year gap between my eldest sister and me might as well have been a generation. And I am now the only surviving woman of my generation in the family.

Long families are typically Irish. My grandmother was eighteen years older than her cousin Marion, who always seemed closer in generation to my mother and aunts. According to Marion's hand-stitched book of pages, bound in brown paper and written in her neat, spiky handwriting, she didn't move from her home in Enniscorthy to London until 1928, twelve years after the Rising. My grandparents took my mother and aunts to live in Enniscorthy in 1921, so for eight of those twelve years she and her sisters must have known Marion well. Which begs a question. On the walk that my mother and I took by the Thames, she told me that Marion had been reticent in old age. But was Marion equally reticent when my mother, as a teenager, lived only a few doors away? Perhaps she avoided political discussion in front of her young cousins. Those were the years of the War of Independence which followed the Rising, and of the bitter Civil War that came afterwards and still haunted the Ireland of my youth. It is possible that Marion continued to be an activist after the Rising. It is even possible that, if she did, my mother knew about it. I'll never know.

The family in Enniscorthy lived close to each other on the steep streets around the cathedral. My grandmother's house still stands below the Fair Ground and the Duffry Gate, opposite what used to be the pig market. When I was small its front door was flanked by two panes of amber glass through which the sun shone onto the foot of the stairs and down the narrow hallway. Unlike the door of the suburban semi in Dublin that I grew up in, it opened straight onto the pavement. From the bedroom where I used to sleep I could hear footsteps in the street outside, and the voices of men out walking greyhounds. The pig market was gone by then, but on a green across the road from my granny's door were three limestone boulders which had once protected a water pump from being knocked against on market days by carts. Three stones in conjunction are significant in Irish mythology; before the pump was installed in the nineteenth century these may have been guardians of a spring well. Each was about three feet high with a sloping surface on the downhill side, polished by generations of children using it as a slide. I can remember hours spent clambering up and sliding down, and my granny's voice calling from the doorway across the road, telling me it was teatime. My mother and her sisters, Cathleen and Evie, had played on the stones in their time. No doubt Marion played on them in hers.

My father's mother died when I was very small, but my Enniscorthy grandmother lived until 1963. We used to visit her with my mother, travelling down on the train from Dublin, crossing the river by the old bridge, climbing the steep hill past the cathedral and the chip shop, and arriving in time for tea with brown bread and salty butter and homemade gooseberry jam. I remember helping my granny to wash up afterwards, and walking down the garden with her, to pick apples. We used to play cards in the parlour in the evenings. She never managed to teach me anything more complicated than Snap but I remember sitting opposite her, banging my cards down on an ugly bamboo table in front of a fireplace with a polished brass fireguard. I wish I had heard her talk about her own childhood – not just about politics but about whether she too had heard men below her bedroom window passing on the hill with the greyhounds, and whether she and Aunt Magger had slid on the stones around the pump. But I was too young then to think of asking. When I knew her, she was an old lady in a lace collar pinned with a citrine brooch, who used to send us apples from her garden each year packed into cardboard boxes. They were collected from the train station in Dublin, brought home on the number eleven bus, and made into tarts by my mother.

When I was a child my favourite season was autumn. My mother's favourite was spring. I once asked her why that was so, and she told me that she loved its sense of expectation. The memory of that conversation still touches me and leaves me faintly angry, because she was one of a generation of Irishwomen whose legitimate expectations for herself and for her children were betrayed. In the absence of written or oral record I cannot be certain what exactly caused twenty-year-old Marion Stokes to go out and fight in 1916. Her primary motivation may have been nationalist, feminist, political or purely cultural. Or something else altogether. In the absence of memory I am left with inference. But two things I do know. One is that the Proclamation of the Irish Republic issued at the outset of the 1916 Rising *'claims the allegiance of every Irishman and Irishwoman'* and *'guarantees religious and civil liberty, equal rights and equal opportunities to all its citizens.'* The second is that a statement issued afterwards by Cumann na mBan asserted that by *'taking their place in the firing line and in every other way helping in the establishment of the Irish Republic'* its members had *'regained for the women of Ireland the rights that belong to them under the old Gaelic civilization, where sex was no bar to citizenship, and where women were free to devote to the service of their country every talent and capacity with which they were endowed'*. That reference to 'old Gaelic civilization' is questionable: it ignores, for example, the fact that for centuries, if not millennia, native Irish society, like many others, used slaves of both sexes as units of currency. But, setting aside bad history and concentrating on political aspiration, it seems fair to assume that Marion and her companions, male and female, were prepared to sacrifice their own lives to secure a state founded on the principle of equal rights and opportunities regardless of gender. Yet I grew up in a state with a constitution that declared the proper aspiration of women to be marriage, our proper function to be childbearers, and our proper sphere the home.

That constitution, drafted for – and to a large extent by – de Valera, who had been a leader of the Rising, passed into law in 1937. So in only twenty-five years the aspirations of 1916 had been eroded to the extent that the rights of half of the state's citizens were reduced. And that is the terrible part. When one section of society effectively becomes second-class citizens, the balance and health of the community as a whole are affected. Among the visible results in Ireland were levels of state-sanctioned institutional brutality which have only recently begun to emerge. Another was the fact that my mother, along with thousands of women of her generation, was told that marriage should be her highest aspiration, childrearing her only creative outlet, and that economic dependence was her civic duty. That in its turn produced levels of misogyny, emotional sterility and civic immaturity still evident in Ireland today. Many women protested in public and in private during the drafting of de Valera's constitution. The Irish Women Workers Union, many of whose members had been involved in the 1916 Rising, expressed outrage; a letter from the secretary to de Valera, quoting the clauses which referred to the position of women, said: 'it would hardly be possible to make a more deadly encroachment upon the liberty of the individual.' But by then women no longer held significant positions of influence in Ireland. The constitution was accepted. And a combination of revisionism and isolationism in the years that followed left the majority of Ireland's citizens ignorant of the legacy we had been denied.

I don't know what first drew Marion to Cumann na mBan. Her mother had married into a family with nationalist sympathies so perhaps Marion grew up hearing and taking part in arguments about what degree of separation from Britain was achievable or desirable. Cumann na mBan itself initially existed to defend Ireland's right to Home Rule. In 1798, after the rebels' unsuccessful last stand at Enniscorthy, a Dublin-based parliament with limited powers was disestablished, after which Ireland was controlled directly from Westminster. Home Rule, which had been edging its way towards the statute book since the end of the nineteenth century, would have re-established a parliament in Dublin and given Ireland Dominion status within the British Empire. The problem was that not everyone in Ireland wanted that and, in 1913, when Home Rule seemed

No!

imminent, activists in the northern counties of the country formed an armed force called the Ulster Volunteers to oppose it. In response, an organisation called the Irish Volunteers was set up to defend it. Cumann na mBan was then formed to support the Irish Volunteers. The role of the women's organisation was to assist in arming and equipping the men, set up training camps, commandeer supplies, carry dispatches and provide first aid. Later, it was agreed that they would give armed support to the men in the event of conflict. With two armed civilian forces on the one island, each opposed to the other's cause, conflict seemed a likely prospect.

Those must have been heady days, when change was on the horizon and everyone had an opinion about what could, should, and might happen. My grandmother, who was married and living in Dublin at the time, probably kept her opinions to herself. I suspect that she was the quiet one in a vociferous family because, according to my mother, she disliked arguments in the home so much that she always kept out of them, announcing roundly that 'in this house they'd pick you up before you'd fall down'. Maybe that was because she had lived through years of passionate debate and had had enough of it. There was certainly plenty around in Ireland in the years before 1916. And when the First World War broke out the goalposts moved, adding to the tension and the debate. John Redmond, who led the Irish Parliamentary Party in Westminster, believed that the struggle for Home Rule should be shelved for the duration of the war. Eoin MacNeill, who had founded the Irish Volunteers, believed that Irishmen should refuse to participate in Britain's fight to protect the rights of small nations in Europe, on the grounds that the rights they sought in Westminster for their own small nation had yet to be granted. Everyone had an opinion, based on strategy, morality, or both. Maybe those were the conversations that my grandmother hated in which 'they'd pick you up before you'd fall down'. Ultimately the Volunteers and Cumann na mBan polled their membership. The vast majority of the Volunteers, about a 100,000 men, voted to support Redmond; only about 10,000 remained loyal to MacNeill. Cumann na mBan issued a statement which read: '*We feel bound to make the pronouncement that to urge or encourage Irish Volunteers to enlist in the British Army cannot, under any circumstances, be regarded as consistent with the work we have set ourselves to do.*' The majority of the women held to that position, though the issue caused a split in the organisation. It was the Volunteer and Cumann na mBan members who remained committed to separatism as their primary aim who would eventually take part in the 1916 Rising.

But what Marion and most of her contemporaries did not know as they drilled in the fields, delivered dispatches, and learnt first aid, was that, along with every other cultural, political and militant nationalist organisation in Ireland, Cumann na mBan and the Volunteers were systematically being infiltrated by a secret society. In inner circles, of which even the founders and leaders of the organisations they penetrated remained unaware, a different agenda was being planned for by a group which claimed direct links with the militants of 1798. To this group, called the Irish Republican Brotherhood and known as the IRB, Home Rule was not the goal. It wanted Ireland to become a fully independent republic. Given that revolutionary movements throughout history have been plagued by informers and spies, the IRB's policy of Byzantine secrecy wasn't illogical. But its culture was rooted in manipulation and its insistence on blind loyalty and obedience required its members to deceive even their closest comrades. This produced a damaging legacy which in my generation, partly because of de Valera's determination to sanitise the past, was never openly recognised.

In 1966, when Marion walked across the hill to watch *Insurrection* with the Tóibíns, Ireland's national television service was only five years old and only 55 per cent of Irish homes had televisions. My own family in Dublin had no television. We watched the coverage of the 1916 half-centenary in our next-door neighbours' sitting room. De Valera was the country's president then, blind and in his eighties. I remember the flickering black-and-white news coverage of Dublin's commemorative parade, and his tall figure taking the salute from a stand outside the GPO, the headquarters of the Rising. It was partly in order for the legend of his 1916 experience to become enshrined in the national consciousness that Marion's story, and those of many other men and women, had by then been smudged, or even completely erased, from the picture. If the passing on of individual, family and communal memory is necessary for a healthy and informed perception of self, then the conscious disruption and corruption of memory on a national scale can only be damaging. In my generation the effects were evident in a disjointed awareness of our parents' experience. Today they remain evident in, among other things, the diminished role of women in Irish society and an enduringly dysfunctional relationship between the citizens and the state.

The 1960s brought a period of new confidence to Ireland after almost forty years of cultural, economic and political stagnation. Much of it had to do with money. Changes in economic policy at home combined with post-Second World War recovery in Europe produced more jobs and more disposable income. I was too young to know what was happening, but I remember a new radiogram on which my sisters played Beatles records, a twin-tub washing machine that my mother filled by hose from the kitchen sink, and the arrival of a rented television set. Admittedly, it arrived at the start of each Christmas holiday and went back again after Twelfth Night, but it still represented previously unknown luxury. It also represented the unstoppable dissemination of new ideas, opinions and attitudes.

By 1966 the economic growth had slowed a bit, so the half-centenary celebrations of the Rising were designed as much to make us feel positive about the future as to commemorate the past. Government ministers gave interviews about the object lessons in citizenship shown by the Rising's participants, and everyone was urged to pull together in a spirit of self-sacrifice and keep on keeping on. *Insurrection* on the television and pageants and parades up and down the country had their effect and, to an extent, national pride was boosted. But people were beginning to question much of what had previously been accepted. De Valera retained his position as President of Ireland after an election later that year but it was a close-run thing.

By the 1970s, when I was at university, the cultural and social repression that had gripped the country for decades was openly being challenged. I might have stayed in Ireland and become part of a growing movement of civil rights activists, feminists, artists, trade unionists and intellectuals demanding, and exploring possibilities for, reform. Instead, a year after I left university, I went to London. By then I had realised that Ireland was not a country in which I could thrive although, at the time I didn't have a simple, clearly defined motive for going. I had left university with an Arts degree in English and Irish language and literature topped up by a Higher Diploma in Education which, in my parents' view, if all other fruit failed, would allow me to fall back on teaching. In a way it was surprising that I had graduated at all, since most of my time at university was spent doing shows in student venues, fringe theatres and festivals. One day I was hitch-hiking to Galway with a rucksack and two prop spears when a car drew in beside me. It was a Friday morning and I had skipped an Old Irish tutorial in order to get myself and the spears over to Galway in time for a performance. As the driver lowered the window I bent down, announced where I was going and, to my horror, recognised my Irish professor. For one insane moment I thought he had tracked me down. Then I realised that he was on his way to Galway to attend the drama festival in which I was about to appear. It was the best of days and the worst of days. I had hitched a lift which took me right to the theatre I'd been heading for; and I spent the entire journey strapped into a seat beside the man whose tutorial I'd just skipped, desperately trying to discuss Old Irish manuscripts with two spearheads jutting over my shoulder.

My ostensible reason for moving to London was to train as an actor. There was a vague sense that, having done so, I would probably come back. I did, in fact, return the year after I completed my training, and worked briefly with the Abbey Theatre Company. But nudging at the back of my mind was an undefined and unexamined reluctance to remain. I know now that one reason for that reluctance was the mixed messages I grew up with. Education was important in our household. It was expected that my sisters and I, as well as our brothers, would have careers. Yet our mother had been expected to give up her job as soon as she married. She had dreamed of being a journalist and of writing books and plays. Instead she settled for what was then the exhausting and isolating role of being a housewife. The message appeared to be that, for women, ambition and education were simultaneously vital and pointless. There was more. In school I had been taught that the British had attempted to eradicate Ireland's native culture. So why, since the establishment of independence, had the works of so many Irish writers and artists been banned? At home I had been taught about a God of love and humility whose care extended even to the fall of a sparrow. Yet the Church I was raised in used threats to exercise power. Had I stayed in Ireland I might have become part of a process of confronting both those mixed messages and their genesis. Instead I felt, rather than decided, that I needed geographical, emotional and intellectual distance.

It was in England that my mother and I had our conversation about springtime. She was always happier to discuss the past while drinking tea in London, eating meringues in Geneva, or wandering through a park in Amsterdam, than at home, where she seemed more reticent. The day we talked about renewal and potential we were walking by the Thames at Richmond, admiring the pale fuzz of green buds on the willow trees. I asked her how she felt about the books and plays she had fashioned in her mind and never written. She didn't answer. Instead she spoke of her pleasure in having children and the satisfaction she had found in reading and typing out books and articles written by my father. She was a clear-minded adviser, a meticulous assistant and amanuensis, and a steadfast support to him throughout his career as a military historian. I believe she had a happy life with him and, though no plaster saint, she was a generous, loving, supportive and creative mother. But I grieve for her lost opportunities, and her stillborn books and plays.

How and why was it that within forty years of the 1916 Rising female representation in Irish affairs of state was almost unknown? Women had presided over republican courts during the War of Independence which followed the Rising, yet by 1927 a law had been passed refusing us the right even to sit on juries. That law remained on the statute book until 1976. Legislation enacted in Ireland in 1933 required female public servants and women who worked in banking to give up their jobs when they married. It was still in force in 1973, and Irishwomen had to wait until 1977 for the Employment Equality Act, which prohibited discrimination on the grounds of gender or marital status in almost all areas of employment. As I write this now, Irish citizens are still protesting about gender inequality, homophobia, and the denial of Irishwomen's basic human rights. Yet, in theory at least, the battle for equal rights was fought and won in Ireland 100 years ago.

When I sat in the Charles Dickens Museum café talking to my agent over lemon drizzle cake, I wondered if, in making my decision not to stay in Ireland, I had simply been driven by ambition. It was certainly a factor. The desire for a career and the freedom to discover my own identity took me away from a battleground where perhaps I should have stood with my contemporaries. I think now, though, that I wouldn't have been much use, and distance has allowed me to go through a process of discovery, analysis and contextualisation which may have some value of its own.

3
A Folded Fist

MY MOTHER'S NAME WAS MARY O'CONNOR. She was born on 31 May 1910, the second of three sisters with an age gap of two years between each. Mary is a typical Irish name, traditionally given in honour of the Blessed Virgin. But my mother, so she told me, was named after Mary of Teck who in 1910 became Queen consort of the United Kingdom of Great Britain and Ireland and the British Dominions, and Empress of India. Both Queen Mary and my mother, with whom she shared a birth month, were given the pet name May by their families, and my mother retained an interest in the British royal family all her life. Her own mother, Mary Bridget Keogh from Enniscorthy, was my grandfather's second wife. I know nothing about his first wife beyond the fact that my grandmother wanted a home that held no memories of her, which seems fair enough. So when my grandparents married, my grandfather rented a house on Washerwoman's Hill near Dublin's Botanic Gardens, where May, Cathleen and Evie were born.

The stories I have uncovered since I attended the event in Enniscorthy Castle move from Ireland to England and back again by way of Flanders Fields and Hitler's Germany. In one way their interest lies in the fact that they span two world wars, a revolution, a civil war, and the founding and development of a republic. What interests me most, though, is how they demonstrate that history at its most fundamental level is made up of shared memories.

My mother's earliest memory was of sitting at a table in the kitchen of the house on Washerwoman's Hill. She must have been about three years old and, wrapped in a large apron, feeling a pleasurable sense of importance, she was polishing a row of brass buttons. When she told me the story in her old age she could still remember the smell of the Brasso, the cushion on the chair and the newspaper spread on the scrubbed wooden table to protect it while she worked. Later on, she remembered, she and her sisters waved from a front window as a tall young man walked down the street with the brass buttons shining on his jacket. Looking back across the years, she supposed that he was her father's cousin who had joined the British army when war broke out in Europe in 1914. At the time, she was too young to know where he was going. Nor could she have known that, as her father's cousin set out to join his British regiment in France, her mother's cousin was awaiting orders to rise up against British rule in Ireland.

There were many shades and variations in the loyalties that permeated Irish life when my parents were growing up. Now, a century later, it can be hard to remember that in the run-up to the First World War a sizeable proportion of the population of Ireland had little or no problem with their country's union with Britain, or that the majority of those who aspired to Home Rule were prepared to support Britain in the trenches. Arthur Griffith, founder of the subsequently ultra-republican Sinn Féin party, even campaigned for several years for a dual monarchy on the Austro-Hungarian model, in which Ireland would become a separate kingdom alongside Britain. Nor was unionism confined to the north of Ireland. Edward Carson, founder of the Ulster Volunteers which opposed Home Rule, was a Dubliner; Eoin MacNeill, co-founder of the Gaelic League and founder of the Irish Volunteers, which supported Home Rule, was an Irish-speaking Ulsterman. Neither of these facts would have been remarkable at the time. And neither unionist nor nationalist opinion was then definable in terms of religion. It is true that the sixteenth-century plantations in Ulster had resulted in a strong Protestant unionist majority there. But it is also true that the Gaelic Revival movement was the inspiration of Anglo-Irish Protestants, both in the north and south of the island, who were wedded to the concept of nationalism. So it is necessary to remember that the definitions of what was desirable and achievable were fluid. The First World War precipitated great change and among the changes, in Ireland as elsewhere, were changes of opinion, aspiration and conviction.

Most people, though, were simply getting on with their lives, just as I was when I left for London in the 1970s. In the period before the First World War, ordinary Dubliners' lives often hung by a thread; only a few miles from my grandparents' rented house, children less fortunate than my mother and my aunts were dying of disease and malnutrition in some of the worst slum conditions in Europe. My grandfather had a pensionable position in the post office, an enviable job at a time when unemployment was high. But had he been a step or two lower on the social ladder he would have been struggling to make a living in a crowded employment market where a steady wage, decent working conditions and even the minimum levels of job security were almost unheard of.

In 1912, in anticipation of the introduction of a Home Rule Bill, James Larkin and James Connolly, both born in Britain of immigrant Irish parents, founded the Irish Labour Party as the political wing of the Irish Trade Union Congress which had then been in existence for nearly twenty years. Connolly and Larkin had worked separately as trade union activists in Scotland, England and in Ireland, where Larkin had started the Irish Transport and General Workers Union. Connolly, who had founded the Irish Socialist Republican Party as early as 1896, had also been active in the US. Larkin's sister Delia, a journalist, actress and trade union organiser, had formed the Irish Women Workers Union in 1911. So the Labour movement in Dublin had begun to gather strength. But while the men who employed Dublin's skilled and unskilled labourers had varying views about the pros and cons of Home Rule, they were united in their

opposition to trade unionism. To them it was a sign of trouble to
come and they decided to nip it in the bud.

So, in 1913, a group of the city's biggest employers agreed to
blacklist union members and in the following weeks hundreds of
men and women suspected of belonging to a union were sacked.
When fellow workers began a sympathy strike they too were
dismissed and employers organised what became known as 'The
Lock-Out', closing the gates of factories, docks and tram stations
and importing blackleg labour. The outcome was horrific. The
Dublin workers held rallies and set up picket lines and the
British Trades Union Congress sent them aid, but the employers
were supported both by the police and the Church and, having
held out for six months, up to 20,000 strikers were starved into
submission. In the course of the Lock-Out a number of men and
women were injured and killed when police baton-charged the
striking workers' rallies. As a result, a workers' militia, called
the Irish Citizen Army, was formed. It remained in existence
after the Lock-Out concluded, and in the years before 1916 its
purpose was redefined.

My mother and I weren't discussing war or politics when she
told me her story about the brass buttons. We were talking about
my own childhood memories of newspaper on our kitchen table
in Dublin, the unforgettable smell of Brasso, and the pleasure
of using a proper lint-free rag to bring up a shine. I remember
telling her how impressed I had been as a child by her masterly
choice of polishing cloths: she knew exactly which old shirt or
worn tea towel would make the perfect rag. Then I undercut
the compliment by saying how irritated I had been by her habit
of rationing the Brasso. She laughed and said Brasso was dear.
It was a typical response. I recall being equally irritated in my
teens by her refusal to buy washing-up liquid; for years she
washed her dishes using slivers of kitchen soap shaken up in a
jar of water which she kept by the sink. So it appears that my
grandmother brought her girls up to be careful with money and,
looking back now, I'm not surprised. The potential for regime

change brings the potential for winners and losers and, while my grandmother had married a man with a good position, by 1916 my grandfather and his co-workers in institutions like the Post Office would have had every right to worry about the certainty of their pensions and the security of their jobs.

Among my inheritances from my mother is a love of fabric. Seventy years or so after she cleaned those brass buttons she could remember the exact texture of the linen apron that enveloped her, the cotton rag in her hand, and the fact that her red hair was tied up off her face by a large ribbon bow. My grandmother must have fancied bows: there is a sepia photo of Cathleen, Evie and May taken about that time in which all three wear huge hair ribbons. It is a studio shot in which the three children pose on a scroll-backed, upholstered chaise longue. Typically for the period, the older girls are dressed in matching kilted skirts and knitted jumpers with high necks, buttoned on the shoulder. Evie, still hardly more than a baby, wears an elaborate pinafore with scalloped sleeves and lace inserts. Cathleen has one foot, in a black, buttoned boot, tucked up under her, revealing dark socks and legs bare to the knee; her arms are casually extended and her head is confidently posed. Evie, in white ankle socks and strap shoes, holds a picture book, a prop provided by the photographer. My mother, sitting forward and a little apart from the others, has one hand doubled into a fist. As they face the camera, Cathleen, the eldest, looks formidable while Evie, the youngest, looks shy. May, my mother, looks round-eyed and reserved. And, if you happen to know the story behind it, that photo throws light on her character.

May could be timid. The surroundings that day had overawed her and my grandmother, aware of the expense of a professional sitting, was nervous and inclined to fuss. No one had explained to the children what was going to happen, so when the strange man posed them in a row and instructed them to sit very still, May panicked. Her mother was out of sight behind the camera. The man had put a big black thing over his head. There was a brass ring round the lens that, for some reason, seemed terrifying. So at exactly the wrong moment she burst into tears. I can imagine the difficulty of keeping the bored older sister and the baby onside while the three- or four-year-old was persuaded to stop crying, sit up and behave. In the end it was the photographer who provided the distraction that did the trick. He produced a half-crown coin from his waistcoat pocket, held it up to the light to make it shine, and told my mother that if she was a good girl she could have it to hold. It took a while to get her calmed down and back onto the chaise longue with the others, her skirt pulled tidily over her knees, one hand touching Evie's book and the other clenched round the half crown. But the photo was taken and the occasion pronounced a success. Afterwards, when she found that she was expected to give the coin back, she was outraged. But she did as she was told because being a good girl meant not making a fuss.

An early meeting to discuss the setting-up of the Irish Volunteers took place in 1913 in Wynn's Hotel, Dublin, in what is now called the Saints and Scholars Lounge. Cumann na mBan's first official meeting was also held at Wynn's and the choice of venue is a clear indication of the two organisations' middle-class roots. Wynn's was a highly respectable hotel just off Dublin's main thoroughfare and its proprietor, Miss Phoebe Wynn, was friends with many of the city's literary figures. Cumann na mBan's founding members were not women who needed to work behind a shop counter or to keep the best side out. Most were related to or associates of the writers, academics and gentlemen of independent means who established the Volunteers, and when they gathered in Wynn's in their sweeping skirts, fur stoles and feathered hats, their agenda was nationalist, not socialist or feminist. Having said that, as anyone who has ever sat on a committee knows, you can have as many agendas at a meeting as there are members around the table.

What is certain is that, at first, Ireland's feminist organisations disapproved of Cumann na mBan. Militant groups such as the Irish Women's Franchise League, equivalent to Emmeline Pankhurst's Women's Social and Political Union in England, accused them of being slaves to the male Volunteers. Moderate groups such as the Irish Women's Suffrage Society, which had links with Millicent Fawcett's English National Union of Women's Suffrage Societies, saw them as irresponsible thrill-seekers. Basically, they couldn't win. But by the time Marion joined a year later, new branches were springing up across the country and Cumann na mBan's membership had broadened. Some new members were workers already involved in the trade union movement who, like James Connolly, had a vision of an Irish Workers Republic with a constitution that would enshrine universal suffrage. Others, particularly in rural areas, may have had less interest in trade unionism but many of them were concerned about women's rights.

Few women in my generation knew the story of Irish feminism. A huge amount of research and publication has since taken place, but when I was at school no one taught us about the Irish Women's Franchise League or the Irish Women's Suffrage Society, both of which were well established when my mother was a child. I was an adult living in England before I discovered that a women's suffrage society had been founded in the north of Ireland in 1871, six years before my grandmother was born, and that a husband-and-wife team had set up a similar society in Dublin four years later. Isabella Tod who founded the North of Ireland Society for Women's Suffrage travelled extraordinary distances around Ireland, speaking at public meetings attended by both men and women, and appeared regularly at suffrage meetings in Britain. The links that she and her colleagues established with British activists were taken up in the next generation and cooperation continued. In 1909, one of the co-founders of the Irish Women's Franchise League spent time working in London for the Women's Social and Political Union and called the experience a helpful apprenticeship for the Irish organisation's campaign in Ireland. But when I was at school the feminist activists of our grandmothers' and mothers' generations did not appear in our history books. We learned nothing of the early links between British and Irish female suffragist organisations, of how growing separatist aspirations in Ireland affected those established relationships, or of how the passage of time changed and refined the various groups' thinking in both countries. No one told us that Irishwomen's organisations had fought to include female suffrage in a Home Rule Bill that was drafted in 1912, or that women were imprisoned for protesting on the streets of Dublin when that effort failed. And no one told us about Irish feminist links with socialism, either. So, inevitably, what we were taught about the founding of the state gave us no hint of how the complexities of Ireland's nationalist aspirations were further complicated by conflicts of aspiration among Irish feminists.

In fact, I grew up with the vague impression that only one woman had a significant part in the 1916 Rising. Others like Hanna Sheehy-Skeffington, who had co-founded the Irish Women's Franchise League, and Kathleen Clarke, a founder member of Cumann na mBan, were referred to solely as the wives of senior men who were executed after the Rising. Their own involvement in politics, which was lifelong and extensive, their involvement in the preparations for the Rising itself, and the fact that Sheehy-Skeffington's husband was an active feminist, were hardly mentioned. The hundreds of other married and unmarried Irish female activists of the period were seldom referred to at all. The woman we did hear about was Constance Markievicz, although the fact that she had been second in command of one of the positions held by the rebels in Dublin during the Rising tended to be reduced to a photo caption. Instead, the photos of her in our schoolbooks, combined with the minimal text that accompanied them, suggested that the most important thing to be said about her was that she liked having her picture taken and had a great eye for an outfit.

To be fair, Constance appears to have made many trips to the photographer's studio, both before and after her marriage to Casimir Markievicz, who was a Polish count. In her early life she had plenty of jewels and dresses to choose from and clearly liked having her photo taken. One of the two photos I remember from my schooldays shows her posed like an actress against a romantic painted backdrop, gazing into the distance with roses and lace on her bosom and a trailing, tiered, scalloped, embroidered skirt. In the second photograph both the backdrop and her outfit are very different. Instead of dreaming among trees by a moonlit lake she stands before a painted column with a severe classical temple in the distance, wearing the uniform of the Irish Citizen Army. It was composed of breeches, polished boots and puttees, an epauletted jacket and a wide-brimmed feathered hat. She designed it herself and the revolver she holds in the photograph wasn't a prop.

Constance Markievicz was born Constance Gore-Booth at Buckingham Gate in London in 1868, the eldest daughter of an Anglo-Irish baronet whose family's colonial roots in Ireland reached back to the seventeenth century. Her father was one of the largest landowners in the west of Ireland and Constance spent most of her childhood and young adulthood living in Lissadell House on the family's estate in County Sligo. When she was about ten years old famine struck the area and her father gave aid to his tenants in the form of food handouts and money to assist them to emigrate. He was considered by many to be a fair and good landlord. Others said that the Gore-Booths were eager to clear their land of elderly, disabled or poverty-stricken tenants who were often hard pushed to pay their rents. It was an accusation thrown at every landlord in Ireland during famine times, regardless of whether they attempted to help their starving tenants or left them to die; and, indeed, the two statements are not necessarily mutually incompatible.

Her association with James Connolly and the Citizen Army began during the 1913 Dublin Lock-Out, when she organised food aid for the striking workers. By then she was Countess Markievicz, having met her husband Casimir when she was an art student in Paris in her twenties. They married in London in 1900, and settled in Dublin three years later. Casimir too was an artist, and an aspiring playwright and theatrical impresario, so while their aristocratic backgrounds brought them invitations to viceregal balls in Dublin Castle they also moved in the city's artistic, literary and theatrical circles. The nationalist and feminist thinking they found in those circles was not new to Constance. She and her sister Eva had founded the Sligo Women's Suffrage Society seven years earlier and W. B. Yeats, also from Sligo, was a family friend. Both sisters were strongly drawn to socialism, perhaps because of the poverty and famine they had seen in childhood on their father's estate. So, although in the next few years Constance became involved in various nationalist and women's organisations, including Sinn Féin and Cumann na mBan, it was James Connolly, who believed that the Labour movement, nationalism and the fight for women's suffrage were interdependent, who gave her specific focus. She worked with him through the Lock-Out and the setting-up of the Citizen Army which, in principle if not always in practice, accepted women into its ranks on an equal footing with men. In the run-up to the Rising she became involved in its strategic planning, provided a safe house in which to hide munitions and have meetings, and subsidised the nationalist boys' group, Fianna Éireann, effectively a training ground for the Citizen Army and the Volunteers. Then, in 1916, when Connolly became part of the inner circle which was planning the Rising, she became the individual chosen to be sufficiently aware of the plans to be able, if necessary, to take his place.

It is no accident that those photos of Constance in her roses and lace, boots and breeches, look like theatre stills; each was contrived to produce a dramatic and erotic effect which, since Constance was an artist, it seems fair to assume was deliberate. When they appeared in my schoolbooks the erotic element wasn't mentioned. Instead they were used to illustrate the legend of the fragile society-woman-turned-freedom-fighter, a story that carried with it more than a whiff of concealed snobbery; this wasn't just a woman, she was a countess, which made her far more interesting than a shop girl or a farmer's daughter. Not only that, but she was near as dammit related to British royalty, which gave her glamour by association, a contradiction which in Ireland has never seemed contradictory, even among hardened republicans.

The fact that both theatricality and eroticism are essential features of warfare was never mentioned in my schooldays either, although the 1916 Rising offers the perfect context in which to consider it. Both before and after the Rising occurred, nationalism – but not socialism – was packaged and sold to the public in terms of a dramatic struggle by Ireland's manhood to free an abused nation personified as a ravaged woman languishing in chains. Constance Markievicz had a foot in both the nationalist and socialist camps. Alongside her involvement with James Connolly, she supported, and occasionally performed in, dramas that attempted to distil the complicated, contradictory aims of the various nationalist organisations into agitprop theatre. To modern sensibilities those plays and pageants seem naive to the point of embarrassment. But they were performed and received in circumstances that make them hard for us to evaluate now, either as art or as propaganda. No one could call them nuanced. Even those written by professional playwrights are about as subtle as a brick, and the pageants produced by Patrick Pearse, a schoolmaster whose dramatic works were written to be performed by his pupils, now seem shocking. They combined flowing cloaks, headbands and his trademark saffron-coloured Irish kilt with the most bloodthirsty features of the heroic cult of the Young Warrior which, encouraged by the turn-of-the-century interest in mythology, was then emerging throughout Europe.

That last point, which is an important one, was also never mentioned when I was at school. The nationalist theatrical, literary and artistic works produced in the run-up to the 1916 Rising had a recognisably Irish flavour but their aesthetic, which belonged absolutely to their time, was not unique to Ireland. The combination of idealism, athleticism, patriotism and quasi-religious self-sacrifice inculcated at Pearse's school in Dublin was also instilled in the English public schools of the period, producing the generation of British army officers that was decimated in the First World War. It was equally present all across Europe in schools, military academies and in the arts. Whether or not artists had a part in creating, as opposed to reflecting, that ethos is an interesting question. In Ireland they certainly tried to, and there is evidence that they succeeded. But the idea that the Irish works belonged to a purely Irish upsurge of national fervour is nonsense.

When I went to London in the 1970s wheeled suitcases had not been invented or, if they had, I hadn't seen one. I took the emigrant boat carrying a long, sausage-shaped bag made of rubberised canvas bought from Hector Gray's in Liffey Street, a bargain shop still remembered with deep affection by my generation of Dubliners. I suppose I must have had my rucksack too, prudently lined with plastic bags, but I don't remember it. The sausage bag was lined with my sleeping bag, which unzipped around the edges to produce a handy quilt under which I slept for years afterwards in various rented rooms and flats. Everything else I took with me went into the bag in layers, like biscuits in a tube, and packing was a fine art because if you got things in the wrong order you could end up with half your worldly goods strewn round you on the pavement while you burrowed like a mole for your train ticket.

Among the objects that I packed and repacked, then and afterwards, was a pencil case made by Evie. She had created it from a single piece of leather, folding the bottom two thirds, whipping them together with a thong to create a wallet, and continuing the whipping round the edge of the top third to make a flap held in place with two press studs. Very much in the manner of her time, it was decorated in pokerwork, and the design she chose was a squiggly, interlaced cat in the style known as Celtic Art. I remember the smell of the thick, dark brown leather and how, if you packed it the wrong way up, things slipped out at either side of the top and disappeared among clothing and books. Once a red biro escaped and leaked into the sausage bag, giving a whole new effect to a tie-dyed T-shirt and spoiling a cheesecloth smock.

I brought that pencil case with me to London because it was a present from my mother, not for its associations with Evie, whom I never knew. Indeed, I hardly know what Evie looked like as an adult. Maybe her attitude to photography was coloured by her first experience of it in that Dublin studio when May cried and everyone got fussed. Or perhaps it wasn't. Anyway, in family snapshots taken in Enniscorthy she usually appears either squinting at the camera or with her face turned away. I don't remember hearing her spoken of much when I was a child, probably because her death had been a shock; later, when I was settled in England, my mother sent me a sheet of paper in my grandmother's handwriting chronicling the unexpected diagnosis and short process of the illness that killed the baby of her family in 1944, at the age of thirty. It is possible that her heart was affected by a childhood bout of tuberculosis. My mother certainly mentioned that the doctors had connected her condition to an illness she had contracted when she was small. But tuberculosis carried such a social stigma when I was growing up in Ireland that it was never spoken of, so I don't know. Indeed, I don't even know what Evie did for a living but it is evident that she was a competent amateur craftswoman, happy to try her hand at anything. A bookcase she designed and built in oak once stood in our house in Dublin. Keeping to the family tradition of thrift and resourcefulness, she made it from offcuts of coffin boards blagged from the local undertaker.

One of my brothers spent time in Enniscorthy during Marion's retirement. He says she had a habit of doodling on

odd scraps of paper. Most of the Stokes family was artistic so
I suppose that isn't surprising. What interests me is that, like
the design on the wallet made by Evie in the 1940s, Marion's
doodles, produced more than half a lifetime after the 1916
Rising, consisted of repeated squiggly motifs in the Celtic Art
style. But perhaps that is not surprising either. Those squiggly
motifs adopted from medieval manuscripts, metalwork and
sculpted stone crosses by nationalist artists like Constance
Markievicz dominated Irish design for more than half a century
and linger still in every tourist gift shop. When I was a child
Celtic Art was considered to be uniquely and exclusively Irish. It
appeared everywhere, from the covers of our school copybooks
to the appliquéd outfits of the ringletted Irish dancers who
bobbed up and down on platforms in Dublin while, ironically,
dancers in rural, Irish-speaking areas wore the latest fashions,
sent home by emigrants in America. The fact that the origins of
Celtic Art appear to be Scandinavian, Coptic or Italian probably
wasn't concealed from us but it certainly wasn't mentioned, and
the idea that the same style characterises Anglo-Saxon and Early
British art would, in the popular imagination of my generation,
have been pretty close to heresy.

That curvilinear style, ornamental, fluid, complex and often
asymmetrical, offers a metaphor for the interwoven network of
cultural, political and military organisations that characterised
Ireland's nationalist movement before 1916. Individual activists,
secretly or overtly, were often members of more than one group,
while groups frequently reconstituted themselves or split. This
produced confusion when each side in a split clung to the group's
original name; I remember the same problem in my student days,
when a split in the IRA resulted in the rest of us identifying the
two groups as 'stickies' and 'pinnies', based on whether the Easter
Lily badges they sold to commemorate the 1916 Rising were
stuck on your lapel by the vendor or came with a free pin. In the
years before 1916 the Volunteers who followed John Redmond
became the National Volunteers while those who supported

their founder Eoin MacNeill remained the Irish Volunteers; but inevitably both sides continued to refer to themselves as 'The Volunteers', adamant that the other side was bogus. And public perception of the nature of any group was often defined not by its constitution but by furious announcements made by former insiders as they marched out in a huff and slammed the door. Indeed, some arguments as to what a particular group stood for at any given time took place at the level of 'oh yes you do' and 'oh no we don't'.

The playwright Seán O'Casey, who came from a working-class Dublin background, was active during the 1913 Lock-Out. After the strike was broken, he wrote the constitution which established the former workers' militia as a citizen army committed to the Labour movement and the creation of an Irish socialist republic. Shortly afterwards he resigned on the grounds that the Citizen Army, and Constance Markievicz in particular, had an inappropriately close relationship with the bourgeois Volunteers. At about the same time, Jack White, the man who turned the Citizen Army into a professional fighting force, and who himself was son of a British army field marshal, also resigned. In his case it was to join the Volunteers. Despite O'Casey's belief that the Citizen Army was too closely involved with the Volunteers, Connolly, the leader of the Citizen Army, was later drawn into the IRB's secret plan for the 1916 Rising, which was hatched without the knowledge of the Volunteers' founder, Eoin MacNeill. Subsequently, Connolly added a further loop to the network of Celtic knotwork by entrusting the IRB's secret plan to Constance Markievicz, the aristocratic artist and amateur actress ... who became a president of Cumann na mBan ... which had been formed to support the Volunteers.

For activists at the time, living with the various levels of knowledge and lack of knowledge must have been a bit like living in the kind of family that the woman I met in Enniscorthy Castle was thinking about when she said that, while her siblings had shared the same experiences, none of them remembered

anything in exactly the same way. Every time I discuss that
remark with an audience it provokes personal stories. Some
people just give amusing examples of the different viewpoints of
different age groups. But others talk about discovering their own
exclusion from family secrets that older brothers or sisters were
privy to, and about older siblings shouldering responsibilities
which younger family members were spared. Most people offer
a great deal of intellectual justification, produced by hindsight:
'I'd say my parents didn't want me causing trouble' ... *'they
probably thought it was best to say nothing'* ... *'my father was
dead so I suppose she felt I was the man of the house.'* Yet, despite
the understanding, a raw sense of outrage or resentment often
remains, in particular among those whose discovery that they
have been excluded from information held by others has left
them feeling humiliated. The same experiences of exclusion and
of isolating responsibility characterised the 1916 Rising, and
the same balancing act between intellectual understanding and
emotional response was required. Indeed, one of the fascinating
things about the Rising and its aftermath is how individuals like
Eoin MacNeill coped with the discovery that senior members
of their organisations had been privy to plans of which they
themselves had been unaware, and how those drawn into the
IRB's inner circle accepted levels of secrecy which forced them
to lie to friends and colleagues in other nationalist organisations
with whom they continued to work.

In 1914, the year that Marion joined Cumann na mBan, most
of those who wanted Home Rule still looked to John Redmond,
the leader of the Irish Parliamentary Party in Westminster, to
achieve it by parliamentary means. But by then the complexities
of political horse-trading and the arming of the Ulster
Volunteers had begun to raise doubts about Redmond's ability
and judgment. Redmond believed that Britain was to be trusted.
Or maybe he thought that saying so would give the Home Rulers
the moral high ground and political leverage once the war in
Europe was over. One way or the other, he urged Irishmen to

join the British army and thousands took his advice. Among them was the tall young man whose buttons my mother polished at the kitchen table in the house on Washerwoman's Hill. I don't know where that young man stood politically. He may or may not have been a Home Ruler. If he was, he may or may not have had confidence in John Redmond. Perhaps he just believed it was his duty to fight for the empire of which his country was then a part, and of which it would remain a part if and when Home Rule was introduced. Many Irishmen believed that. Others, since times were hard, enlisted in the British army for the pay, and for the separation allowances paid to their wives at home while they were fighting overseas.

When I was at school certain repeated features in Irish history were summed up in handy, chanted reminders for use in exams. One was 'Too little Too late And In The Wrong Place', applicable to foreign aid for Irish rebellion in any period from the Elizabethan age to the present day. The other was 'England's Difficulty Is Ireland's Opportunity', a slogan guaranteed to garner a few marks if crowbarred into an essay on the 1916 Rising. It was coined when the IRB, which claimed political descent from the rebels who made their last stand in Enniscorthy in 1798, was established after a failed rising in 1848 and sums up the IRB's position at the outbreak of the First World War: in their view the time was right for another rising because the concentration of British troops in the trenches offered better odds for its success. But while IRB plans for a rising were already under way in 1914, many conflicting aspirations and loyalties had to be reconciled or negotiated before they had any chance of finding widespread support. Not only that but while it was one thing to define the kind of freedom that could or should be achieved, and another to create persuasive works of art that linked a perceived past to an imagined future, planning a military operation was something else again. Then, as now, artists and activists were willing to work for nothing while arms dealers worked strictly for cash.

Compared to their counterparts in Ulster, the Irish Volunteers were poorly armed. This was partly because the British were more vigilant about intercepting imports of arms to the south of Ireland than to the north – a fact that contributed to nationalist doubts about Redmond's judgment. So, for those who were secretly planning the Rising as well as for those determined to defend Home Rule whenever it should be introduced, sourcing and paying for munitions was a major issue. That issue of finance wasn't foregrounded in my schooldays. Nor was the manipulative role of the IRB. Our received version of the 1916 story fused Christian and Iron Age mythology, combining the image of Christ's sacrifice on Calvary with the high deeds of Cú Chulainn, the Irish Achilles. In my schoolbooks the Rising was presented as the heroic enterprise of an austere group of visionaries whose sacrificial courage had laid upon their successors the responsibility of living up to their values – although by the time I was at school the government was in the business of emphasising self-sacrifice rather than blood sacrifice. The trouble with any simplified version of history is that once it is found to be incomplete it tends to be rejected out of hand. When I left Ireland in the 1970s it had already begun to be fashionable to find reasons to cut the heroes of 1916 down to size. But the Rising was, in many ways, an expression of remarkable courage, self-sacrifice and vision. It was also a bit of a mess, which makes the courage of its participants even more remarkable.

The underlying reason for most of the messiness had to do with the sourcing of arms. By the time the Volunteers came to vote for or against John Redmond's judgment, most of those who voted against him had already lost confidence in Home Rule and were becoming committed republicans. This was what the IRB had been waiting for. They looked to their contacts with powerful Irish-American organisations for money to fund a rising and, still acting without MacNeill's knowledge, accelerated their planning. MacNeill's own position was that a rising should be attempted only if he saw adequate reasons and likelihood of success. In the meantime he continued to train the Volunteers so that any attempt to disarm them, to introduce conscription to the British army, or to abandon Home Rule could be successfully resisted. Which meant that he too needed access to arms and money to pay for them. So in the summer of 1914 the Volunteers made contact in London with the representative of a Belgian arms dealer and arranged to import guns from Germany. The deal was funded by a loan from Alice Stopford Green, the daughter of an Irish Anglican rector – another woman who was seldom mentioned in my schooldays.

Part of the 1914 shipment of arms was landed at Howth, near Dublin, nine days before the war broke out in Europe. They were brought in a private yacht owned by Erskine Childers, an English supporter of Home Rule who, disturbed by demonstrations of support for Ulster unionists both from senior British army officers in Ireland and Conservative politicians in Westminster, had agreed to assist in the Volunteer's gunrunning. Alice Stopford Green's loan, which didn't quite cover the cost, was supplemented by money raised by two other women, Mary Osgood and Mary Spring Rice. Mary Osgood, an American, was Childers' wife. Mary Spring Rice was another Anglo-Irish aristocrat, the daughter of Baron Monteagle of Brandon in County Kerry. Both women were part of the yacht's crew. So was Sir Roger Casement, an Irishman knighted two years earlier for human rights work in South America undertaken at the request of the British Foreign Office. Two years later, at Easter time when the IRB's plans were coming to a head, it would be MacNeill's concern about the consequences of rising without adequate arms that ultimately caused the Rising to go off half-cocked.

Although the authorities attempted to intercept them, the Howth guns and the remainder of the shipment, landed a week later farther down the coast, were successfully hidden in safe houses, and in Patrick Pearse's school. By then Pearse, who was both a member of the IRB and the Volunteers, was centrally involved in IRB planning. He was also utterly persuaded by the idea of blood sacrifice, an aspect of the Rising that many of my generation found weird. Actually, that's an understatement. While some of my generation regarded Pearse as close to holy, others found him deeply creepy. This was partly because of his poetry which hovers occasionally on the verge of paedophilic, and partly because of his iconic portrait which was said to have been painted in profile because he had a squint. The squint, of course, is irrelevant and the poems may derive from medieval Irish praise poems celebrating the beauty of young warriors. But, as 1970s teenagers, many of us were unwilling to give him the benefit of the doubt.

As well as bringing in guns from abroad, nationalists gathered munitions at home: guns and explosives were stolen or bought from British soldiers stationed in Ireland, or from the police, home-made bombs were assembled in cellars and sheds, and blacksmiths forged pikes to be used by those who had no other weapons. In Enniscorthy, Cumann na mBan and the Volunteers took delivery of their share of the arms paid for by the efforts of Alice Stopford Green, Mary Osgood and Mary Spring Rice. I don't know how those guns were transported from Dublin to Enniscorthy or if Marion was personally involved in receiving them; if she was she would have waited for orders and acted accordingly, having been told no more than she needed to know, for her own sake as well as for her comrades'.

I don't know what uniform Marion wore, either. Everyone's gear and weapons were paid for out of their own pockets or subsidised by officers. So, unlike Constance Markievicz who could afford her elegantly tailored breeches, jacket and fetching feathered hat, many Cumann na mBan, Volunteer and Citizen Army members drilled in mismatched uniforms or civilian dress. But while I suspect that Markievicz was rather pleased with the effect of her hat, she didn't necessarily design it with an eye to vanity. As an officer in the Citizen Army she needed a uniform which made her identifiable in battle. In that sense, her feathers were literally fetching; like the plumed and polished helmets of officers throughout history, they were intended both to identify her to her followers in the field and, by showing no fear of drawing attention to herself, to demonstrate contempt for enemy marksmanship.

In many ways war works like theatre. In battle, gestures need to be unambiguous, music has to be audible and emotive, and flags, emblems and uniforms must be attractive and instantly recognisable. Uniforms are designed to give weight and stature to whoever wears them, and to suggest that the power of the group is invested in the individual. And in the ancient heroic tradition invoked at the time of the Rising, power is underpinned by the concept of deliberate self-sacrifice. The hero is the mediator between God and the people, offering his life in exchange for the wellbeing of his community and his own immortal fame; and the more lightly he holds his life the longer he is likely to keep it, since the immortal gods are moved by mortal courage. Looking back now, it's easy to dismiss the dramatic quasi-religious version of the 1916 Rising that my generation of schoolchildren imbibed in the 1960s and 1970s. Yet it contains grains of truth. Many of the individual men and women who prepared for and took part in the Rising drew inspiration and courage from the concept of self-sacrificial heroism, and from the plays, poems, ballads, emblems and flags that attempted to encompass their aspirations. It may even be that the reality of the world they lived in, the visions of the future they aspired to, and the individual turmoil they experienced, were so complex that the only satisfactory way to express them was through archetypal imagery.

But heroes of myth and legend don't live in a world of kitchen tables and polishing rags, or worry about wages and pensions. The men and women who took part in the 1916 Rising did, and each would have known that, whether they lived or died, their involvement would affect others besides themselves. For many, the real conflict of loyalties must have been personal, not political, and the reality of what that means can only be found in an awareness of the complexity of their times.

The photo of Constance Markievicz dreaming in lace and roses includes two other figures. One is a little boy who leans against her in a dark suit with a wide, white collar, looking imperious. Or bored. He's her stepson Stanislas, Casimir's son by a previous marriage. The other is a little girl in a short frock, who smiles shyly at the camera. She's Constance and Casimir's daughter Maeve, born in 1901. Hardly older than Evie is in the shot of my mother and my aunts, she clings to her mother's neck, with her head against Constance's cheek. A single ringlet on her forehead is held in place by a ribbon bow and her gathered skirt reveals white socks and little kid shoes with ankle straps. In the context of fashionable photography of the time, the fact that Constance is posed gazing into the distance simply adds to the sense of dreamy romanticism: in the context of what was about to happen, the suggestion that she is ignoring the children is painful. Before Maeve was eight years old her mother had gone away to become a revolutionary and her father, who had no interest in his wife's nationalist activism, had left as well. Stanislas later joined him in the Ukraine. Maeve was raised in her grandmother's care in Sligo. She was a fifteen-year-old in an English boarding school when she read the newspaper reports of the Rising, which denounced her mother as a traitor to her king and country. Some years later she met Constance again in a London hotel. They had to be introduced because Maeve didn't recognise her.

Maeve Markievicz died in 1962 at her home on Parliament Hill, London. Her adult life was spent in England where, after 1945, she took up reclaiming and planning urban gardens which, during the war years, had been left to run wild.

4
The Filly-Foal

I FIRST CROSSED THE TOWERING mountain range at the western end of the Dingle Peninsula as a student in the 1970s. From the moment I arrived there on a muddy road by starlight, I fell in love with the place, its people and the cultural life I found there. It became a focus that unconsciously informed my writing and a place to which I repeatedly returned on holiday, on my own to begin with and then with Wilf. So, some years after my mother's death in 1990, when Wilf and I decided to divide our life and work between London and Ireland, we didn't look to Dublin, where I grew up. Instead, we found a stone house at the end of the Dingle Peninsula where Irish is still the first language of everyday life. Part of the reason for the survival of the language there lies in the remoteness of the area. As a student hitch-hiking to the peninsula in the 1970s, I could reckon on a full day's journey starting at the crack of dawn, and I remember many a tense hour on country roads with traffic churning past me in the dusk, while trickles of rain ran down my neck and seeped through the back of my rucksack. Rucksacks were canvas in those days – at least the one I could afford was – so you quickly learned to pack everything in plastic bags and to line the back with a towel.

Irish as the first language declined from the nineteenth century onwards. It survived longest in rural parts of the west, and today a broken ribbon of Irish-speaking, or Gaeltacht, areas still stretches the length of the country's Atlantic seaboard. There are three distinct dialects, spoken respectively in the south-western, western and north-western regions. The Dingle

Peninsula, which in Irish is called Corca Dhuibhne (which is pronounced something like 'Kirka Gween-ah'), is in the south-west. Its name translates as 'the territory of the people of the goddess Danú'. Danú is a Celtic fertility goddess: as The Maiden, The Mother and The Crone she represents the circularity of the Ancient Celts' world view, which perceived the universe as a cyclical stream of energy in which death is the womb of life. Echoes of her triple aspects appear throughout Celtic folklore and mythology: as the Irish Saint Bríd the imprint of her naked feet brings life back to the fields in springtime; in Scotland she is The Washerwoman At The Ford, the hag who washes bloodstained grave clothes after battles; as the matriarchal Good Goddess, versions of her name survive in place names across Europe, from the Danube to the Don. The name itself means 'water', because water is the basic requirement for life itself.

Gaeltacht areas have long been among Ireland's most impoverished regions with resultant high levels of emigration. When I first visited Corca Dhuibhne I discovered that the people who lived there had far more experience of life and work outside Ireland than the average Dubliner of the time. Many of my neighbours today took their first trip to England, America or Canada when they were hardly out of their teens, and some continued to travel to and fro for the rest of their working lives, unfazed by the contrast between a world where meals were still prepared over open fires and the slick world of fitted kitchens and fridges. Some, only a few years older than myself, had set out without much fluency in English. Like emigrants anywhere throughout history, they found work and accommodation with the help of those who had made the journey before them. Shared language was a huge factor in their shared experience but what ultimately defined their sense of identity was the physical landscape of the peninsula from which they came. Now, forty years later, that detailed knowledge of the land their families farmed and the seas they fished still underpins my neighbours' consciousness of who they are. For incomers, this can be baffling. Almost every Gaeltacht conversation involves place: each description of an event begins with a description of where it occurred, and each individual is referred to in terms of the house in which he or she was born, lives or was married into. When more than one place or individual is mentioned in conversation, a complex web of relationships, all defined by place, provides reference points that are meaningless to an outsider. To anyone born and bred there, such ignorance must be tiresome; I know that some of my older neighbours in Corca Dhuibhne find it almost incomprehensible. For them, shared memory is almost as important for communication as is language, and when apparently intelligent adults turn out to have one without the other it just seems inexplicable.

That profound sense of place is preserved in the Irish language in a specific genre of storytelling known as *Dindsenchas*, which translates as 'the lore of places'. Written collections of Dindsenchas occur in medieval manuscripts but the genre itself is much older. It evolved as a series of prose tales and poems about the origins of place names in Irish myth and legend, and its purpose was to bolster the territorial claims of kings and chieftains by establishing their descent from heroes and gods. At the folk level it appears in detailed communal memory of family and individual relationships to specific places, expressed in story, songs and poems, and reaching back for generations. To a greater or lesser extent, the same traditions survive in many parts of rural Ireland – and, indeed, across the world – but in Gaeltacht areas they continue to inform daily life to a degree now lost in other parts of the country.

After centuries of colonial rule, the revival of the Irish language was seen as an obvious starting point for a resurgence of national identity. If you're in the business of colonising someone else's country the first thing you need is superior military force, but the real work begins after you have fought your wars, established control and set up strongholds from which to administer your authority. Successful invasions – as opposed to hit-and-run pillaging – require colonists who, in return for money or grants of land, organise the exploitation of the conquered country's resources. What you need as a colonist are systems that allow you to control the conquered population without military back-up. That requires ways of establishing that your superiority is innate, not just based on military strength. To do this you need to convince the natives that their own cultural identifiers are now a liability, while yours, being superior, are something to aspire to. That way, while denying them access to most of its facilities, you ensure that they want to join your club.

But while devaluation of native language and culture is the starting point of effective colonisation, physical distance and unreliable communications systems between colonists and the authorities in their country of origin can undercut the effect. As early as the twelfth century, Anglo-Norman settlers in Ireland were accused by worried administrators in London of becoming more Irish than the Irish themselves. You can see why they would be worried: a significant number of the colonists had become culturally assimilated, adopting Irish social and legal systems, marrying into the native aristocracy and speaking the language. Inevitably, the real picture would have been more nuanced than it appeared from London, and the cross-fertilisation must have worked in both directions, although perhaps that wouldn't have pleased the administrators either. One way or the other, the next colonists sent by England's monarchs appear to have arrived with stricter instructions to remain 'on message'. So, despite occasional interruptions and backsliding, the process of denigrating the native Irish culture really began to achieve results.

By the nineteenth century, associations with inferiority and poverty had produced the desired negative reaction to the Irish language which, for millennia, had preserved the native culture. Although many native speakers continued to cling to the language, others were literally beating it out of their children, convinced that a command of English would enhance their chances of survival as emigrants. In Marion's lifetime, children were often sent to school with wooden tally sticks hanging round their necks: a notch was cut in the stick for each Irish word the child was heard to use and, at the day's end, he or she was caned according to the number of notches accumulated. Although Irish was later taught in schools, the devaluation process continued. In rural English-speaking areas where Irish had been commonly spoken until comparatively recently, the language was often seen as a barrier to social betterment and in the cities, where Irish had long been extinct, it was widely perceived as a cause for mockery. In fact, the revival of interest in the Irish language, which spearheaded the revival of interest in native Irish culture, was based in Dublin and London and initiated by scholars who were not native speakers.

My mother, who grew up on the east coast, had little or no Irish; I don't even know if she learnt it at school. My father, who was from the west, grew up with the dialect spoken in the countryside around Galway city, although his family spoke English at home. But by sheer chance the Irish I learned in my Dublin school belonged, more or less, to Corca Dhuibhne. When I was a teenager, University College Dublin was accustomed to receiving students who combined decent standards in written Irish with a mishmash of pronunciation and idiom learned from schoolteachers whose first language had been English. So, like sheep separated into pens, those of us who arrived in that condition were categorised according to the predominance in our spoken Irish of one dialect or another and dispatched during the Easter holidays to the appropriate area, where we lodged with local families and were expected to spend our time talking with and, more importantly, listening to native speakers. It was one of the positive and formative experiences of my life.

Mixed messages are part of the Gaeltacht experience too, however. Life in rural Ireland has traditionally been dominated both by the Catholic Church and by the particular kind of misogyny which Christianity has encouraged for centuries. But, just as life in Gaeltacht regions is lived in two languages, traces of the profoundly pagan sense of spirituality inherent in native Irish culture live on there in parallel with the Christian world view, subtly informing issues that might otherwise appear unambiguous. Within living memory, women's lives here were dominated by the worth of the land that their male relations could or would give them as marriage portions. On the face of it, therefore, women in Gaeltacht regions, like women in subsistence-farming communities throughout the world, have traditionally been regarded as chattels. Yet men too could be required to bring a portion with them into a marriage, and it was never the case that the men here made all the running. Perhaps Ireland's ancient matriarchal culture survives in its purest form in Irish-speaking areas. Certainly, while many of the elderly women who are my neighbours had marriages arranged by their families, it was possible, at least in some cases, for a girl to send a relative to make an offer to the partner of her choice. And, while women here are characteristically deeply religious, many put as much value on their own sense of spirituality as on Church dogma, which to some degree was and is seen as alien. As a teenager I wasn't aware of those subtleties. What I saw were communities in which everyone, male and female, worked backbreaking hours to support their families, experienced the constant threat – or promise – of economic emigration, and lived in what seemed to me to be the most beautiful place on earth. From that first visit, although it took me almost thirty years to achieve my aim, I knew that one day I would come back to Ireland and live in Corca Dhuibhne. Part of the reason I stayed away so long was purely practical: my career was based in England, and London had become my home. But among the reasons why I left in the first place was the increasing complexity of my relationship with the Irish language.

Both Cumann na mBan and the Volunteers had roots in a cultural organisation called the Gaelic League so, although I don't know if my grandmother or Aunt Magger had any Irish, Marion would certainly have been involved in attending and

organising Irish-language classes in Enniscorthy. Twenty years
before he founded the Volunteers in 1913, Eoin MacNeill,
who was a professor of early and medieval Irish History at
University College Dublin, had co-founded the Gaelic League
with Douglas Hyde, who became the university's first professor
of modern Irish and, eventually, the first president of the Irish
Republic. Establishing the Gaelic League was an active attempt
to draw Irish people of different religious and political loyalties
into a common awareness of native Irish culture. And far from
being chauvinist or isolationist, it emerged from a European-
wide growth in Celtic Studies that happened to be booming at
the time. What complicated matters as time went on, however,
was the shift from cultural nationalism, which underpinned
the Home Rule movement, to militant republicanism, which
consciously annexed Ireland's native language and culture for
use as political weapons.

Douglas Hyde, who was the son of a Church of Ireland rector,
was a great man for setting up organisations. In 1982, the year
before he set up the Gaelic League with MacNeill, he co-founded
the Irish National Literary Society with the poet and playwright
W. B. Yeats. It was the focus of a group of writers, known as Gaelic
Revivalists, who were influenced by translations of material that
had been preserved both in medieval Irish manuscripts and in
the oral heritage of the Gaeltacht areas. The word 'Gaelic' can
be a dodgy one to define, but Yeats and his contemporaries
used it to describe the culture that existed in Ireland before the
arrival of the English. Establishing the actual characteristics of
that culture continues to cause much table-thumping among
scholars. However, the Irish National Literary Society was led
by creative artists, whose business is to explore the potential for
meaning in imaginative connectivity, not the scientific evidence
that establishes whether or not actual connections exist. So they
weren't particularly bothered by questions of archaeological,
or sometimes even historical, accuracy. Yet, regardless of the
differences in their approaches, the relationship between the

scholars and artists of Marion's generation was fruitful. Their work was central to the shaping of Ireland's nationalist cultural perceptions in the years that led up to the 1916 Rising, and the plays written by the Gaelic Revivalists were the seed bed of what became the Abbey Theatre, now Ireland's national theatre, which, as it happened, was established and funded by an Englishwoman, Annie Horniman from London.

There is no native theatrical tradition in Ireland. When I was at university I tried, in a woefully under-researched essay, to prove that the contemporary Irish-language theatre I was involved in had roots in the ancient native tradition of bardic poetry which may or may not have been composed for public recital with musical accompaniment by professional performers. I'm not sure if I imagined that establishing a connection would justify my habit of bunking off tutorials to hitch to drama festivals. Anyway, I convinced no one, not even myself. Ireland's theatrical tradition actually began with the arrival of productions from England in the seventeenth century. But by the middle of the eighteenth century Dubliners had become avid theatre fans, and Irish playwrights and performers were being applauded in fashionable London. There were strong links between theatre and politics in Britain during the eighteenth century and, as it happened, Richard Brinsley Sheridan, one of London's most successful playwrights and theatre managers, was both an Irishman and a politician. So the idea that theatre could be a forum for political debate was already well established in Ireland by the time that Revivalist playwrights like Yeats began dramatising their vision of a new nation reborn from a half-forgotten past. In the years before 1916, the Celtic Revivalists also produced plays and pageants in Irish, and the Gaelic League's language classes were remarkably successful. However, many of the Irish National Literary Society's members, including Yeats himself, could neither speak nor read Irish. That fact made them and their work no less Irish in the eyes of the nationalist revivalists of Marion's generation. Sixty years or so later, by the

time I began working in Irish-language theatre, there had been a
cultural sea change.

I remember a night in the Damer Theatre in Dublin in the
1970s. The theatre was housed in the basement of the Unitarian
Church on St Stephen's Green, in the heart of the city, and had
been set up in the 1950s to produce professional and amateur
plays in the Irish language under the auspices of a non-political
cultural organisation called Gael Linn. Damer shows were
produced on shoestring budgets so everyone's latent skills
and talents tended to get pressed into service, whatever their
actual job description might be. I can't recall what play was in
rehearsal but I do remember that the designer had worked
late into the evening to get the set right and that I was among
a group of volunteers who had stayed to help him paint it. He
was an Irishman who had spent much of his career in theatres
in England, where he had picked up an English accent. And,
as it happened, he had no Irish. I daresay his main reason for
doing shows at the Damer was that work was hard to come by
in Dublin so he took whatever was going. But it was evident
that he also enjoyed the enthusiasm that characterised the
Damer's shoestring productions. Whatever his reasons, we were
lucky to get him; he was a professional with years of practical
experience, and a generous teacher, happy to pass on his skills.
The fact that he found most of the conversation that went on
around him incomprehensible didn't bother him and the rest of
us shifted from Irish to English and back again when necessary,
often without consciously registering which language we were
speaking at any given moment.

That evening we kept going till the job was done, so it was
late when we scrubbed the paint off our hands under a cold tap,
turned out the lights, shut the door, and decided that a pint was
in order. Around the corner was a club which we referred to in
English as the Conradh Club because it was run by the Gaelic
League, which in Irish is called Conradh na Gaeilge. At that time
of night it was likely to be less crowded than a pub so, as we often

did, we went there for a drink. When we arrived, the others who
were with us went to the bar while the designer and I looked for
a table. Eventually we found one, claimed the necessary number
of chairs by piling bags and coats on them, and sat down to wait
for our drinks. Everyone around us was speaking Irish. Our own
conversation was in English and we were chatting quietly about the
work we had just completed when I realised that a man at a nearby
corner table was staring at us. As soon as he saw that I'd noticed
him he got up, came over, planted his hands on the table top and,
looking straight into my eyes said, in Irish, 'watch your language'.
Then he turned to the designer, pointed a finger at him and, once
again in Irish, said: 'Irish is the language spoken here.' Beyond the
man's shoulder I could see a group of his friends at the corner table
watching him approvingly. The designer hadn't understood what
was said but he got the message. I was so taken aback that I said
and did nothing. Then, as the man turned away and strode back
to his friends, our companions arrived with the drinks. Once they
sat down the majority of the conversation round our table was in
Irish, but as soon as I got my head around what had happened
I continued to speak loudly in English. The designer, who was a
lot older than I, kept his eye on the table in the corner and, at one
point, told me gently to keep my voice down.

That idiocy, the inevitable result of defining being Irish as
not being English, has roots that reach back to an annual general
meeting of the Gaelic League in 1915, when a group of members
who were also members of the IRB pushed through a motion
committing the League to a political agenda. Hyde resigned
immediately on the principle that language should be above
politics. MacNeill, then unaware of the IRB's policy of infiltration
and manipulation, reluctantly took over as president of the
League, and from that point onwards increasing politicisation
of Ireland's native culture led to increasing levels of chauvinism
which reached their zenith in the isolationist years after the
Second World War. So, while most people in Gaeltacht areas
continued to speak Irish simply because that was the language

they spoke, by the time I was growing up, much of English-speaking Ireland identified the Irish language with de Valera's personal vision of Irishness which had become overtly linked to his political agenda. One bizarre outcome of this process was that my generation of Irish schoolchildren came to hate an elderly woman called Peig Sayers with a passion so intense that it still sizzles today in Internet chat rooms.

Corca Dhuibhne's mountain spine dips into the Atlantic Ocean at its western end, and rises again as a group of six offshore islands, called the Blaskets. Peig Sayers was one of the many women from the villages west of Dingle town who married men from the largest of the islands, called the Great Blasket, and went to live there. Hardly two square miles in area, the Great Blasket's name in Irish is An Blascaoid Mór; locally it's called An tOileán, which just means 'the island'. The form of words used in Irish to describe travelling to the island translates as 'going into' it which, by chance, reflects the semi-mystical quality it acquired in Ireland's national cultural consciousness in the first half of the twentieth century. Although life there was actually very similar to life in the mainland villages, the extreme physical beauty of the island's position, combined with the perceived cultural and spiritual purity of its isolated community, made it a lodestone both for Gaelic Revivalists and scholars specialising in Celtic Studies. Among those who visited were Irish, Danish, German and British writers whose interest in the language led to warm friendships with the families with whom they stayed, and those friendships led to a canon of books written or dictated in Irish by members of the island community, including Peig Sayers. As part of the huge body of material collected over the years by Irish folklorists, the Blasket Island books are fascinating, not least because their authors, who belonged to a dying community, were aware of the irony and complexity of a situation in which their duty to their oral culture demanded that they turn to writing. But as a schoolbook for teenagers, Peig's memoir, drearily subtitled 'An Old Woman's Reflections', was a disaster.

It was a compulsory part of my generation's education, remained required reading in Irish schools until the 1990s, and probably did more than anything else to undermine what the founders of the Gaelic League had tried to achieve.

I am not sure how I managed to emerge from my schooldays with a love of the Irish language. I suspect that initially it was just that I liked the look of it when it was written down. Mine was the last generation of Irish schoolchildren that learned to read and write Irish in the flowing script derived from medieval manuscripts. We only used it briefly. When I was about six or seven, a new, official version of the language was rolled out through the education system, with the aim of making it easier to teach and to print. It involved a sudden changeover to new, standardised grammar and spelling, and to the Latin script which up to then we had only used when writing English. I found the process confusing and as a consequence I am unable to spell accurately in either language today. But the memory of the enchanting shapes I had encountered in my first school copybooks must have had its effect, because I survived the upheaval and continued to enjoy my Irish lessons. That, however, might just have been luck. Most Irish schools at the time were run by one of the religious orders which fused a particularly joyless, authoritarian form of Catholicism with de Valera's isolationist ideal of an Ireland in which cultural and moral purity was preserved by rural poverty. My siblings were all taught by priests and nuns. I, as it happened, was not.

If you trawl Internet chat rooms for references to Peig Sayers today, most search engines turn up negative memories of the experience of learning Irish in general, and of her book in particular. What interests me is how many people remember her as 'whingeing', 'whining' and 'miserable'. Her reminiscences – significantly edited in the book that made it to our schoolrooms – do in fact begin and end with reflections on death which, considering she dictated them in old age to her only surviving son, is not surprising. But the majority of her story – though it describes a lifestyle that had little in common with the experience of most mid-twentieth-century Irish teenagers – is not miserable. And while the book has none of the erotic comedy, grotesque exaggeration and irreverent irony which belongs to the native Irish tradition of storytelling and in which, according to local people, Peig actually delighted, it offers a window on a world in which neither rural poverty nor a sense of spirituality implies lack of sophistication. The opening chapter in which she describes her own first day at school offers a wonderfully assured verse composed by one of her neighbours about the village schoolmistress. '*He who would view this filly-foal / strolling beneath her parasol; / Beads of gold in her ear-lobes, ringing like the bells of Rome; / Saffron silks on her shoulders, her cheeks like the bloom of roses; / Fairer than Niamh the Beautiful at the death of Talc Mac Trone.*' The life Peig Sayers was eager to describe is hard, but her language is robust, the surroundings she describes are beautiful, and the communities she depicts are characterised by warm-hearted spontaneity. But somehow, preceded by a pious foreword by her son and presented as the apotheosis of an Irishness that most of us found alien, her book produced exactly the opposite effect to the one that she intended. I didn't hate it when I read it myself as a teenager. But the truth is that I didn't begin to understand it until I came to Corca Dhuibhne. And in the years that have followed that first starlit night, I've come to recognise that while, on the one hand, my neighbours here speak Irish simply as a practical means of communication, a sense of duty towards the language and the culture it preserves is part of their sense of identity.

A few miles from Peig Sayers' birthplace in Baile Bhiocáire near Dún Chaoin, the last village at the western end of the Dingle Peninsula, is the house where Wilf and I live. We found it after months of searching: a long, low building with a slate roof, set low in the landscape in the foothills of the last mountain on the peninsula. It was built a year or so before 1916 under a scheme run by the Congested Districts Board, which was tasked with improving housing conditions and alleviating poverty in the west of Ireland at the turn of the twentieth century, part of a policy referred to in Westminster as 'killing Home Rule with kindness'. So, while Marion and her colleagues in Cumann na mBan were drilling in the fields outside Enniscorthy, here in Corca Dhuibhne local men working under a foreman appointed by the government she planned to overthrow were raising the fieldstone walls that shelter me now as I sit here writing this book.

My neighbours remember the story of this house. As soon as it was built, a young woman called Neillí Mhuiris Ní Chonchubhair and her widowed mother were relocated to it from a thatched cabin farther down the hill. Like everyone else born in the area, then as now, their first language was Irish. Neillí's mother, who had no English, could read but not write Irish. Neillí could speak, read and write in both languages; the standardisation I struggled with in my own schooldays had yet to be introduced, so when learning to write she had mastered two different scripts. It appears that she was the scholar in the family because, when the 1911 Census was taken in Britain and Ireland, it was she who entered her family's information on the form. Douglas Hyde, then a professor in Dublin, chose to fill in his census form in Irish, consciously making a cultural and intellectual statement about his personal sense of identity. In a mud cabin in Corca Dhuibhne, Neillí Mhuiris Ní Chonchubhair chose to make the same statement, completing her form in script as beautiful as the lettering in a medieval manuscript. In her case the sense of identity she affirmed had been inherited, rather than rediscovered, and was deeply rooted in a sense of place.

In 1914 the British government's decision to shelve the introduction of Home Rule for the duration of the First World War added to the tension in Ireland. During the hiatus, party political horse-trading continued in Westminster where the balance of power between Britain's Conservative and Liberal parties often hung on the floating votes of unionist and nationalist Irish MPs. In Europe millions died in the mud and blood of the trenches. In Ireland the IRB systematically infiltrated the nationalist movement. Rightly or wrongly, Marion and many of her contemporaries came to the view that the political process couldn't be trusted. The rest, literally, is history. After the 1916 Rising and the War of Independence and the Civil War that followed it, the Irish Free State was established in 1922. Six, largely unionist, counties in the north of the country immediately seceded from it, exercising their right under the agreement by which it was set up. The result was the partition of Ireland which continues to this day.

When I was growing up, echoes of that decision-making still rumbled, so it is true to say that I encountered the same kinds of passionate arguments that may have troubled my Enniscorthy grandmother. But it is also true that in my childhood and teens most people in the Republic were content to know that we were beginning to emerge from years of isolationism and to share in post-Second World War regeneration. Partition, to a large extent, had become part of the status quo. Then, at the beginning of the 1970s, a civil rights movement began to be active in Northern Ireland. I remember marches, protests and speeches reported in the newspapers and on television (which had, by then, arrived to stay in our house). I remember the first time I heard the word 'gerrymandering' in student debates. The unrest in the north provided an opportunity for an IRA separatist campaign there, and the rights and wrongs of partition began to be discussed in a new context. Then, in January 1972, a civil rights march in Northern Ireland ended in the massacre of civilian marchers and bystanders by the British army, which ostensibly was there to keep the peace. Four days after that event, which became known as Bloody Sunday, an official day of mourning was declared by the Irish government and there were organised protests all over the country. Looking back now, I know that I was present at a recognisable turning point in history. All I saw at the time was how it affected myself.

I hadn't planned to walk the several miles from University College Dublin to the British embassy waving a placard, but the events of Bloody Sunday had whipped up such outrage that the entire campus was seething. At the age of eighteen, I was unaware of the emotional and political complexities that Marion's generation had wrestled with, and my combined obsession with the theatre and distaste for the politicisation of culture had left me pretty ignorant of contemporary politics as well. So, as far as I can remember, I marched that day, in platform clogs and a maxi dress, mainly so as not to be left out. I remember that it was raining. If you wear a maxi dress in the rain, no matter how high your platforms are, you eventually get rising damp. We marched into town past banks, shops and hotels that were all shut because it was a day of mourning. As we got closer to the embassy, the crowds got bigger. Our column of student marchers combined with other definable groups – trade unionists, civil rights organisations, a band playing the Dead March led by men carrying coffins draped in black. I remember displays of anger and grief, but the main sensation, as I recall it, was excitement. An estimated figure of between 20,000 and 30,000 people converged on Merrion Square where the embassy was housed in an elegant Georgian terrace. Those of us who could crowded into the roadway and onto the pavements between the square's railed gardens and the terraced houses that faced them. The crowds kept arriving behind us, funnelling into the square from the main street along which we had marched.

As more and more people forced their way into the road outside the embassy, a friend and I managed to wriggle our way to the railings surrounding the square's central gardens. Each upright bar, set in a low stone plinth, was topped with a point like a spearhead. So, having reached the railings we weren't going to get past them. The mass of people jammed into the space in front of us was now unable to move. My face was pressed between the shoulder blades of the person in front of me, and the stone plinth was cutting into the backs of my calves. There was no room to turn round properly but, hitching up my damp skirt, I reached back to grasp an iron rail, wriggled sideways, got one foot on the plinth, and pulled myself up to stand on it. Then I realised that my platform clog was immovably wedged between the lower bar of the railings and the plinth. At that moment a tide of new people tried to force its way into the square. My friend scrambled up beside me. The crowd in front of us swayed. For a moment I thought my ankle would be broken as the combined weight of hundreds of jam-packed bodies swung me sideways with my foot still stuck in the clog. Then I managed to wrench free and reposition myself. Now, with each foot uncomfortably jammed in a narrow space between two rails, I was facing the gardens and away from the embassy. But the extra height made me feel safer and, by twisting my upper body and hanging onto the railing with one hand, I could see over the heads of the crowd. And there I saw how easily one group can be infiltrated by another, and how efficiently the weight of a mass movement can be used to the advantage of a smaller one.

Emerging from a street at the corner of the square, a file of figures jostled its way through the crowd, fanning out to positions at intervals in front of the embassy. I was aware of them mainly because of the purposeful way they moved. Across the road on the crowded steps of the terraced buildings, voices began to chant nationalist slogans. On the march the sense of excitement had seemed to be fuelled by a sense of pride in our shared determination to demonstrate our outrage. No one had shouted 'Brits Out' or 'Burn the Embassy'. We were angered by what had happened and we blamed the British army, but I don't believe that the majority of the 30,000 people who joined that Dublin march did to so protest about partition. Yet, as I watched, the shouting grew louder, and the mood of the crowd changed. There was a crash of breaking glass and a spurt of flame from a petrol bomb. Members of the Garda Síochána, the Irish police force, who until then had just preserved a presence, began to move forward. The individuals who had fanned out through the

crowd began to push to the front of it. Hindsight makes me want
to dress them in black berets and balaclavas. Maybe they were
just muffled up against the rain. But they certainly came armed
with petrol bombs and when they pushed their way to the front
of the crowd they acted as a unit. Inflamed by their actions, the
crowd was turning into a mob.

That was enough for me and my friend. I don't remember
how we got down from our vantage point or how we got out of
the square. What I recall is the swelling sound of the violence
behind us as we walked away. Within a few blocks of the square
you could hardly hear it. Shops, banks and hotels may have been
closed for the day of mourning but ordinary life still went on.
The only indication of what was happening less than half a mile
behind us was the distant sound of approaching sirens. We didn't
talk much. I think we were both shocked. By the time I got home
my parents were watching the scene in Merrion Square on the
evening news, and the chanting crowd on the screen was dancing
by the light of the flames from the burning embassy.

At some point when I was growing up I seem to have
absorbed my father's hatred of the Irish kilt, an anomaly invented
by Patrick Pearse, the most iconic leader of the 1916 Rising,
whose personal image of Irishness dominated the cultural
landscape of my childhood. When I was a teenager Pearse's kilt
seemed to me to symbolise everything that was naff about Irish
design. I suspect that to my father it symbolised the triumph of
the cult of personality over the evidence of history. In the 1970s
that cult seemed on the verge of being toppled, and it might have
been interesting to see what would happen once it was gone.
But two things made me decide there was no point in staying
in Ireland to find out: various versions of that experience I'd had
at the Conradh Club, and the burning of the British Embassy.
What happened on that march wasn't cataclysmic; a beautiful
Georgian building was destroyed but the Garda response was
moderate, no one in the crowd was injured, and the embassy
staff got out long before the first petrol bombs were thrown.

What might have happened is a different matter. While I was trying to wrench my platform clog from between the plinth and the railings, a ministerial meeting taking place in a building a few blocks away was deciding how to respond to a demand from the British government that the Irish army be called out to defend the embassy. The chief of staff of Ireland's defence forces informed the minister that his troops could save the building but that they must be authorised to use live ammunition in their own defence and that of the unarmed Gardaí. In the end, despite pressure from Britain, the Irish government decided that taking action likely to precipitate armed conflict would be playing into the hands of the IRA. The result, it was thought, might be the precipitation of a new civil war, this time fought on both sides of the border. History turns on such decisions and on the judgement of those who make them.

The Damer Theatre had a wonderful smell. It was a combination of church hall, cigarette smoke and the fine clouds of dust that rose from the knackered tip-up seats if you happened to sit on one suddenly. In the background there was always the greasy smell of Leichner 'Five and Nine' makeup, and a hint of bacon and cabbage from the caretaker's flat, which was accessed from a backstage corridor. In the years since the theatre's inception it had produced a significant body of new work in the Irish language, including Brendan Behan's play *The Hostage* which had its premiere there in 1957 as *An Giall*. The stage saw its fair share of spears, sheepskins and súgán chairs, but it also saw plays that explored contemporary themes in settings other than cottage interiors or the High King of Ireland's banqueting hall. In my own brief time there I played in an adaptation of Rabelais' *Gargantua et Pantagruel*, translations of one-act plays by Chekhov, and pantomimes full of contemporary political satire. It seemed then that the Damer might go on to provide Dublin with a viable, professional Irish-language theatre company, genuinely reflective of contemporary life. I had colleagues at university who believed that it would and, thinking that I might

be part of it, I wondered if they were right. But 1972 proved to
be the beginning of the prolonged period of brutal violence, now
known as The Troubles, which ended with the IRA ceasefire of
1994 and the Good Friday Agreement of 1998. None of us could
have known that at the time. What I knew was that, with the
upsurge of new militant nationalist feeling, speaking Irish had
begun to reveal connotations which I found disturbing.

Along with those connotations came arguments about what
was or wasn't *fíor Gaelach*, stupid late-night wrangles which I
always wanted to avoid but seldom managed to stay out of. *Fíor
Gaelach* means genuinely or truly Irish. Applying it to a work of
art or literature, or to intellectual discussion, implies an accepted
set of values, a process for formulating them, and an accepted
system for their ongoing re-evaluation. Achieving even one of
those conditions is a non-starter in a free society. Who defines
the criteria that define true Irishness? What happens to those who
don't accept them? But by then the idea that the Irish language
was a holy vehicle, suitable only for the communication of specific
subject matter and sentiments, had become ingrained in the
minds and policies of much of the country's cultural establishment
and provided a seed bed for the belief that separatist nationalist
activists had a monopoly on the use of it. Both ideas would have
been anathema to the Gaelic League's founders, and most native
speakers, then and now, would simply find them daft.

And so, for those reasons and half a dozen others, less
portentous but equally important to me at the time, I went to
London, trained as an actor, began to become a writer, met Wilf
and got married. Forty years or so later, the dynamic between
Ireland's oral Irish-language culture and its written English-
language inheritance still seems to me to contain the greatest
potential for creative exploration of who I think I am. And
our life balanced between London and the western end of the
peninsula now seems to me to be the best expression of who I
have become. In each place I am a 'blow-in', someone who has
arrived from elsewhere; and no one I have encountered either

in London, the city of immigrants, or Corca Dhuibhne, where almost everyone has been an emigrant, has seemed bothered or threatened by that. For me, being a blow-in and being able to consider the world in two languages and in terms of two different cultural inheritances offers endless opportunities for growth. By the time Wilf and I found the house in Corca Dhuibhne I had spent more than half my life in London and come to terms with my relationship with the Irish language, though I had lost much of the fluency I had once had in it. On various visits to the area over the years Wilf, who is an opera director, had fallen in love with the area's physical beauty and became interested in Irish traditional music. He hasn't learnt the language yet but he has learned to play the concertina, and the differences and similarities between the classical music he grew up with and Corca Dhuibhne's native musical tradition produce endless food for exploration and argument. Sometimes, when I sit listening in a pub or beside someone's fire, I realise that, without anyone noticing, the conversation is moving between English and Irish, with the musical instruments providing illustration and translation across the meeting of minds.

I was a child myself when my mother told me that she and Cathleen and Evie had been born in a house in a place called Washerwoman's Hill. As I began to write this book, I wondered if perhaps I had remembered the name wrongly. But, remembering that she had also told me how she and her sisters had played in the Botanic Gardens, I Googled 'Dublin', 'Botanic Gardens' and 'Washerwoman's Hill.' I didn't find a street name but I found a pin on a Google Map on TripAdvisor marking Washerwoman's Hill Restaurant on Glasnevin Hill. Beside it was the wide, green expanse of the National Botanic Gardens. So I rang the number and, as it happened, the woman in the restaurant who picked up the phone was a local who lived just round the corner. She couldn't remember a time before the new name appeared on the street signs. But she knew that the old people in the area still use the name Washerwoman's Hill.

5
Secret Stitching

MY FATHER'S NAME WAS Gerard Anthony Hayes McCoy. He was born on 15 August 1911 in a house in Eyre Square, Galway, on the west coast of Ireland. Galway, which in Irish is pronounced Galliv, takes its name from a twelfth-century fort built by a local king at the mouth of the River Corrib. A hundred years after the fort was built, the settlement that grew up around it had become a compact walled city. It was colonised during the Norman invasion and in time became dominated by a group of Hiberno-Norman merchant families who developed it as a trading centre with links throughout Europe and beyond. By the fourteenth century the city was Ireland's principal port for trade with France and Spain. The merchant families who controlled it, then and for a long time afterwards, ensured that the native Irish in the countryside beyond its walls kept their place and kept their distance.

I have few childhood memories of my father's home city. After my parents married and settled in Dublin his parents and his sister Marguerite remained in Galway but by the time I was born both my grandfather and Marguerite had died and my grandmother was living in Dublin with us. She herself died only a few years later. I remember her as a restless, resentful presence in the house and a spellbinding storyteller on whose bed I used to sit for hours while she talked and sang to me and I combed her hair. I have no memory of her speaking Irish, but I believe that she may have grown up in an Irish-speaking household. And I think that the rhythms of her speech and her songs and folktales were what laid the foundation for my own love of folklore and of the language.

Most of what I know about my father's youth was told to me by my mother, and much of it may have been coloured by the difficult relationship she had with her mother-in-law. It was hard for my grandmother, having lost her husband and her only daughter, to lose her home in Galway but there was no help for it since she couldn't, or perhaps wouldn't, live alone. I don't know what family discussions took place before she came to live with us in Dublin in the mid-1950s, but I know that as soon as she arrived in the house she took to her bed and refused to get up again. The only time I remember her on her feet was the occasion when, bitterly angry at some perceived slight, she rose up, dressed herself and, putting on her hat and coat, went and sat on the wall by the front gate, demanding to be taken home. Since she knew perfectly well that her house in Galway had been sold, the gesture was both pathetic and infuriating. And, since much of her time in our house was spent pretending not to know who my mother was, I imagine that the task of coaxing her back indoors that day must have fallen to my father.

My grandmother doted on my father, apparently to the extent that, when he was growing up, she frequently took him for picnics by the river instead of sending him to school. This was partly because her firstborn, Ignatius, had died at the age of eight, when my father was just six months old. She kept a photo of Ignatius, known as Nacie, by her bedside in our house in Dublin. It shows him kneeling by a crucifix with his hands joined and his eyes cast up to heaven, wearing a tunic and short trousers, like a sailor suit, with a neckerchief and a broad leather belt. Despite his suitably pious expression, he gives the impression that he is rather enjoying the drama of his setting. Judging by his age in the photograph, it must have been taken shortly before he died

Nacie's death was said to be my grandmother's great tragedy, not just because she lost him so young but because, after he died, all the doses of medicine he was supposed to have been given during his illness were found on the shelf of a mantelpiece behind the headboard of his bed. According to the family story, my grandmother had allowed him to order her out of the room so that he could take the medicine himself 'like a big boy'. This seems highly unlikely but it may be true. If it was, the discovery must have tortured her; though it's doubtful that the medicine, which apparently was a cough syrup, would have saved Nacie's life. I was told that he died of diphtheria – either an accurate statement or a euphemism for the tuberculosis which still carried a stigma in Ireland in my own generation. I can't remember when my mother told me about Nacie's death but I know that the story came with an unspoken sense of disapproval of my grandmother: I'm not sure if she was being dismissed as a drama queen who had invented the medicine story or a besotted mother who had allowed an eight-year-old to dictate to her about something so vital. One way or the other, my mother clearly felt that her own mother, my Enniscorthy grandmother, would have had more sense.

Nacie died in 1912, two years before the Volunteers and Cumann na mBan were established in Galway. My grandfather had inherited his father's hairdressing business but by then the shop was run by a manager, and my grandfather spent much of his time reading books upstairs in the rooms occupied by the family. The square was originally a medieval marketplace in front of one of Galway's gates, and in the early eighteenth century the land that it consisted of was formally presented to the city by Mayor Edward Eyre. By then it had been planted with ash trees and enclosed by a wooden fence which was later replaced by a stone wall and, later still, by cast-iron railings. But despite the various stages of gentrification, the space between the railings and the row of houses which included my grandfather's Hairdressing Rooms continued to be used as a cattle market. My grandmother disliked the noise and the smell and the presence on her doorstep of men from the country spitting on their hands and striking bargains. She had married into the city from the countryside herself and perhaps didn't want to be reminded of it. She certainly saw herself as a step above the barefoot shawlie women who walked miles to market carrying fish or vegetables in baskets on their heads.

My mother was fond of my Galway grandfather. He came on occasional visits to Dublin when my parents were first married and once, she told me, he mended a wireless for her. It seems that he was a quiet presence in the Eyre Square household while my grandmother ruled the roost. I don't know where either of my father's parents stood on the Home Rule question. Perhaps they didn't discuss politics. My grandfather grew up in a family that had supported the Land League, the nineteenth-century political movement dedicated to breaking up the estates held by Anglo-Irish landlords, such as the Gore-Booths at Lissadell, and restoring the land to the native tenant farmers. My grandmother, on the other hand, was the daughter of a British army pensioner who worked on a landed estate as a gatekeeper. Memories of what was known as the Land War were still raw so I imagine that families like my father's didn't discuss it. I have no idea where either of my paternal grandparents stood on women's suffrage either, though I suspect that if my Galway grandmother had had the vote she would have guarded it jealously. What I do know is that, while her own father was unable to write, my grandmother was literate from childhood, worked in her youth as a seamstress, and encouraged her only daughter to graduate from university with degrees in both Arts and Law, and a PhD.

In the summer of 1914, branches of both the Volunteers and Cumann na mBan were established in Galway, and Eoin MacNeill, Roger Casement and Patrick Pearse visited the city to address meetings. When the organisations' membership was polled in September that year, the vote was equally split between those who backed MacNeill and those who accepted Redmond's policy of supporting the British in the trenches. At least, that was the paper result: in fact there was little public support for militant nationalism in Galway city so, there at least, the Redmondites effectively came out on top. Nationalist feeling in the west of Ireland was strongest in the countryside. This was because rural poverty had been perpetuated by a system that allowed landlords to raise rents if tenant farmers improved their holdings, and to evict families and tear down houses when rents couldn't be paid. Photos of those evictions, black-and-white shots of battering rams guarded by armed policemen and pitiful family groups crouched by the roadside with their few sticks of furniture, featured prominently in the history books of my childhood.

As the IRB's secret plans for a nationwide rising continued to escalate without MacNeill's knowledge, organisers, including James Connolly's 22-year-old daughter, Nora, were sent from Dublin to Galway to mobilise the Volunteer and Cumann na mBan members who had rejected Redmond. Many of those they made contact with had recent memories of the Land War and of the Land League, which had been founded on the west coast. Maud Gonne, an IRB activist, had a track record in campaigning against rural evictions and organising aid for evicted families. Gonne was the founder of Inghinidhe na hÉireann, a separatist women's organisation which predated Cumann na mBan and had recently been amalgamated with it. The link between her work in rural communities and the Land League's work less than twenty years earlier was a significant factor in encouraging Cumann na mBan membership in the west.

Pretty much the sum total of what I learned about Maude Gonne in my schooldays was that she had blighted the life of the poet W. B. Yeats. Like Constance Markievicz and the other female activists of her time, she was relegated to brief paragraphs in our schoolbooks, and the fact that Inghinidhe na hÉireann translates as 'The Daughters of Ireland' made her seem fairly cringeworthy to 1970s teenagers. So there was little to spark our interest. Maud Gonne's role as the poet's muse came up in discussions of English literature but in history lessons she was generally dismissed as a noisy self-publicist who hung round the fringes of the 1916 Rising, making a bit of an ass of herself.

This image, projected in some of Yeats' most powerful poetry, ignores so many facts that the memory of how it was sold to us still infuriates me.

Maude Gonne was born in England in 1866 and died in Roebuck House in Dublin in 1953, the year before I was born. Her house was up the road from the newly built semi that my parents moved into when my grandmother came to live with us. The area, then on the outer fringe of the city, was rapidly being developed, and Roebuck House, which had originally stood in open fields, was soon demolished to make way for new housing. But I remember it from my childhood, and the fact that Sadie, who came in once a week to help my mother scrub our kitchen floor and clean the oven, had worked there at some point and told voluble stores about Gonne, whom she always called 'Madam'. I remember too that our next-door neighbour ran the auction at which the contents of Roebuck House were eventually sold, and that my mother came home from it with a wonderful set of faded red velvet curtains. Yet I never connected Sadie's stories of Madam MacBride with Maud Gonne, the poet's muse. No one told me that Roebuck House had at one point been shared by Maud Gonne and Charlotte Despard, an English Communist and feminist activist whose embarrassed brother was, at the time, the British Viceroy in Ireland. Nor did I know that Despard, who served time in prison for feminist activism in Britain, had first come to Ireland at James Connolly's invitation on behalf of the Irish Socialist Republican Party, and had subsequently joined Sinn Féin.

My ignorance was probably due to the fact that, from the point of view of the establishment, Maud Gonne was mad, bad and fairly dangerous to know. According to her autobiography, her father's family originally came from Mayo but her great-great grandfather was disinherited and went abroad to trade in Spanish wine. Her mother, who was Irish, died young and Maud was sent to school in France. Her father, she says, was educated to inherit the wine business. Instead, he became a British army officer and, when Maud was sixteen, he was posted to Dublin where she went to live with him. After his death a few years later, Gonne returned to France and began a love affair with a married, anti-Semitic, right-wing politician with whom she became active in French and Irish nationalist organisations. This politicisation eventually led to her involvement with the IRB. She and her lover had two children, one of whom died in infancy, the second of whom, she said, was conceived in a mystic attempt to reincarnate the first. The dead child was a boy. Gonne raised her surviving child, Iseult, without help from her lover, often passing her off as her niece to avoid the stigma of illegitimacy.

Gonne met W. B. Yeats when she was twenty-three and still involved with her French lover. She and Yeats were both interested in the occult and he introduced her to the Golden Dawn, a quasi-Masonic magical order of which she became a member. Having proposed several times and been refused, he appears to have remained infatuated with her for the rest of his life despite his subsequent, apparently happy, marriage and her own, apparently abusive, one to John MacBride, a leader of the 1916 Rising. It is debatable whether Yeats was in love with Gonne or with the image he invented of her. Certainly he hated the idea that his muse was a political activist. In 1917, when it finally dawned on him that Maud wasn't going to marry him, he proposed to Iseult, then aged twenty-two, having first asked Maud's permission. Iseult didn't marry him either. Maud remained friendly towards Yeats throughout his life, announcing that the world owed her a debt for having broken his heart, since she'd provided inspiration for his poetry. Presumably she thought that the facts of her political career would counterbalance the vitriol with which he dismissed it: if she didn't, she must have had a surprising lack of concern for how she might be remembered.

Not a lot of Maud Gonne's story made its way into my schoolbooks. Nor did much about W. B. Yeats' interest in the occult. However, a general impression of Gonne as a vain, selfish woman given to striking poses did. Her political campaigning was hardly mentioned, while our sense of her cringeworthiness was reinforced by production photos of her in the title role in *Cathleen Ni Houlihan*, an agitprop play by Yeats which projected the image of Ireland as a female figure whose wrongs required blood sacrifice from her menfolk. That play was presented to us in history lessons as a landmark on the road to the Rising. Yet the fact that Maud Gonne performed in it, conflated with the fact that she made impassioned speeches about rural evictions, was used to dismiss her as a drama queen. Looking back now, I'm baffled by my own failure to see the double standard. Perhaps we were all so used to mixed messages that it didn't occur to us to question them.

Judging by photos and portraits of Gonne in her youth, she had an eye for fashion and, like Constance Markievicz, she could certainly strike a pose. At this remove it is impossible to tell if, or how much, she enjoyed dressing up and making speeches on stage. But in terms of her career as an activist, the question of whether she did or not is unimportant, except insofar as it may have made her a more effective communicator. And the idea of evaluating her political worth solely by the extent of her theoretical enjoyment of a position in the limelight is ridiculous. Yet both Gonne and Markievicz's work was dismissed on those grounds by many of their contemporaries, and in my generation's schooldays their contributions to the founding of the Irish state were trivialised on the same basis. There is no doubt that, if you fancied a quiet night in, Gonne might have been wearing company. But the same could probably be said of Robespierre or of Steve Biko, or many another male revolutionary. What my generation, and many women who came after us, failed to see was that dismissing female activists as self-dramatists is the oldest trick in the book. Sadly, it continues to be played today, and not just in Ireland. What is sadder still is that it continues to be effective.

By 1915 an IRB Military Council had been set up, tasked with planning a rising the following year. The council consisted of five men, including Patrick Pearse, all of whom continued to work with their colleagues in the other nationalist organisations without revealing their new role within the IRB. In Enniscorthy and across the rest of the country, Marion and her militant nationalist colleagues openly continued to drill in the fields and to stockpile arms. Meanwhile the authorities made sporadic arrests and broke up nationalist printing presses but failed otherwise to intervene effectively for fear of political backlash. In Dublin, Cathleen, Evie and May played in the Botanic Gardens while, within half a mile of their home on Washerwoman's Hill, guns and ammunition, conveyed in bread vans, on bikes and in babies' prams, were hidden in corner shops, sheds and private houses. And in poverty-stricken rural communities like Corca Dhuibhne and Connemara, the idea that independence from Britain would bring down the landlords continued to take root and grow.

The funeral of a veteran IRB man called O'Donovan Rossa provided another landmark on the road to 1916. Shortly after the failed rising of 1848, Rossa had been sworn into the IRB, colloquially known at the time as the Fenians. Some years later he took part in another attempted rising after which he and other ringleaders were imprisoned and subsequently forced into exile. Rossa died in America in 1915 and the IRB, spotting the propaganda value of an Irish funeral, arranged to have his body brought home. The coffin was conveyed to Dublin in a carefully staged progress, and a funeral procession, escorted by Volunteer, Citizen Army and Cumann na mBan members, marched through the city to Glasnevin Cemetery, beside the Botanic Gardens. There Patrick Pearse delivered a eulogy attacking the supporters of British government in Ireland. Fifty years later, my generation of schoolchildren learned that speech by heart. Well, actually, that's not true. We didn't learn all of it; just the peroration, which was calculated to be memorable and which those of us with a parrot's memory still can quote today. '*The Defenders of this Realm have worked well in secret and in the open. They think that they have purchased half of us and intimidated*

the other half. They think that they have foreseen everything,
think that they have provided against everything; but the fools,
the fools, the fools! – they have left us our Fenian dead, and,
while Ireland holds these graves, Ireland unfree shall never be at
peace.' It was a brilliant combination of theatre and propaganda,
produced and performed at a psychological moment in history.
Unquestionably, it affected the course of events that led up to
the Rising eight months later, and did much to establish Patrick
Pearse's reputation for posterity. I can't recall any teacher in my
childhood dismissing Pearse as a drama queen.

I had no adult relationship with my father, who died after a car
accident in the 1970s when I was still at university. I remember
him as charming and funny, a brilliant lecturer with an energetic
personality that resisted both humbug and compromise. I was
five years old when he became a professor of history in Galway
in the late 1950s. Up to that point he had worked in the National
Museum in Dublin. When he accepted the new post, my parents
decided that, since my older siblings were settled in school and
studying for various exams, the family would continue to live in
Dublin while my father commuted to Galway each week during
term time. I'm not sure how happy my mother was in her role as
part-time single mother but I'm sure she kept the best side out.
My father's departure on Tuesdays and return at the end of the
week became part of the rhythm of my childhood. I remember
him setting off with a bulging briefcase full of work to be done
on the train, and coming home with comics bought from the
station newsagent, *Bunty* and *Judy* for me and my sisters and
The Beano and *The Dandy* for my brothers. He was a dedicated
scholar and teacher and, along with his work on numerous
boards, institutions and committees, wrote books and articles,
radio plays and television scripts. But, despite his workload, I
spent a good deal of time in his company in the holidays and
at weekends, going for walks, listening to stories and talking
books. I remember insisting that, instead of holding my hand,
he linked me as he often linked my mother; since he was very

tall and I was small at the time, it wasn't particularly comfortable but it made me feel grown up. Frequently the subject matter of whatever he happened to be writing would find its way into our conversations, and often the second-hand books which he collected like a magpie would migrate from the table where he kept his current research material to the bookcases from which I chose my reading.

But that was when I was a child. By the time I was a stroppy student in the 1970s, his health was failing and he was worried and irritated by my tendency to bunk off lectures and take to the roads with spray-painted spears on my shoulder. He and my mother had sacrificed a lot to provide five children with university educations, and what he regarded as my lack of focus troubled him. At the same time, my mother's concern about his health expressed itself in an anxious determination not to permit him to be agitated. As a result, he and I hardly talked at all when I was a student. And by the time I gained my degree and had sense enough to converse without precipitating arguments, it was too late.

My father, who was known to his family as Gerry, was five years old in 1916, so perhaps he was too young to know what was happening beyond the doorstep of the house in Eyre Square. But perhaps not. I have clear childhood memories of the National Museum in Dublin where he worked before he became a professor in Galway. I remember sitting on the floor under his desk in a room that he shared with a colleague, drawing pictures of the skeletons I'd seen in the museum's display cases. Now I am ambivalent about exhumed burials in museums but then I was very fond of them and liked their bony fingers and the naked planes of their skulls. I remember porters who spoke Irish and smelled of tobacco, and being shown a Victorian doll's house with dark, heavy furniture and bed-curtains that frightened me. I don't know why I was occasionally in the museum during working hours: this was before I went to school, so perhaps my father had been pressed into service as a childminder because of some emergency at home. I remember walking with him from the museum in Kildare Street to Bewley's on Grafton Street, where we sat on bentwood chairs at a marble-topped table while he drank tea and I concentrated on not spilling my milk, which came in a glass on a saucer. One of the wonders of that day was that we shared a plate of Goldgrain biscuits brought on a tray by a waitress. Another was that my father reached under the seat of his bentwood chair and left his hat on a round shelf there which he said was designed for the purpose. It was the first time I became aware of a relationship between form and function: and I was delighted by it.

I can't have been more than five years old when I marvelled at the chair with the hat shelf. So perhaps my father was aware of the Rising as a five-year-old in Galway, or at least had a child's sense of the tensions leading up to it. I don't know because I never asked him. It's unlikely that my aunt Marguerite, who was twelve in 1916, was unaware of the turmoil outside the house in Eyre Square that Easter; but she was dead by the time I was born, and my mother, my principal source of stories of my father's family, seldom mentioned her. In fact, I have no stories at all about Marguerite's childhood. And practically the only thing that my father told me about his was that he owned a plush monkey called Benjy.

I don't think that my father and I ever had a serious conversation about politics, though I do remember him announcing that no party, however enlightened its policies, should be allowed to hold power for extended consecutive periods. Knowing what I know now about the period he lived through, I wish I had had the opportunity to discuss it with him. Instead, alongside his published and unpublished work, I've inherited a ragbag of memories interrupted by his early death and coloured by my mother's narrative. It is a nuanced legacy which reveals as much in silence as in story.

When Wilf and I drove back across the country from the event in Enniscorthy Castle we crossed the county border into

Kerry around sunset. The landscape changes as you cross Ireland from the east coast to the west. The houses and field patterns are subtly different from one county to the next and, as you drive down the Dingle Peninsula, the daylight hours lengthen. In places where EU money has run out or was never applied for, the rural Irish roads are as narrow and twisted now as I remember them forty years ago when I toured shows to village halls in the Gaeltacht. In other places the broad highways that cut through the valleys and mountains are desolate as deserts. Outside the tourist season you can drive for miles without passing another car.

It was about six miles from Tralee, at the entrance to the Dingle Peninsula, that the plans for a nationwide 1916 Rising were scuppered. By this stage, James Connolly had become a member of the IRB Military Council. No one knows how he felt about watering down his aspirations for a socialist republic by throwing in his lot with the IRB, but presumably he had decided that if a rising was going to happen it was vital that the Citizen Army be a part of it, and influential in the changes that would follow. The shipment facilitated by the Belgian dealer was not sufficient to arm the Volunteers and the Citizen Army, many of whom continued to drill with wooden guns and hurleys, so the military council of the IRB made direct contact with the German government. The plan – itself the cause of internal IRB controversy – was to buy arms and to recruit Irishmen from the British army prisoners of war there to support a rising in Ireland. The attempt to raise an Irish Brigade from the German POW camps proved to be a damp squib, but the Kaiser saw the value of what, in terms of the First World War, amounted to an attack on Britain's rear, so a ship called the *Aud* was dispatched to Tralee Bay with a cargo of 20,000 rifles. Roger Casement, who had been one of the IRB's negotiators, returned to Ireland separately in a German submarine. He was to rendezvous with the *Aud,* and the arms were to be landed on the Kerry coast at a remote location called Fenit, which translates from Irish as 'The Wild Place'.

In Dublin, using a leaked document which had been sexed up to make it look as if danger was imminent, the IRB convinced MacNeill that the British authorities had immediate plans for mass arrests of Volunteers. They also informed him of the arrival of the *Aud*. Taken together, the two statements convinced MacNeill that a rising was both necessary and practicable. But, within hours, the IRB heard that Casement had been arrested and that the *Aud*, captured by the British before the guns could be landed, had been scuttled by her German captain. They concealed the bad news from MacNeill and decided to press on with their plans.

After that things happened quickly. The chosen date was Easter Sunday. In keeping with the quasi-religious nature of the propaganda that led up to the Rising, the intention was to link the idea of the resurrection of Christ with the resurgence of an independent Ireland. In Dublin Pearse, Connolly, Markievicz and their colleagues began to implement the plans that for months had been hatched in secret. The leaders of Cumann na mBan were put on alert. Weapons, supplies and first-aid equipment were assembled at the Citizen Army headquarters in the Irish Transport and General Workers Union premises, Liberty Hall. So that his men would be poised to take action on command, MacNeill issued orders for Volunteer manoeuvres to take place throughout the country on Easter Sunday. Then, on Easter Saturday morning, he discovered that his closest colleagues had once again conspired to deceive him: Bulmer Hobson, a senior IRB member who had also been kept unaware of the Military Council's plans, managed to alert him before he himself was kidnapped on Pearse's orders and held at gunpoint to keep him quiet. Ironically, it was Hobson who had originally sworn Pearse into the IRB. Horrified, furious, and convinced that the Rising had no hope of success without the German rifles, MacNeill placed an advertisement in the Sunday papers and dispatched messengers around the country to countermand his order for manoeuvres.

But once again the Military Council decided to go ahead. The more pragmatic among them, like Connolly, hoped to hold out long enough to raise international awareness of their aims. Pearse, the most iconic of them in the years that followed, continued to take the view that blood sacrifice was valuable, in and of itself. Among the leaders of the Rising were individuals who believed that the Military Council's decision to go ahead was wrong, but felt they had no option but to stand with their comrades. They included the Director of Arms of the Volunteers, known as The O'Rahilly, who died in the Rising having spent the previous weekend desperately travelling around the country delivering MacNeill's order to prevent it. On Easter Monday, a day later than originally planned, the Rising began in Dublin, where it lasted till the following Sunday. About 1,000 insurgents mobilised in the city, among them about 100 women and girls. MacNeill's followers elsewhere in the country had been thrown into confusion by his last-minute attempt to avoid Volunteer involvement. In the end, despite gallant efforts by isolated local units and the seizure of a post office and police barracks to the north of Dublin, which was followed by a five-hour gun battle, the only significant mobilisation outside Dublin happened in Galway and Wexford.

None of this messiness makes for good memories, which explains why many of my generation grew up with the false belief that the Rising was conceived as a glorious, sacrificial gesture, and was intentionally confined to Dublin. In an era when wounds were still raw, the transmutation of a story of confusion, division and deception into a heroic myth may have been understandable, but the creation and promotion of the myth required the suppression of many other stories. Marion's was only one of them.

My mother had no childhood memories of the Rising and my aunt Cathleen who may have had, since she was older, didn't do girly chats any more than Marion did. I wish I had been old enough to talk to my Galway grandmother about what happened that Easter week because, whereas my mother's home on Washerwoman's Hill was several miles from the centre of Dublin, the house on Eyre Square was in the centre of Galway and, during the Rising, the square became a focal point. But, though my Galway grandmother saw out that week in the eye of the storm, perhaps she wouldn't have talked about it either. Galway city did not support the Rising; afterwards, when public opinion swung in favour of the defeated rebels, Galwegians faced recriminations and reprisals. Such memories strike deep and, though she was a great one for dramatic stories, they might have kept my grandmother silent. Yet what happened in Galway wasn't unique; in fact its story illustrates two characteristics that were typical of a picture that was repeated across the country. The first was lack of public support for the Rising. The second was the militants' inability to agree on what they were fighting for.

Unsurprisingly, as soon as news of the Rising in Dublin reached Galway, people panicked. In Dublin, public buildings had been seized and were under fire, shops and businesses were being looted and property commandeered. In the countryside around Galway groups of Volunteer and Cumann na mBan members, coordinated by the IRB mobilisers from Dublin, were organising attacks on British army patrols and on barracks. There seemed every likelihood that rebels would soon make for Galway city. Although pro-Redmond Volunteers gathered in force to support the authorities, the walls that had once protected the inhabitants were long gone. The Rising in Dublin had interrupted communications; telegraph lines had been cut and travel restricted so, as the week went on, no one knew for certain what was happening. As rumours flew and fighting continued in the countryside, Galway's shopkeepers and business people boarded up their premises and formed teams to help the urban district council erect barricades on the roads. To them, the Rising spelled anarchy.

Over the course of the next five days, crowds gathered round Eyre Square, anxious for news. The combination of concern for

friends and relatives in the countryside and fear of an attack
on the city was nerve wracking. A committee for public safety
was set up and civilians enrolled as special constables. Despite
his own family's nationalist leanings, my grandfather must have
been as anxious as anyone. He had a business in a prominent
position on the square and a wife and two children living over
it. With barricades on the roads, it wasn't possible to evacuate
his family and, besides, there was no way of knowing where they
might safely be taken. For that week Galwegians lived as if under
siege, though their homes, shops and businesses were actually
in no danger. The Volunteers who rose in the west in solidarity
with Dublin had little ammunition and only about fifty service
rifles between 500 or 600 men. Instead of attempting to take the
city, they fought a guerrilla action over five days, falling back to
new positions across the county between engagements. And,
whether through loyalty to the Crown or to Redmond, or as a
result of MacNeill's countermanding order, not everyone in the
countryside supported them either.

    And even among this small group of rebels there was
disagreement. The IRB mobilisers were in the business of
throwing out the British but, like the workers' movement in
Dublin, the militants in the west wanted more. As far as they
were concerned, they were fighting for an egalitarian system of
government which would enshrine the rights of small farmers
and agricultural labourers. At several points during the week,
officers fell out over whether or not livestock should be seized
from the large estates. Ultimately, the IRB's agenda prevailed but
the lack of coherence made for lack of discipline. Having grown
up in a family that worked for a landlord, my grandmother had
every reason to fear for her family's safety.

    The Botanic Gardens are about four miles from the General
Post Office in Dublin city centre where the headquarters of the
1916 Rising was established. As a postal worker, my mother's
father took a dim view of the rebels' choice and, according to
my mother, the fact that by the end of the week the building

was a burnt-out shell went a long way towards convincing him that whoever had planned the Rising was fundamentally irresponsible. Six buildings and several outposts were taken over in Dublin that Easter Monday. For the rest of the week, while the rebels held out and the British army tried to dislodge them, the flames and smoke in the city centre were visible for miles. The authorities blockaded the roads and proclaimed martial law but word spread quickly, and many Volunteers and Cumann na mBan members who had obeyed MacNeill's countermanding order for Easter Sunday made their way into town to join the Rising. In all, about 1,700 rose in Dublin. Initially, women were turned away by the commanding officers of some of the rebel garrisons. Many Cumann na mBan members quoted the Proclamation of the Republic, read out by Pearse at the outset of the Rising, and claimed their right to fight. Pearse and Connolly eventually circulated an order confirming the women's equal status. Some acted as couriers and first-aid workers, others as combatants. According to Cumann na mBan evidence, de Valera flatly refused to admit any women to the garrison he commanded.

I remember making the train journey from Dublin to Enniscorthy to visit my grandmother in the 1960s. It involved sandwiches wrapped in sliced-pan paper, thermos flasks of tea, and milk in a corked medicine bottle which usually went sour before the train passed the copper mines at Avoca. Nowadays the short trip on the motorway hardly justifies a coffee break. On Holy Thursday of Easter week 1916 a Cumann na mBan member called Eily O'Hanrahan took the 6.00 a.m. train from Dublin with a dispatch for the Enniscorthy Volunteers sewn into the lining of her fox fur. She was a trained courier so, although she had a sense that the Rising was coming, she had asked no questions about what she carried. It appears to have been an order to rise on Easter Sunday, written and signed by Pearse. Having received it, senior Volunteer and Cumann na mBan members in Enniscorthy coordinated with their colleagues in

Wexford town and elsewhere in the county, and prepared for action. But although MacNeill's countermanding order had yet to be issued, other messengers besides Eily had come through from Dublin and the officers in Wexford seem to have been uncertain about exactly what was required of them: so on Good Friday an Enniscorthy Volunteer travelled to Dublin and returned next day with confirmed orders to rise on Easter Sunday. Then, within hours of that confirmation, MacNeill's messengers were dispatched throughout Ireland, and the following morning his notice appeared in the Sunday newspaper. So the plans to rise on Sunday were cancelled and senior Volunteer and Cumann na mBan members in Enniscorthy attempted to make sense of what was happening.

On Easter Monday, unaware that the Rising had been scheduled, aborted and, by then, rescheduled, Eily O'Hanrahan took another message from Dublin to Enniscorthy. This time she had instructions to travel on to Wexford town and deliver a second dispatch there. Starting at 6.00 a.m. again, she made her delivery in Enniscorthy. But she couldn't find the man she was supposed to meet in Wexford town so, having eaten lunch there in White's Hotel, she returned to Enniscorthy for advice. When the train drew into the station, there were armed members of the Royal Irish Constabulary (RIC) on the platform. Eily stayed put. Then, when the train was held up farther up the line, she heard someone shouting that the streets of Dublin were 'running with blood'. She made her way down the train to the lavatory, took the undelivered dispatch from her fur and tore it up, flushing some of the pieces down the lavatory pan and eating the rest to make sure that the torn pages couldn't be found and reconstructed. She then travelled on to Dublin, went home to collect her sister, and they reported to the GPO. For the rest of the week Eily took responsibility for issuing arms and acted as a courier between the Dublin garrisons, where her two brothers were fighting as Volunteers.

Word that the Rising had begun seems to have reached Wexford on Easter Monday evening, by the late train from

Dublin. Jennie Wyse-Power, a founder member of Cumann na mBan, had arrived earlier in the day hoping to establish the extent of the support that the rebels could expect from the Wexford area. Although Volunteer officers in the county had been attempting to liaise with each other by bicycle, at that stage it was still impossible to tell. By Tuesday night it became clear that if Wexford rose it would do so without support from the surrounding counties. At that point the leaders in Enniscorthy had difficulty in restraining Volunteers who wanted to march to Dublin. Then a message got through from Connolly in the GPO, ordering the Enniscorthy Volunteers to hold the railway line from the east coast port of Rosslare, to prevent British reinforcements reaching Dublin. This was when Marion and her companions were ordered to prepare to seize Enniscorthy town the following morning.

I have only one photograph of Marion, an inch by an inch and a half in size. It's a colour print, mounted on a memorial card produced for her funeral in 1983. Memorial cards used to be a feature of every Irish funeral, printed pasteboard slips the size of a playing card, usually with a prayer or religious quotation on one side and a photo of the deceased on the other, along with his or her name, age and date of death. They were given to mourners to be kept in missals as prompts to pray for the dead. I remember my grandmother's prayer books bristling with them. Marion's card makes no mention of her role in the Rising. Her memorial photo shows a severe, elderly lady wearing a white top under a black dress with a draped neckline, and a pair of 1970s spectacles. She looks directly into the camera and her face gives nothing away.

What did she think about that Wednesday night in 1916 as she prepared herself for the morning? Or was she too busy carrying messages, guns and first-aid equipment to think about anything at all? Everything still had to happen in secrecy and by then, given the situation in Dublin, the RIC were on full alert. The militants worked to a prearranged plan. Foodstuffs and bedding were collected or commandeered. Boys in their teens, members of the Fianna organisation founded by Constance Markievicz, acted as lookouts and helped to issue arms. I don't know if Marion talked to her mother about what was going to happen, or if she had any sleep that night. Unlike Markievicz in her breeches, the Cumann na mBan and many of the Citizen Army women wore skirts, fuller and longer but of the same weight and texture as the one I hung onto as a child when I followed Marion up the castle turret stairs. I don't know if she brushed her uniform skirt that night or made a will or wrote farewell letters, or ironed a shirt and polished her boots for the morning. I imagine that she did if she had time. She knew she might be going out to die and she was always a stickler for procedure.

The loss of the German guns was a game changer in Enniscorthy. As in Dublin and Galway, the militants were under-armed and lacked ammunition. Marion would have been trained to use a gun but she and her Cumann na mBan comrades probably set out that morning without them; many of the Volunteers were armed with handguns and pikes. They assembled before dawn and marched to the Athenaeum, where they took the keys from the caretaker at gunpoint. The castle was commandeered from the family that was living in it at the time and Volunteers were posted on the roof. The rest of the town was taken over, shops, pubs and businesses closed, a curfew imposed, and any arms in private hands were demanded in the name of the republic. The Athenaeum over which Gretta Comerford, Una Brennan and Marion raised the tricolour was intended to be only a temporary headquarters. Without the firepower to attack the town's RIC barracks, the plan was to starve the police into surrendering the building and the munitions that were stored there. There was also the hope that if Enniscorthy held out long enough and things went well in Dublin, the RIC men, who were Irish themselves, might change sides and join them. Whatever else might happen, the fact that Enniscorthy had risen would, it was hoped, divert British troops from Dublin, lessening the pressure on the rebel garrisons in the capital. Carrying out orders from Dublin, Volunteers blew up railway tracks to prevent British reinforcements being brought to Dublin by rail from the Wexford port of Rosslare. In the event, troops were not diverted from the capital and British reinforcements landed elsewhere.

I don't remember if the Rising in Enniscorthy was depicted in Hugh Leonard's TV drama series, *Insurrection*. But perhaps we didn't really watch every single night. It was an eight-part series of hour-long episodes. Maybe Mrs O'Connor, our neighbour with the television, had to go out one night or perhaps, after the initial excitement, I lost interest. I don't remember. But Marion watched it, as did other survivors of the Rising, some of whom had first been introduced to nationalism through propagandist drama. I don't know if Marion was the kind of woman to be moved by music or poetry, or impressed by theatre. Her beady eye and massive calm make me doubt it, yet the fact that she joined Cumann na mBan in the first place suggests she had an imagination to be stirred. Whether or not Hugh Leonard's television series dramatised her immediate personal experience, I'm not surprised that she was interested in *Insurrection*. It was designed to provide an overview of the course of the entire Rising, which she didn't have as a participant and may not have gained in the intervening years.

Insurrection had a huge cast which included 300 members of the country's defence forces. It portrayed the story of the Rising as it might have been seen by an Irish TV news team, had such a thing existed at the time. Dramatisation was interspersed with on-the-spot 'reporting,' and links and explanations were provided for the audience by the actor Ray McAnally in the character of a news anchorman. As she watched it, Marion must have been remembering the actual drama she had lived through. I doubt if she had difficulty in distinguishing fact from fiction. Now, however, in the absence of memory and distanced even farther by time, it is dangerously easy to confuse one with the other. At the same time, it is useful not to be too dismissive of play-acting. Revolution has to be played out in imagination before it can be achieved.

As Commander-in-Chief of the rebel forces, Pearse signed an unconditional surrender in Dublin on Saturday 29 April 1916. But the flag raised by Marion and her two companions flew until late the next day. When word of the Dublin surrender was brought to Enniscorthy, the rebels refused to believe it. In the end, two Volunteer officers were taken to Dublin under safe conduct and brought to Pearse in his cell. There, while the authorities were inspecting his written confirmation of the surrender, Pearse whispered to the Volunteers to hide their arms because they'd be needed again. On the officers' return to Enniscorthy they tendered an unconditional surrender with regard to themselves, provided that the rank and file were allowed to go free. The commander of the British troops in Wexford refused to accept it and both officers and men were imprisoned pending trial. The Fianna boys and the Cumann na mBan women were released.

In *Man And The Echo*, a poem about the 1916 Rising written in 1938, W. B. Yeats struggles with the outcome of agitprop drama, asking *'Did that play of mine send out / Certain men the English shot?'* The answer, and he knew it, is 'probably'. The poem is powerful and his troubled sense of guilt is touching. Yet he fails to recognise that women too made deliberate choices to risk death. In Dublin, where nearly 100 women took an active part in the Rising, British army officers initially refused to accept the surrender of rebel garrisons from women, even when the highest-ranking surviving officers were female. Some women who surrendered were told by the British to go home. Many did so, either thanking their lucky stars for their escape or perceiving their value for the future. Or both. Others refused, and in the weeks after the Rising some were sentenced to death. The death sentences were later commuted to life imprisonment and many women endured solitary confinement and hard labour. Others, who had risen or prepared to rise but escaped imprisonment, took central roles as organisers, spies and combatants in the War of Independence and the Civil War that followed.

In 1916, after the Dublin rebels had been forced to retreat from their burning headquarters, Pearse's offer of surrender was carried to Brigadier General Lowe, the commander of the British forces, by a Cumann na mBan member called Elizabeth O'Farrell who had been among the last of the insurgents to leave the GPO. There were three Cumann na mBan women in the retreat, which took place under heavy fire. In the shambles that followed it, O'Farrell acted as an intermediary as Pearse attempted to negotiate terms and Lowe demanded unconditional surrender. Ultimately Pearse accepted the inevitable. O'Farrell then carried his orders to the other rebel garrisons in the city, where the fight was still continuing. Later, at the formal acceptance of the unconditional surrender, she was photographed standing at Pearse's side. As it happened, the angle of the shot largely obscured her presence. Which was unfortunate. But later prints of the photograph show Pearse in his slouch hat and military greatcoat standing alone and defiant before the British officers. Someone made the deliberate decision to airbrush O'Farrell out of the picture. Which is outrageous.

6
The Soldiers' Song

I CANNOT PASS A SHOP that sells stationery. This is a trait inherited from my father who spent much of his life in search of the perfect pencil. He also loved gold Indian ink and red sealing wax, stout brown paper and string. I remember frequent trips into town on the number eleven bus with letters and parcels sealed with blobs of red wax, each carrying the imprint of a tag that he carried on his key ring. We posted them in the General Post Office where, while he bought stamps, I stood and admired the sole of Cú Chulainn's foot.

Cú Chulainn is the hero of one of the earliest cycles of Irish storytelling. His statue in bronze, by Oliver Sheppard, now stands in a window of the GPO in Dublin. When I was a child it stood on a plinth in the high central hall there, and you could walk all around it. I can't remember a time when I didn't know his name, and the story of how he took up arms in boyhood appeared in my first school reader:

Once, when Cú Chulainn was chasing a ball across a green plain, he came upon the Boy Troop of Emain Macha gathered round a druid who was teaching them. 'The boy who first takes up arms on this day,' said the druid, 'will have fame forever in the mouths of the men who come after him.'

'Then I will take up arms on this day,' said Cú Chulainn.

'If you do,' said the druid, 'your time will be short. That is the fate that is fated,' he said, 'for the boy who takes arms on this day.'

'I care not if my days be long or short', said Cú Chulainn, 'if my name is remembered forever in the mouths of the men of Ireland.'

So he takes up arms and dies gloriously in battle and his name has been remembered to this day.

The legend of Cú Chulainn preserves an ancient world view in which to be forgotten is the ultimate disaster. Along with many other early societies, the pagan Celts appear to have imagined no afterlife; only by constantly speaking of and praising the dead can their descendants preserve the presence of the ancestors whose spiritual energy is a vital part of what animates and empowers their community. So the immortality of the dead relies entirely on the memory of the living, who condemn them to annihilation if they allow them to be forgotten. And the community that takes that risk, risks its own annihilation as well.

Sheppard's statue shows the figure of a young warrior, naked except for a headband, a loincloth around his hips and a cloak which has fallen from his shoulders. A bronze shield hangs from his left arm and a sword trails from his right hand. His upper body slumps to the left against a strap that binds him to a tall stone; his right foot rests on the ground while his left leg, twisted sideways, reveals the underside of the left foot where patches of the bronze on the heel and toes are rubbed to dark gold. I can't remember how high the plinth was at the time when I first saw the statue but I know that the figure's bronze feet were exactly at the level of my eyes.

I remember the wonder of that twisted bronze foot, the lean, muscular legs, the slumped body and the drooping head. Perched on the naked right shoulder is a huge raven with beady eyes, a hooked beak and half-spread wings. An inscription near the statue today explains that the wounded hero tied himself to the stone so that he could die on his feet; so long as he lived, his enemies still feared him, and not until a bird flew down and perched on his shoulder could they muster the courage to approach. I learned that version of the story of Cú Chulainn's death when I was at school. It isn't wholly accurate. In the version handed down across millennia in Ireland's written and oral traditions, the bird on the hero's shoulder is Badhb, the ancient

Celtic goddess of fertility, in the third of her three aspects, which is Death.

Despite the increasing interest in family history sparked by television and the proliferation of online genealogy services, most people lack the time, money and know-how to comb through official databases. Instead they generally turn to family records preserved in old letters, passports or certificates, photographs, newspaper cuttings, or the bill for great-granny's funeral that somehow never got thrown out. Along with that kind of ephemera, many families still have Victorian family bibles with blank front pages in which names, dates and rites of passage were once faithfully inscribed; it is not unusual for the layout to be unmethodical or the inscriptions inaccurate, but information handed down that way is often valued and given more credence than official records. Indeed, even if people do acquire official data, many prefer a family version, which they feel belongs to them, to contradictions offered by officialdom. That fact, and the reasons for it, interests me. Contradictions and inaccuracies can be revealing in themselves.

Before I sat down to write this book I contacted Maria Nolan, the woman who originally invited me to Enniscorthy to speak about *The House on an Irish Hillside* and had hosted the castle event. I wasn't quite sure what I was looking for but I hoped that another event, focused this time on the town's experience of 1916, would offer both a forum for a discussion of the absence of memory and a sense of whether and how far my own family experience was replicated. Maria, a regular contributor to one of Enniscorthy's local newspapers, made arrangements for an event in the town library and placed a piece in the paper. In addition, as a founding member of Enniscorthy's literary festival, Focal, she publicised the event on the festival's Facebook page. Which was how, once again, via a trip to Enniscorthy, the Internet led me to new insights into Marion's story.

Almost as soon as Maria posted on Facebook I began receiving messages on my own Facebook Author page. One was from

a woman I hadn't met since I had played with her on my visits
to Enniscorthy as a child; she invited Wilf and me to stay in her
family home while we were in town, and offered to introduce me
to Wexford's county archivist. Another message, saying that her
mother had stories about Marion, came from the daughter of a
woman called Katherine Kavanagh who had known my mother's
family. Katherine, known as Katch, was one of the first to arrive at
the event, which was hosted by the town's librarian. It was a rainy
winter's day and everyone turned up in raincoats, shaking out
umbrellas. Katch, a smiling, keen-eyed lady with beautifully set
white hair, arrived wearing a dark coat and a wonderful wide silk
scarf in shades of powder blue, pale pink and amber. Around her
neck, beneath the scarf, she wore a string of pearls that had been
left to her by Marion. She brought Marion's birth certificate, a Red
Cross medal, copies of the memorial card – one of which she gave
me – and a sheaf of papers.

A photographer arrived to take a few shots for a local paper.
He hadn't heard what the event was about but within moments
it emerged that he himself was related to Marion. His branch of
the Stokes family had been painters and decorators, he said, and
always had an interest in art and photography. He wasn't aware
that the family had any connection with the Rising; if they had,
he had never heard it spoken of. As more people arrived and the
photographer left to cover his next story, we moved upstairs and
settled in the room provided by the librarian. I was introduced,
gave an outline of what this book was going to be about, and
people began talking. Much of what was shared that day was
general. But some was specific. One man towards the back of
the room named the land where Cumann na mBan and the
Volunteers had drilled in the months before the Rising. When I
asked if they had drilled in secret he said that the RIC members
in the town at the time belonged to three local families, so of
course they weren't going to interfere, not unless they had no
option. I don't know if he meant that they wouldn't have wanted
to or that they would have known better than to try. Probably

both. The fact that British authority in Ireland in those years was upheld by an Irish police force produced tensions that, with the right pressure at the wrong moment, can still erupt today.

Like me, Katch Kavanagh is related to Marion. But, unlike me with my urban upbringing and emigrant experience, Katch has lived her life in the rural community in which she was born, and has the shared memory of her generation. So, like any of my neighbours in Corca Dhuibhne, she established the setting of her story before she began to talk. *'Marion's mother was an aunt of your grandmother. Your great grandfather was James Kehoe of Cathedral Street, which was then Duffry Street, and Marion's mother was his sister Cathleen Teresa Kehoe, therefore Marion and your grandmother were first cousins. Marion was also a first cousin of my grandmother, Katie Stokes, which makes you and me the same relation to Marion but on opposite sides.'* This is the kind of information I need to write down and reproduce as a diagram. I can't take it in otherwise. But that day everyone in the room over the age of sixty-five absorbed it immediately and waited for the next bit.

After she returned to Enniscorthy from London, Marion spent many Christmases with the Kavanaghs and was a close family friend. Yet Katch's memories match my mother's. Marion never talked about her experience in the Rising, she said; none of them did, and few people in the town talked much about the troubled years that followed the Rising, either. People around the room nodded. It was clear that this fact was a given. Katch's description of Marion was familiar to me: an intelligent woman with an air of quiet authority; not someone you would cross. She remembered Marion as being close to my grandmother, and had stories about the house near the Duffry Gate; the clock in the hall that always chimed just before the bell in the Cathedral tower struck the hours, and the cut-glass biscuit barrel on the sideboard that I remember from my own childhood.

Then the discussion opened out again and returned to the absence of memory. Did anyone recognise the scenario in which different siblings had different versions of the same story? Everyone did and the question produced a buzz of laughter and chat between individuals. At some point I asked how people felt about the contradictions and lack of information that shrouded the early years of the country's independence. There was little response. Maybe it was crass of me to have asked. Perhaps speaking about the silence was seen as implying criticism of a previous generation. Or perhaps things happen when they happen, not when an author clicks her fingers and asks for them. That day we moved on to talk of other things, equally valuable to my purpose and offered with generosity and enthusiasm. Then in the weeks that followed I began to receive emails and tweets about untold stories and unpublished memoirs, and scans of recollections printed in early twentieth-century magazines. One elderly man who hadn't been able to attend the event gave his phone number to the librarian some weeks later, asking if I would call him. When I did so he told me that too many memories had been lost.

At the close of the discussion in the library I went and joined Katch who was talking to a friend. She was tucking away the material she had brought with her when a question about a distant branch of the Stokes family caused her to take it out again. The moment she unfolded her sheaf of papers I recognised them. They were photocopies of pages from Marion's hand-stitched book, which wasn't strange in itself, given Katch's close relationship with Marion. But the sight of those photocopied pages reminded me that I'd only skimmed through the book when my mother gave it to me in London more than twenty years earlier. The layout is complex and in places the writing is cramped so I had laid it aside, intending to come back to it. Now seemed an appropriate time.

So, back home at my desk, I dug out the slim book with its scuffed brown paper cover and turned the pages, struck again by the blackness of the ink and the neat, spiky handwriting. Marion didn't lay out the names in the conventional family-tree format; instead she lists different branches of the family on

separate pages, and information in one list is sometimes filled
out in more detail elsewhere in the book. The details express the
same profound awareness of the relationship between family
and place that I am aware of now in Corca Dhuibhne. *'Paddy
Stokes, Borris, told me that when Marion Stokes, Drumderry,
married she reminded her husband to always call on the Stokes
when passing through Borris. The farm in Drumderry was sold
later but the name is still remembered ... I believe there are strange
names amongst the Stokes graves in Kiltennel, such as Turnbull
and Burbage, and in one grave there is a seven foot coffin.'* Among
the lists of names and dates are stray, unfinished stories. Two
nineteenth-century brothers, John and Thomas Stokes, went to
America but '*... they did not live in the same state in the USA and
John arranged a meeting place half way for both of them. Thos
went to the appointed place. John had not arrived and, in spite of
all the efforts to trace what happened on his journey, nothing was
ever heard of John again.'* One story about a later John Stokes,
who was a farmer, refers to Marion's own father. *'John Stokes was
very successful in the curing of cancer. He left detail of the "cure"
with my father who hadn't the same gift with regard to Herbal lore
and it was lost after my father's death.'*

She makes no mention at all of her own involvement in the
Rising but in turning the pages that day the kaleidoscope shifted
again and I discovered another lost thread in my family's story.
The date and place of Marion's parents' marriage appear at the top
of a page which gives the names of her eight siblings, presumably
in order of age, indicating that the first child in the family was
a girl and the second a boy. His name was Thomas and he was
three years older than Marion. I know that because, although she
gives no birth dates, either for herself or her siblings, she records
the date and circumstances of this brother's death. *'Thomas J.
Stokes. Unmarried. Arrested after Easter 1916, finally interned at
Frongoch Camp. Bala. N. Wales. Released Christmas Day 1916,
his health impaired. He died at home in Cathedral St. about 7am
Sept 29th 1917, aged 24 years. R.I.P.'*

Thomas J. Stokes, Tom to his family and friends, was a painter and decorator. He joined the Volunteers when the Enniscorthy branch was established and was one of the forty or so Volunteers in the area who supported MacNeill and rejected Redmond. At some early point in his involvement with the Volunteers he was sworn into the rank and file of the IRB. So, like Marion, he was a militant separatist nationalist. In 1915 he marched in his Volunteer uniform to Glasnevin Cemetery in Dublin behind O'Donovan Rossa's coffin and heard Pearse's graveside eulogy. I don't know if Marion was at Rossa's funeral as well. If she was, she and Tom could have had time to drop in on my grandparents before catching the train home to Enniscorthy; Washerwoman's Hill was just around the corner from the cemetery. Of course, my grandmother might not have welcomed two young cousins armed and in uniform on her doorstep. Still, blood is thicker than water. Perhaps she would have let them in, shown them where the loo was, and offered tea with biscuits served from her cut-glass biscuit barrel.

In the year of O'Donovan Rossa's funeral Pearse and The O'Rahilly inspected A and B Companies of the Enniscorthy Volunteers at the foot of Vinegar Hill, in a place known as the Barley Field. As part of the occasion Tom, who was a member of A Company, sang 'The Soldiers' Song', a Volunteer marching song which would later be popularised by the men who ended up in Frongoch. Later still, after a certain amount of controversy about the suitability of its martial lyrics, 'The Soldiers' Song' became Ireland's national anthem. It is a good, stirring tune and usually sung in Irish, which most people don't follow, so the issue of suitability has now pretty much gone away. In 1915 in the Barley Field Tom must have sung it in English. He was dead before the translation came to be made.

After the surrender in Enniscorthy, where the Volunteers had managed to carry out Pearse's order to hide their arms, much of the male population of the town was rounded up. Eventually the men accused either of being combatants or their

THERE WERE No
TRIALS
INTERNMENT

supporters were weeded out and sent to Dublin. Those convicted
were then sent to Frongoch Internment Camp in Wales or to
prisons in England. Tom was among those who ended up in
Frongoch. Until I found his name in Marion's handwritten book
I had never heard of him. I had heard of Frongoch, though. It
featured in my schoolbooks as a 'republican university' where,
in the wake of the 1916 Rising, new bonds were forged between
nationalists from all over Ireland, the cultural activities of the
Gaelic League flourished, and plans for the War of Independence
were conceived and hammered out. That picture of hearty lads
playing Gaelic football, dancing to traditional Irish music, and
cunningly outwitting their boneheaded British captors, was
Ireland's version of the Second World War prisoner-of-war films
like *The Colditz Story* or *The Great Escape*. To a certain extent it
was true, but it omits the fact that Frongoch was a collection of
jerry-built huts on a muddy, rat-infested site where men went
mad and became seriously ill in the foul-smelling, crowded
conditions. One of the camp's doctors 'worried by statements
concerning the treatment of prisoners' drowned himself in a
nearby river.

In the immediate aftermath of Easter Week the authorities
acted quickly to round up actual and suspected rebels. Having
failed to act decisively in advance of the Rising, they were
determined to avoid a replay of it: understandably, since they
still had the Great War to get on with. In Dublin the leaders
were tried for treason as soon as possible. The starting point for
identifying them was easy: there were seven signatories to the
Proclamation of the Republic read out by Pearse when the Rising
began. They were Thomas J. Clarke, Seán MacDiarmada, Thomas
MacDonagh, P. H. Pearse, Éamonn Ceannt, James Connolly and
Joseph Plunkett, whose names appeared in that order on the
proclamation. None of them had expected to survive and all were
executed. Connolly was the last of the signatories to be shot and
with him died both the Citizen Army and his dream of Ireland
as a socialist workers' republic. De Valera, whose death sentence

was commuted to life imprisonment, seems to have avoided a firing squad largely because he was tried later than the others, although it was also the case that, having been born in America to a Spanish father and an emigrant Irish mother, he had US citizenship and by the time he came to trial Irish-American outrage at the executions was running high. Others were executed too whose names are less well remembered, including Patrick Pearse's brother, Willie, and Michael O'Hanrahan, brother of Eily O'Hanrahan who had carried dispatches to Enniscorthy sewn into her fox-fur stole.

In 1966, as part of the fiftieth anniversary commemorations, the Irish Department of Education printed reproductions of the 1916 Proclamation, to be framed and hung with appropriate ceremony in every school in the Republic. Many schools did hang them; others, as I suspect happened in the case of my own school, just never got round to it. One way or another, reproductions of the proclamation were present at the time, but not ubiquitous. Pearse's iconic portrait, however, appeared everywhere, often draped in the tricolour and flanked by religious imagery. His profile was reproduced on medals and memorabilia and displayed, as if on an altar, surrounded by flowers. What few people knew at the time was that this elevation to near holy status produced a furious letter to Seán Lemass, then Taoiseach, or Prime Minister, of Ireland, from Kathleen Clarke, the widow of one of the proclamation's signatories.

Kathleen Clarke's letter claims that Pearse took advantage of the confusion in the GPO to sign himself 'President' in his communications during Easter Week, whereas the President of the Irish Republic in 1916 had in fact been her husband Thomas J. Clarke. Then, having stated her case, she threatens to go public if, during the upcoming commemorations, there should be any official reference to Pearse as President. From the government's point of view, the half-centenary commemorations were about promoting a positive future for Ireland, not reopening old wounds. So I doubt if the Taoiseach welcomed the letter,

especially since the order in which Thomas J. Clarke's and P. H.
Pearse's names appear on the proclamation suggests that Kathleen
Clarke's claim might be valid. He replied to Clarke saying that
he had nothing useful to add to the discussion and, presumably,
took judicious action behind closed doors. At no point during
the year of commemoration was Pearse officially referred to as
President. His image, taken from the iconic portrait, did appear
on a specially minted ten-shilling coin, though, and the design
for the reverse of the coin was taken from Sheppard's statue of
Cú Chulainn.

Kathleen Clarke's letter pulses with the anger, frustration
and pain that characterise real-life revolutions as opposed
to their sanitised legends. According to her, Pearse – who she
claims knew as much about commanding as her dog – wasn't
satisfied with his role as Commander-in-Chief. As a result,
she says, his time in the GPO was spent writing, largely, in her
view, to establish his own legend by issuing communications
over a signature to which he had no right. To substantiate her
allegation she quotes Seán MacDiarmada, another signatory of
the proclamation, who, she says, was always complaining to her
husband that Pearse wanted to grab honours due to others. I
don't know if any of that is true, and at this remove nothing can
be proved one way or the other. What interests me is the fact
that while Clarke's letter reminds the Taoiseach that the issue is
a matter of historical record, she declares that for fifty years she
has remained silent in public.

Kathleen Clarke, a founder member of Cumann na mBan,
was one of the small inner circle aware of the plans for the 1916
Rising. Both her husband and her brother were executed after
Easter Week. Immediately after the executions Clarke, who was
pregnant, lost her baby. Within weeks of her miscarriage she
founded the Volunteers Dependents Fund which, reconstituted
as the Irish National Aid and Volunteer Dependents' Fund, gave
practical aid to prisoners and their dependents and provided a
rallying point for the activists who masterminded the next stage

of the nationalist campaign. Along with other female nationalist activists, including Constance Markievicz, Hannah Sheehy-Skeffington and Maud Gonne, Clarke, who had three small children, was arrested and imprisoned in Britain during the War of Independence. On her release she continued to act for the rest of the war as a key operator in nationalist intelligence systems.

Clarke, who was a district judge of the republican courts and subsequently served as the first female Lord Mayor of Dublin, remained active in Irish politics until the late 1940s and when she died, aged ninety-four, in 1972, she was given a state funeral. In her letter to the Taoiseach in 1966 she declared that she knew more about the events both before and after the Rising than anyone else then alive. Given her close involvement with the work of the IRB's Supreme Council, that seems more than likely to have been true. Yet, bound by loyalty to friends, former friends and colleagues, fearful of destabilising the fledgling state that her husband had died for, or simply because she understood realpolitik, for fifty years she had judged it her duty to keep her mouth shut. And, even in 1966, having delivered her shot across the Taoiseach's bows, she continued to remain silent in public.

The average Irish person under the age of fifty today, if asked for a list of the leaders of the Rising, would probably grope for half-remembered lines from W. B. Yeats' poem 'Easter 1916', which, with its repeated refrain 'a terrible beauty is born', has entered international, as well as national, consciousness. The poem ends with a roll call of the executed leaders which, while it excludes all but three of the proclamation's signatories, includes Maud Gonne's husband, John MacBride. But the name doesn't appear in Yeats' poem because MacBride had a prominent position among the 1916 leaders: it is there because he happened to steal the poet's muse. In fact, though MacBride was an active nationalist, he joined the Rising by chance. Unaware of what was about to happen, he was walking up Dublin's Grafton Street on Easter Monday 1916 when he saw Thomas MacDonagh at the head of a troop of Volunteers, offered to join him, and ended up as second in command of one of the rebel garrisons. Afterwards he was tried and shot. His name sticks in the memory because Yeats wrote it out in a verse, but both his involvement in the Rising and his execution were as arbitrary as de Valera's survival. Had others lived or died, or been commemorated differently, Ireland would have had a different legacy of memories and, with them, a different sense of identity.

On Easter Monday 1916, Michael Mallin who, with Hannah Sheehy-Skeffington's pacifist feminist husband, Francis, had co-founded the Irish Socialist Party, established a rebel stronghold in St Stephen's Green in Dublin city centre. On pacifist grounds, neither of the Sheehy-Skeffingtons fought in the Rising. Francis, known as Frank, attempted to control civilian looting during the week and was executed on the command of a British army officer who was himself a native of Cork. Hannah, who had refused to join Cumann na mBan because she believed they lacked enough feminist conviction, acted as a messenger for the insurgents; she had been assured by Connolly that the proclamation's guarantee of equal rights and opportunities for women would be honoured should the Rising succeed. She had also been chosen as one of a five-person provisional government which was to have been set up if the insurgents had managed to hold out against the British for an extended length of time. Mallin's second in command was Constance Markievicz. His force of about 160 men and women, mostly members of the Citizen Army, approached along Grafton Street, entered the railed park through the arch at its northwest corner, cleared it of strolling Dubliners, and locked the gates. The original plans for the Rising had presumably involved the takeover of the buildings around the park. But that didn't happen. So, finding themselves exposed to sniper fire on all side, the rebels had to retreat to the nearby College of Surgeons. The wounded they took with them had been treated under fire in the park's octagonal bandstand.

Suppressed and distorted, the practical and emotional consequences of what my parents' and grandparents' generations went through in the process of achieving separation from Britain constantly ripples beneath my own generation's perception of who we are. I grew up in an Ireland which, leaving aside the continuing issue of partition, had achieved political independence. With that separation, and bolstered by the consequences of de Valera's policy of isolationism, came a clear sense of separate cultural identity. But my parents' and grandparents' generation had a different, more complex experience. The Ireland into which they were born was politically and, to a large extent, culturally identified with Britain and many had proud family histories of service in the British armed services, another fact that could hardly be acknowledged in de Valera's Ireland.

The arch that Mallin's rebel troops passed under in 1916 is a monument to the members of an Irish regiment in the British army who died in the Boer War. I remember standing under it with my father in the 1960s, reading the lists of the dead carved in limestone on its massive inner curve. The names of the battles they fell in were tarnished by the time I stood gazing up at them but in 1907, when the arch was erected, they were inscribed in gold. I remember my father pointing up at them with his walking stick, and saying that it was called Fusiliers' Arch because the name of the regiment it commemorated was the Royal Dublin Fusiliers. I'm not sure if it was then or later that I learned it was also known as Traitors' Gate. I occasionally referred to it that way myself, when talking to friends. Not out of any sense of outraged nationalism but because to a teenager it sounded like a pretty cool name.

On the day that my father and I stood in the shadow of the arch reading the inscriptions, he told me the hoary old joke about a baffled mother who received a letter from her Fusilier son saying his regiment had 'made a shift for Lady Smith'. Then, seeing my blank face, he explained that the siege of a town called Ladysmith was a turning point in the Boer War, and that a shift was an old fashioned word for a lady's vest. When I still didn't get it we came to an unspoken agreement to let the matter rest and walked on through St Stephen's Green to visit the bandstand. There, like generations of Dublin children before me, I swung my way around it in satisfyingly dizzying circles, using the slender iron columns that support its pointed octagonal roof. In 1916 they had enclosed a first-aid station where Cumann na mBan members tended the wounded while British soldiers on leave from the trenches, many of whom were Irish, sniped at them from the nearby Shelbourne Hotel.

After the surrender in Enniscorthy, the town filled with British army troops and Marion and her colleagues began organising aid for prisoners and their dependents, the role which had been envisaged for them at the beginning by the founders of Cumann na mBan. For several days the Volunteers were held under guard in the town, first in the RIC barracks and then in the Athenaeum. While they were there their families were allowed to send them food. They were guarded by members of the Connaught Rangers, an Irish regiment of the British army. Since the regiment had had substantial losses at Ypres and Gallipoli, the soldiers might have been expected to despise the rebels; but some of the soldiers were Enniscorthy men themselves, so the officer in charge may have felt the need to assert his authority. One way or the other, he refused to allow his prisoners to receive overcoats. So when Tom and his comrades were placed on a train to Dublin, many of them were in shirtsleeves. From Amiens Street station (now Connolly station) in Dublin they marched for an hour in the rain to Richmond Barracks, where they slept twenty-five to a room in wet clothes on the bare floor. After a week in those conditions with little food, they and scores of others were marched to the docks under a hail of stones and abuse from some Dubliners and cheers of support from others. Then, packed into a cattle boat, they were taken to Britain. They spent the next six weeks in Stafford Prison, constantly hungry and in solitary confinement for twenty-three hours at a time. While there, they were not permitted to speak to each other and had half an hour's exercise a day, walking in circles in the yard. Then they were sent to Frongoch.

It could be said that to militant nationalists the phrase 'England's difficulty is Ireland's opportunity' expressed common sense, to the Dubliners who stoned the rebels after the Rising it was the slogan of an irresponsible minority who didn't give a damn about other people's lives, and that to the British public it was treachery. But beneath the surface things were far more complicated. Some individual gaolers and guards encountered by Tom and his comrades in prison and in Frongoch Camp treated them sympathetically. To an extent this came down to personality – both the prisoners' and the guards'. But it was more than that. In the weeks and months that followed the Rising the story of the executions in Dublin produced international outrage. In London Roger Casement was sentenced to death for his part in the German gunrunning. Despite a campaign for his reprieve supported by influential members of the British public, and a last-minute petition on his behalf to the king, he was hanged in Pentonville Prison. Meanwhile, for a growing section of the British public, the gung-ho patriotism with which the war in Europe had begun was turning to disillusionment. So while the Irish rebels might be despised they could also be admired, both for the courage with which they had fought against the odds and the fact that they opposed the government that continued to herd young men off to the trenches. The treatment received by the individual prisoners must have been a matter of chance – if you were lucky you were slipped a cigarette, if you weren't someone spat in your food.

I don't know when Tom's experiences as a prisoner began to affect his health. Perhaps, having endured cold, hunger and solitary confinement, he was already ill when he arrived in Frongoch. After the Rising, the camp had been cleared of German prisoners of war to make room for the Irish rebels. It was a disused distillery, divided into two lesser camps, North and South, dominated by a tall chimney and connected by muddy paths. The vermin were a constant presence, so much so that the prisoners called the camp 'Francach', which is the Irish for rat. The huts were cold and in the crowded conditions infectious diseases from scabies to tuberculosis spread quickly. Although contact with Kathleen Clarke's prisoners' aid organisation was soon established and food parcels were permitted, rations were small and fruit and vegetables seldom appeared in the prisoners' diet. There were about 2,000 men confined there and none of them knew what might happen to them next.

During Easter Week, faced with the complexity of the breaking news, the British press had described the rebels as Sinn Féiners. While this name, which was inaccurate, must have saved a lot of printer's ink it also drew the attention of the British public to the fact that conscription still had not been imposed in Ireland. This was because the Sinn Féin party, which now backed the idea of an independent Irish Republic, required their elected candidates to abstain from taking their seats in the Westminster parliament, an overt rejection of Westminster's authority to legislate for Ireland that, by definition, rejected Britain's right to introduce conscription on Irish soil. It was decided in Westminster's corridors of power that an attempt to impose conscription in Ireland immediately after the Rising would swing Irish public opinion towards the rebels. So the government held back. But among the prisoners in Frongoch were men who had travelled from Britain to Ireland to join the Rising and they, if they could be identified, could legally be conscripted at once. One of them was a man from Cork called Michael Collins, who was two years older than the 24-year-old Tom Stokes.

Collins, who had been sworn into the IRB in England where he had gone to work as a clerk in the post office service, had avoided conscription in January 1916 by moving from London to Dublin. There he joined a branch of the Gaelic League, became aide-de-camp to Joseph Plunkett, one of the signatories to the proclamation, and having been closely involved with the preparations for Easter Week, fought under Pearse's command in the GPO. After the surrender, knowing that he was a likely candidate for execution, Collins managed to move from one group of prisoners to another during a selection process. Unidentified as Plunkett's aide-de-camp, he was sent to prison in England and ended up in Frongoch. Having arrived in the camp he took a leading role in the process of welding the prisoners into an effective unit to protect those among them who were in danger of being sent to the trenches.

Life in Frongoch must have been a weird mixture of boredom, discomfort, excitement and stress. Some men, like Collins, responded well to the team sports, wrestling and races which were organised by the prisoners themselves, and to the route marches imposed by the camp commandant. Others who were older or less physically fit found them difficult. The Gaelic League members in the camp organised concerts of traditional music and Irish language and history lessons. Largely organised by Collins, an intelligence network operating both in Ireland and England began to be formed. As time went on, guards were bribed or cajoled into smuggling letters in and out and contact was established with other prisoners, including de Valera, who were imprisoned in gaols in England.

Frongoch was a melting pot in which the prisoners, who came from all over Ireland, regrouped and made plans. Their leader, Michael Staines, the senior surviving officer of the Rising, who had been Quartermaster General and part of the GPO garrison, had ended up in Frongoch because, like Collins', his rank had not been identified during the selection process in Dublin. He and Collins, the senior IRB man in the camp, had been perfectly placed to see what went wrong in Easter Week. In a letter written in Frongoch about his experience in the GPO, Collins expressed admiration for the men and women in the ranks, and recognised the courage of the leaders. But he deplored what he described as the air of Greek tragedy about the Rising, the memoranda couched in poetic phrases, and the lack of organisation and cooperation. Connolly, he said, was a realist while Pearse, the Commander-in-Chief, was the direct opposite. Having seen the result, Collins began to apply his own realism and organisational skills to the task of imagining a new and very different fight for independence. But first he had to stay out of the trenches and get out of Frongoch.

I don't know how much Collins' influence in Frongoch impacted on Tom. To ensure that individuals eligible for conscription couldn't be identified, Staines and Collins ordered the prisoners to give false names to the authorities and to confuse them by standing by the wrong beds during roll calls. In attempts to establish the men's prisoner-of-war status and to avoid their being classified as criminals, disruptive campaigns were organised, resulting in solitary confinement and loss of privileges, such as letters and food parcels from home. Immensely fit himself, Collins made enemies among his comrades by accusing them of faint-heartedness and unwillingness to stay the course. I have no idea how Tom responded to the orders or the bullying but, given the fact that his health broke down completely within months of his release, he can't have been well placed to cope.

Some of the prisoners were released before the others, but Tom was one of about thirty Enniscorthy men held in Frongoch until it closed in December 1916. By then hunger strikes were being held in the camp to coordinate with a growing propaganda war outside for the prisoners' release. Some prisoners were seriously ill and one, terrified of conscription, went mad. In late November the commandant, declaring that he would have discipline in the camp even if it was filled with nothing but dead bodies, instructed the doctors not to treat prisoners who refused to give their names. That was when one of the two doctors committed suicide.

In its original English-language version, the song, which in an Irish translation became Ireland's national anthem, begins

with the line 'Soldiers are we, whose lives are pledged to Ireland.'
In the translation now most commonly sung, this line appears
as 'Sinne Fianna Fáil' which can be translated either as 'We
are the warriors of destiny' or 'We are the warriors of Ireland'
because the word 'Fál', which is associated in Irish mythology
with destiny, appears in early texts as an ancient name for
Ireland itself. 'Fianna Fáil' is a reference to a legendary Irish
warrior band called the Fianna, which was invoked in the choice
of name for the nationalist boys' organisation co-founded by
Constance Markievicz in 1909, and in the umbrella name of
'Fenians' for Irish-American nationalists and the IRB; the letters
FF were later used as an insignia for the Volunteers. The stories
of the Fianna, like those of Arthur and the Knights of the Round
Table, celebrate comradeship, honour, courage and loyalty to an
almost superhuman leader. In Ireland the concept of 'warriors
of destiny' resonates with the older stories of the Cú Chulainn
cycle in which the individual hero, by embracing his inevitable
and allotted fate, is preserved from annihilation and achieves
immortality through the faithfulness of his descendants. The fact
that a precursor to the Fenian boys' organisation was called the
Red Branch Knights, a nineteenth-century English translation
of the collective name for Cú Chulainn's companion heroes,
demonstrates that the actual and emotive links between the
two story cycles were consciously being invoked for political
purposes in the years before 1916.

In 1926, when Éamon de Valera founded the political party
that would hold power in Ireland for most of the twentieth
century, he gathered those poetic and political resonances into
his own armoury by naming his party Fianna Fáil. Then in 1935,
when he had become President of the Executive of the Irish Free
State, he requested that Sheppard's bronze statue of Cú Chulainn,
on a plinth inscribed with the proclamation and the names of
its signatories, be placed in the central hall of the GPO as the
national 1916 memorial. There were several objections, which he
smoothly overrode, and in the end he got his way. Presumably,

he knew exactly what he was doing. Sheppard's statue expresses all the numinous power of the Cú Chulainn legend, and by installing it in the GPO de Valera perpetuated the links between his own 1916 legend, Pearse's iconic role in the Rising, and the greatest legendary hero of Ireland's ancient past. Later, 'to avoid party political connotations', it was suggested that the words 'Fianna Fáil' in the national anthem be changed to 'Sinne laochra Fáil', which means 'we are the heroes of destiny' (or 'of Ireland'), and is how 'Soldiers are we' appears in a second translation, from the 1930s. But when I emigrated in the 1970s the emotional links between de Valera's Fianna Fáil party, the 1916 Rising, and Ireland's ancient cultural heritage of storytelling were still consciously being invoked. The complexity of the history of the adoption of the national anthem has now been largely forgotten.

Sheppard's statue, called *The Death of Cuchulain*, was inspired in part by the writings of Lady Augusta Gregory who, when I was young, was remembered largely as a motherly figure who encouraged the exhausted poet W. B. Yeats, also a Cú Chulainn fan, to put his feet up and eat fruit cake. Which in fact she did, bringing the cake with her to Dublin by train from her large estate on Ireland's western seaboard. But more recently it has become clear that Gregory, not Yeats, wrote much of *Cathleen Ni Houlihan*, the agitprop play that Yeats later feared had sent men out to die. She was an influential Gaelic Revivalist who was first introduced to traditional Irish storytelling by her Anglo-Irish family's tenants and, having learned to read Irish, produced the first English-language collection of the Cú Chulainn stories based on written and oral versions. Like the lore of place names contained within them, the original stories were produced at a time when Ireland had no central authority, and were intended to bolster the territorial claims of kings and chieftains by establishing their descent from heroes and gods. The written versions from which Lady Gregory worked are preserved in medieval manuscripts, but the form of Irish in which many sections of them are written is far older. They deal with the heroic exploits of the Ulaid, who inhabit an area in what is now north-eastern Ulster and north Leinster, and chronicle their battles with the tribes that surround them, which include the men of Érainn. The Érainn are identified as inhabitants of Ireland in a second-century text written by the Greco-Egyptian scholar Ptolemy, whose sources include Greek, Roman and Persian texts. Éireann is the modern Irish word for Ireland. This series of facts gave rise to another hoary old joke, told to me by my father when I was at university.

According to the story, at which I can still hear my father chortling, a working party of civil servants was set up in 1935 to organise the ceremonial installation of Sheppard's Cú Chulainn in the GPO. One of the matters on the agenda was the inscription on the plinth, to which someone suggested adding intellectual weight and authority by including Cú Chulainn's last words as they appear in the earliest medieval text. So a letter was sent to Eoin MacNeill, who by then had returned to his career in the field of Early Irish Studies. His reply was a line of Old Irish taken, as requested, from the earliest version of the story, and accompanied by the literal translation, 'I die as I have ever lived, fighting against the men of Ireland'. The civil servants thought it best not to mention this to the politicians so the idea was quietly dropped. Presumably that story is apocryphal. But the fact that it was told in Ireland in the 1930s and remembered and passed on in the 1970s is interesting.

Marion's book says that Tom was released on Christmas Day 1916, which cannot be accurate. I think she must mean that that was the day he came home. The last of the Enniscorthy men were released from Frongoch in the forty-eight hours before 25 December. By Christmas Day the camp was closed. Along with their companions from Galway, Dublin and other parts of Ireland, the men travelled by train to Holyhead and boarded the boat for Dublin at 1.30 in the morning. Every Dubliner of my generation who emigrated to England experienced that rough stretch of sea. I remember years of coming home on the bucketing mail boat with a rucksack full of Christmas presents, and the miserable hours of nausea in my childhood when my mother tried to ward off my seasickness with dry arrowroot biscuits, which travelled in her handbag in an envelope. They didn't help much. Tom and his comrades endured a stormy passage at Christmas 1916. Because of the weather, the journey took an hour longer than scheduled, and many of the men spent it in the bar. The combination of seasickness and the effects of a night's drinking after months without alcohol meant that they arrived at the docks in Dublin in bad shape.

From Dublin the released prisoners made their way back to their homes. I don't know if Tom broke the journey in Dublin. He might have stayed with my grandparents in the house on Washerwoman's Hill, or with one of the Dubliners whom he'd known in the camp. Probably he just wanted to get home to his mother. I hope the family had a happy Christmas that year because Tom didn't live to see another one. The train from Dublin to Enniscorthy departs from a station which was then known as Westland Row and is now called Pearse Station, having been renamed during the 1966 commemorations. For the first part of the journey the railway track curves along the coast. I remember the intense childhood pleasure of watching seabirds wheeling over the waves, followed by the moment of atavistic fear when the train hurtled into a long, dark tunnel hollowed out of the cliff. At Christmas 1916, if Tom sat in a left-hand seat he would have had the same view of heaving waves, felt the same sudden shock of entering the darkness and emerging again into the light. On the way to the copper mines of Avoca, the railway line passes through the suburban seaside town of Dún Laoghaire, which means the Fort of Laoghaire. In Tom's day the name had been changed to Kingstown, and the king it referred to was George IV of England, not Laoghaire, the legendary fifth-century High King of Ireland. The name was changed back again in 1920, in the lead-up to the creation of the Irish Free State. Beyond Kingstown, Tom's train travelled

on down the east coast through County Wicklow and into
County Wexford, stopping at little towns, like Woodenbridge
and Camolin, which no longer have railway stations, and larger
ones, like Arklow.

On my childhood journeys to visit my grandmother I used
to chant the names of the stations we had yet to rattle through.
Arklow ... Inch ... Gorey ... Camolin ... Ferns ... Enniscorthy.
When the train approached Arklow station my mother used
to start packing up the tartan flask and the medicine bottle of
milk, and folding away the paper that had wrapped our tomato
sandwiches. At Christmas in 1916 Tom's train passed over tracks
where, in Easter Week, explosives had been laid by Volunteers
from the towns and villages around Enniscorthy. As it clattered
along the Slaney valley, he would have seen roads marched by
the Volunteers and Cumann na mBan, and the fields that they
drilled in. Before the Rising, Volunteers from all over the county
trained together: on one occasion the Ferns and the Enniscorthy
Companies held a sham battle at Scarawalsh Bridge, where my
grandmother's family, the Kehoes, had relatives. Among Tom's
comrades were Doyles and Kehoes, Rafters and other men
from Ballindaggin and Gorey, names and place names that
belonged to the web of family and community relationships that
underpinned the Irish rebels' sense of national identity.

I don't know what illness Tom brought home with him from
Frongoch. Many men were broken by the camp's conditions and
he was among those who were imprisoned the longest. Marion,
who was a nurse, just refers to his health as 'impaired'. It was on
the hill that leads up from the town towards the Duffry Gate
that my mother's sister Evie felt the exhaustion that first warned
the family of her fatal heart condition, so I hope that in 1916
someone met Tom off the train from Dublin and helped him
to carry his gear. Perhaps Marion, working for the prisoners'
aid organisation, had written to him when he was in the camp,
and sent parcels. Women all over Ireland threw themselves into
the task of collecting and sending money and food parcels to

Frongoch. But if Tom was one of the men who went on hunger strike he wouldn't have been allowed to receive them.

And maybe he didn't take the train alone. Perhaps he returned to Enniscorthy with a crowd of his comrades, one of whom carried his gear up the steep streets towards the Duffry Gate. As the returning rebels walked out of the train station they would have seen Vinegar Hill above and to the left of them, facing the castle on the far bank of the river. In Easter Week the Volunteers had climbed Vinegar Hill and taken potshots from the summit at the RIC barracks below. That particular manoeuvre was fairly pointless but it consciously invoked the town's memories of the rebellion of 1798.

7

The Intelligent Woman's Guide to Socialism and Capitalism

IT WASN'T UNTIL I MOVED to London in the 1970s that I realised the extent to which the First World War had been presented to my generation of Irish schoolchildren as a mere backdrop for the 1916 Rising. We knew that the catalyst for the war in Europe had been the assassination of Archduke Franz Ferdinand of Austria who, judging by his photograph, was a man who was proud of his moustache. We were taught about the deep irony of Britain's eagerness to protect the rights of poor little Belgium while trampling on the rights of poor little Ireland. But why Franz Ferdinand and his wife Sophie (whom nobody mentioned) had been targeted by assassins, and how that led to the invasion of Belgium was never placed in a European or wider world context. The primary message that 'England's difficulty was Ireland's opportunity' overshadowed everything else.

We did learn British history, though. I remember astonishing English friends by being able to reel off the dates of Disraeli and Gladstone's recurring administrations and lists of England's monarchs, starting with Henry II who began the process of Britain's colonisation of Ireland. I could also hold forth knowledgeably on the Repeal of the Corn Laws, the Hanoverian Succession, and the ticklish relationship between Charles II and his brother James. And I could bore for Ireland on the subject of how Richard Brinsley Sheridan's career in the English theatre was coloured by his Irish nationalist leanings. To my own astonishment, most of my English contemporaries at drama school had no idea that Sheridan was Irish, and many

of them didn't seem to realise that George Bernard Shaw came
from Dublin; they simply identified all playwrights writing
in the English language as English. Which suggests that the
unconscious assumption that one's own country is the centre of
the universe is not uncommon.

As far as I can remember, I discovered the Fabian Society,
Britain's oldest political think tank, through a combination of
reading Shaw's *The Intelligent Woman's Guide to Socialism and
Capitalism* and flogging dramatisations of Early Irish texts to
BBC radio. When I left drama school one of my first jobs was
with the New Shakespeare Company at the Open Air Theatre in
London's Regent's Park. I was lucky to get it because, with the
insane arrogance of youth, I hadn't bothered to learn an audition
speech; instead I improvised what I declared was a monologue
from a newly written Irish play. I figured that David Conville, the
producer, would assume that he just hadn't heard of my fictional
up-and-coming foreign playwright. What I hadn't considered
was the possibility that I might be asked to repeat the speech at a
callback. So when that happened, as to my great surprise it did,
I had no option but to confess. The callback was held onstage
at the theatre where, if silence fell when the wind was in the
right direction, you could hear the lions roaring in Regent's Park
Zoo. After my confession I stood in silence for several moments
listening to lions while Conville eyed me cynically from his seat
at the back of the amphitheatre. Then he said thank you and I
went home.

However, the New Shakespeare Company played Shaw as
well as Shakespeare, and it happened that season that there was
a role in one of their Shaw plays for an Irish actress more or less
my age, size and shape. So – possibly because Conville had been
impressed by me but probably because rehearsals were just about
to start – I got the part. The play was set in Ireland during the
First World War and, still squirming from the experience of
my audition, I threw myself into research. Given that my part
consisted of one small scene and one big speech, I didn't really

need to read *The Intelligent Woman's Guide to Socialism and Capitalism*. But once I began I got interested. And then, in some other book I discovered the Fabians.

Shaw joined the Fabian Society when it was still a small group of writers, artists, socialists and feminists meeting in each other's back parlours. One of its stated objects was '*to persuade the English people to make their political constitution thoroughly democratic and to socialise their industries sufficiently to make the livelihood of the people entirely independent of private Capitalism.*' As the First World War drew to a close, this idea and its implications were being thrashed out all over Europe, and the publication of books like Shaw's reflected a growing assumption that women should be part of an international process of decision making which would create a new, post-war world. Shaw was introduced to the Fabian Society by a journalist called Hubert Bland who was untypical of the other founding Fabians in that he opposed female suffrage. Bland's wife, the writer E. Nesbit, was equally opposed to it, despite the fact that she too was a Fabian and the principal breadwinner in her own family. But then Nesbit, whose first name was Edith, had a fine disregard for contradiction. She was a committed socialist whose houses and numbers of servants got larger from year to year. And she was an affirmed feminist whose family included two children, passed off as her own, who were actually the illegitimate offspring of Hubert Bland and Alice Hoatson, Edith's own best friend. Shades of political opinion and social behaviour could be as complex and varied in early twentieth-century England as they were in Ireland.

Looking round for more acting work when the New Shakespeare Company season was over, I wrote and pitched a script to BBC radio, consciously exploiting the fact that I could speak Irish which was a Unique Selling Point in a crowded marketplace. The script was a dramatisation of one of the legends of the Fianna and their superhuman hero Fionn Mac Cumhaill. I was lucky. Broadcast for schools' radio, complete with whiz-bang sound effects, it kick-started a series of writing commissions which I cunningly sprinkled with words in Irish, thus ensuring that I got hired to work on my own scripts as a voice artist. In time I moved on to writing and playing in shows that no longer required the USP that had first got my foot in the door, and worked with producers in schools radio, drama, the BBC World Service, and in BBC and commercial television. Along the way I met Peter Fozzard, an unassuming powerhouse of creativity who, in his tweed jackets, V-necked pullovers and round glasses, looked exactly like the 1950s English schoolmaster he had been before joining the BBC.

By the time I worked with him, Fozzard was a senior radio producer. His approach to production epitomised the ethos that the corporation's entire resources should be equally available to each programme it made, a democratic, if not socialist, vision now long gone from the BBC. It coincided at the time with a policy of allowing producers to commission work themselves without going through a drawn-out pitch-and-selection process. The usual procedure was for a writer with an idea to ring up a producer and talk about it. If the idea grabbed the producer's imagination and seemed right for a particular slot, it was often commissioned on the basis of a single phone conversation. If it hadn't come in at the right moment, one producer might hand you on to another for whom it might be more suitable. I was passed on to Peter Fozzard by the producer who commissioned my Fianna scripts and, after continuing to work from Middle and Early Irish material for a while, he and I worked occasionally on ideas which reflected my growing awareness, and his encyclopaedic knowledge, of English social history.

It was Fozzard who jolted me into realising how little I knew about the levels of contact between early twentieth-century feminists in Britain, Ireland and beyond. He also drew my attention to the sloppy thinking which informed my own 1970s feminism. One day when we were discussing a script I had written he mentioned that several of the incidental characters were designated MAN #1, MAN #2, and so on. One-liners and small parts in a radio play are usually 'doubled', which means that several or all are played by the same voice artist. Doubling requires experience, skill and flexibility as a single performer has to create, sustain and remember a series of different voices for incidental characters who sometimes are heard within moments of each other. That day, as he flicked through the pages of my script, Fozzard looked at me mildly through his glasses and asked why I'd chosen to make all my incidental characters male. I was taken aback and, groping for a reply, said something about voices in the crowd representing the man in the street. But in fact, since the gender of the characters concerned didn't particularly matter, I'd typed MAN #1 and MAN #2 without a moment's thought. There was a pause in which I considered both the world I had chosen to project to my audience and the job opportunity for a woman which I'd mindlessly failed to create. Then Fozzard, producing a pencil, neatly changed the names of 50 per cent of the incidental characters in the cast list from 'Man' to 'Woman'. I had been slightly apprehensive about our discussion of my script, which was structurally idiosyncratic, but that was the only change he made.

During those early years in London I found myself reading about Constance Markievicz's sister, Eva Gore-Booth. Unlike Constance, the militant nationalist, Eva was a pacifist mystic poet. She published nine books of poetry, seven plays and several collections of spiritual essays. This might suggest that Constance was the practical sister and Eva the airy-fairy one but in fact Constance was a romantic with practically no political judgment while Eva was a clear-minded and effective political activist. Working in Britain for the Labour movement, Eva and her lifelong companion Esther Roper campaigned for workers' rights and international feminist cooperation: what they aspired to was a joined-up world in which politics driven by universal suffrage and balanced debate would be informed by spiritual values. Constance, on the other hand, threw all her energy into violent separatism. Yet the sisters remained devoted to each other throughout their lives and, during Ireland's War of Independence, Eva's campaign to reform conditions in women's prisons was boosted by data smuggled out by Constance from her prison cells in Britain.

I learned nothing about Eva Gore-Booth while I was growing up in de Valera's Ireland. Given that she was an Anglo-Irish pan-pacifist feminist woman working in England, that isn't surprising. What is interesting is that, despite her significant political presence in Britain before, during and after the First World War, none of my English friends had heard of her either. This is partly because the vision of a post-war world of international cooperation, social justice and universal suffrage promoted by men and women like Eva Gore-Booth and the Fabians wasn't achieved. It is also because the popular legend of the suffragettes provides a less complex version of Britain's feminist history.

I have always disliked the word 'suffragettes,' almost as much as I dislike the concept of 'herstory'. The term 'herstory' became popular in the 1970s among feminists attempting to highlight the extent to which the role of women in history had previously been ignored. The point is valid but the term is daft. The name 'suffragette,' which was invented by a journalist as a term of derision, was embraced by early twentieth-century feminists who, emphasising the letters 'get' in the middle of the word, announced that, as suffragettes, they were fighting to 'get' votes for women. That is not just tortuous it is perverse, because it requires that the 'get' in suffragette be mispronounced to make the point. So it is fair to say that I don't come to the suffragettes without a certain bias. But it is equally true that the name has become a lazy catch-all term for a complex grouping of political activists, many of whom disliked the word 'suffragette' as much as I do.

Like Redmond's Irish Home Rule party, the National Union of Women's Suffrage Societies founded in Britain in 1897 was committed to constitutional, not militant, activism. It was a broad grouping of women's organisations with affiliations throughout mainland Britain, Ireland and abroad and, as the Westminster parliament was slow to respond to its demands, some of its members soon became restless. In 1903 Emmeline Pankhurst, who advocated more radical activism, founded the Women's Social and Political Union. This was the organisation that embraced the name suffragettes.

Pankhurst established and controlled the Women's Social and Political Union along with her daughters Christabel and Sylvia. Before the split with the National Union of Women's Suffrage Societies the Pankursts had viewed the struggle for women's rights in the wider context of the Labour movement and trade unionism. They were introduced to Gore-Booth and Roper through Christabel who attended lectures given by Eva and, according to Sylvia, adored her. But soon they moved away from the Labour movement and Eva Gore-Booth's influence, and focused on the militant Votes For Women campaign that people remember today.

That campaign is remembered largely because of its drama and because Emmeline and Christabel Pankhurst were brilliant self-publicists. Inevitably, smashing windows and blowing up postboxes produced more martyrs and memorable images than the philosophical, cultural, economic and political theories discussed in pamphlets issued by the Fabian Society or the journal founded by Gore-Booth and Roper, which explores the complexities of gender and human sexuality. The suffragettes had impressive physical and moral courage and the Pankhurst name, like Constance Markievicz's, has become legendary. But, like the dramatic gesture that was the 1916 Rising, the drama whipped up by the suffragettes has elbowed out a more detailed and nuanced awareness of the issues of the time.

When Frongoch camp closed, the war in Europe still had two years to run. It had begun in a clash of superpowers – Franz Ferdinand's Austria-Hungary, Britain, France, Germany, Italy and the Ottoman and Russian Empires. But by 1917 it was clear that a new world order might take the place of the old model of imperialist expansionism. At the outset of the war, Emmeline Pankhurst, like Redmond, had accepted the idea that issues like Votes for Women and Home Rule for Ireland should be shelved for the duration, and while Redmond was urging the Volunteers in Ireland to join the British army the Pankhursts were handing out white feathers as symbols of cowardice to British men and boys who had yet to enlist. As it happened, Millicent Fawcett, founder of the National Union of Women's Suffrage Societies, shared her former follower Emmeline Pankhurst's patriotism and insisted that the members of her own society should support the war effort. As a result, after much debate, Eva Gore-Booth and Esther Roper broke away and set up a separate organisation, composed of pacifist socialist feminists.

This led to their involvement in the International Committee of Women for Permanent Peace, which emerged from a congress of over 1,000 participants organised in The Hague in 1915 by Dutch and German pacifist feminist suffragists. The president of the newly formed committee, an American activist called Jane Adams, had already been working with US feminists to provide a forum for mediation between the belligerent countries in the European war. Had these women's efforts been successful the course of world history could have been different and, history suggests, far better. In 1919 they tried to influence the terms of surrender and subsequently denounced the punitive terms of the Treaty of Versailles which ended the war in Europe, warning that it would provoke another world war. Looking at what might have been is often a fairly pointless exercise. Yet the fact remains that, twenty years after the Treaty of Versailles was signed, the International Committee of Women and those who agreed with them were proved right.

But in 1917, with all still to play for, the coming peace process offered the potential for a new world order, and these were the circumstances in which the released republican prisoners and their growing numbers of supporters in Ireland were planning to achieve recognition of Ireland's right to independence. And when the United States entered the war in April 1917 the odds in their favour increased. American politicians would now have a significant voice in the post-war peace process, and Irish-American opinion had serious clout.

Although the camp at Frongoch had been closed and some Irish prisoners who had been held in Reading Gaol had been released, those identified by the British as the more senior figures involved in the 1916 Rising, including de Valera, were still in prison in Britain. At home, the disruption to ordinary lives caused by the Rising and its aftermath meant that Kathleen Clarke's Irish National Aid and Volunteer Dependents' Fund was working at full stretch. All over the country Cumann na mBan members were rattling collection boxes, writing letters and holding sales of work, dances and concerts as fundraisers. Meanwhile, on the other side of the Atlantic, Irish-American organisations were raising thousands of dollars for the cause.

The month after Tom Stokes returned to Enniscorthy from Frongoch Michael Collins, who had spent Christmas in Cork with his own family, arrived in Dublin looking for work. Kathleen Clarke's organisation had decided to recruit for the position of a salaried secretary and Collins was invited to apply. One member of the interview panel thought that he was outrageously cocky, but Clarke approved of the administrative experience he had gained when working in London before the Rising. So he got the job, which soon came to involve far more than acting as secretary to a charity.

In 1917, with an eye to the international situation, new aspirations and alliances were hammered out in Ireland. It was vital to ensure that the fight could continue if post-war diplomacy should fail, so, building on the intelligence network he had established in Frongoch and on the executed leaders' contacts and data supplied by Kathleen Clarke, Collins set about reorganising the IRB. It must have been a bit like the arrival of a new CEO who combined micromanagement with a blue-sky approach. His experience as a soldier and his immense energy impressed the old guard and encouraged recruitment to the Volunteers. But he also recognised that, if a credible claim to independence was to be made at the end of the Great War, Ireland's nationalist organisations needed a new, shared political strategy. With this in mind, he readdressed the constitutional battle, to be spearheaded this time not by John Redmond's Home Rule party but by Arthur Griffith's Sinn Féin.

After the Rising Arthur Griffith had been picked up and imprisoned in Reading Gaol but in early 1917 he was free and back in Dublin. In January Count Plunkett, father of the executed 1916 leader Joseph Plunkett, stood as Sinn Féin candidate in a County Galway by-election. Three of Plunkett's sons and two of his daughters had been involved in the Rising. Joseph, aged twenty-nine, whose aide-de-camp had been Michael Collins, was married in prison and, ten minutes later, marched to face his firing squad. The fact that he was already dying of tuberculosis had added to the poignancy of his presence in the GPO, where he fought with his neck swathed in bandages, having just had surgery. In the circumstances, the count, who with his wife, Joseph's mother, had also been imprisoned after the Rising, was swept to victory on a sympathy vote. Sinn Féin's policies at the time were so fluid that it was unclear whether or not the count would take his seat at Westminster or what he would do when he got there. But this was the party's first parliamentary victory and it marked a turning point in the newly evolving republican strategy. The next thing, Collins decided, was to get one of the prisoners in Britain elected to Westminster on a Sinn Féin ticket. The candidate he selected was a man called Joe McGuinness who had a niece called Brigid Lyons.

In 1915, the year after Marion joined up in Enniscorthy, Brigid Lyons had established a branch of Cumann na mBan in Galway city. Her family were country people who had been involved in the Land War and one of her earliest memories was of her father displaying his Land League membership card emblazoned with a quotation from a popular ballad recalling the 1798 Rebellion. The same ballad with its invocation of the claims of the dead was in one of the first poetry books I had at school.

Brigid's uncle Joe was an officer in the Volunteers and her aunt, known as Aunt Joe because there were several Aunt Kates in the family, was a founder member of Cumann na mBan. They adopted Brigid unofficially after her mother died and paid for her boarding-school education in a Sligo convent. In both Ireland and England at the time the number of women with degrees in medicine was infinitesimal but Brigid, who was determined to become a doctor, was encouraged to apply for a university scholarship by a nun who taught her at school. Having gained it, she spent the summer of 1915 in Dublin where she marched with Aunt Joe in O'Donovan Rossa's funeral procession before setting off for her first term as a medical student in University College Galway. During the summer Aunt Joe had enrolled her in the Dublin branch of Cumann na mBan so she was already trained in first aid and field medicine.

In Easter Week 1916, when my grandfather was boarding up his barber's shop in Eyre Square while my grandmother urged five-year-old Gerry and twelve-year-old Marguerite to keep away from the windows, Brigid Lyons was in a rebel garrison in Dublin with her uncle Joe. News of the Rising had reached Galway by the midnight train on Easter Monday and Brigid reached Dublin on the Tuesday. Joe McGuinness was stationed in the Four Courts, as a lieutenant under the command of Kathleen Clarke's brother, Ned Daly. The Four Courts, an imposing eighteenth-century building which housed the courts of justice, was strategically placed on a major route into the city, and the fighting there was heavy. Aunt Joe, carrying supplies and dispatches from one garrison to another, led Brigid there safely through the back streets and left her to help the other Cumann na mBan girls, who were cooking by candlelight in the basement. Though the garrison was undermanned and under-armed and communications with headquarters were soon cut off, the sound of heavy shelling boosted rumours of a German landing to support the rebels. So morale was high. Later they were to discover that the sound of shelling had come from a British gunboat pounding the rebel headquarters in the GPO from a position on the River Liffey. That night, as the fighting continued around them, Brigid and her Cumann na mBan companions discovered a cupboard full of judge's robes and slept on the floor on mattresses, wrapped in velvet and ermine.

They were woken by an officer asking for two Cumann na mBan members to move to a new outpost. Brigid and a Dublin girl called Katie Derham offered to go and, escorted by the officer, crawled through a hole in the Four Courts wall and ran under fire to a nearby house with orders to convert it to a first-aid post and canteen. The householder, a Volunteer, made them a stretcher out of a hearthrug nailed to a stepladder before leaving them alone in the house and returning to the fight. Within half an hour he was their first casualty, and a stream of others followed. Brigid treated them, helped Katie to cut up meat with a bayonet and made endless pans of chips and stacks of sandwiches. At one point, being an undomesticated boarding-school girl, she emptied a pot of used tea leaves into the fire. Katie, who was used to cooking in Dickensian conditions smacked her with a spoon and said that she'd 'bring crickets'. Years later Brigid told John Cowell, her biographer, that with rumours of the Germans on the Naas Road, a naval battle in Dublin Bay, and the might of the British Empire outside the door, she couldn't see what harm a few crickets might do.

When the rebels in Dublin surrendered, Brigid and Katie were still tending wounds and making sandwiches. Brigid was sharpening a knife and Katie was drying teaspoons when they suddenly realised that the shooting had stopped. But no one came to tell them anything so they kept on working. A little later, when Brigid was chopping wood for the fire, a group of Volunteers crashed into the house and began to break a hole through the wall of the back yard. They were desperate to escape to carry on the fight and to avoid having their weapons fall into British hands, so several of them gave their revolvers to the girls with instructions to hide them. One of them snatched Brigid's hatchet and tried to destroy his rifle. When the men left, scrambling through the hole in the wall, Katie and Brigid kept on making sandwiches.

It was Elizabeth O'Farrell who brought Pearse's order to surrender to the Four Courts. As would happen later in the week in Enniscorthy, the Volunteers first thought that it was a trick. Having been cut off from headquarters for more than forty-eight hours they were certain that the rest of the country must by now be up in arms. Some believed that the Irish regiments in the British army had mutinied and defected to the rebels. Many were still convinced that the Germans had landed to support them. Back at Brigid and Katie's first-aid post, Katie left, hoping to make it home through the burning streets to her mother. Brigid gave the remains of the food to starving local people who had been trapped in their homes during the fighting. Then she picked up a discarded oilcloth cape, put it on, stepped into the street, and closed the door behind her. She had kept back a loaf of bread, some butter and some ham in case anyone else from her uncle Joe's battalion should need feeding. Walking through the shattered streets, she met a Volunteer from the Four Courts coming to fetch her. He was hungry and thirsty so they went back to the house together and she made him tea and sandwiches. Then they returned to the Four Courts where she surrendered with the others.

The British army officer to whom Commandant Ned Daly surrendered the Four Courts had undertaken to release the Cumann na mBan members of the garrison. Instead, Brigid and the rest of the women were held there overnight and taken next day, as the Enniscorthy men were taken later in the week, to Richmond Barracks. On the way Brigid managed to dump the revolvers she had been given the previous day. In the square at Richmond Barracks she watched the leaders of the Rising being

weeded out for court martial; one of the few that she recognised
was Constance Markievicz in her breeches and plumed hat.
Later Markievicz was placed at the head of the captured women
and they were marched under guard to Kilmainham Gaol; the
British soldiers had to close ranks to protect the women from the
missiles thrown by the crowd of angry Dubliners that followed
them. Brigid said later that Kilmainham was all right during
the day but that once it got dark she was terrified. On three
consecutive nights, at 3.00 a.m., she heard firing parties carrying
out the executions in the yard below her cell.

Nine days after the surrender in Dublin Brigid and her
Cumann na mBan companions were released. Her uncle Joe, who
had been among the Volunteers she had watched being chosen
for court martial, was sentenced to five years' penal servitude
in England. And, in 1917, while still serving out his sentence
in Lewes Gaol, he was proposed as a Sinn Féin candidate for
election to the British parliament in Westminster. For the most
part, the citizens of Galway had reacted to the surrender with
relief so when Brigid returned to university after the Rising
she had little in common with most of her fellow students.
Although she still wanted to become a doctor, an opportunity to
get away from an atmosphere of disapproval and back to active
service must have been exhilarating. She abandoned her lectures
and took to her uncle Joe's campaign trail, stuffing envelopes,
running errands and hanging posters while the candidate
himself remained in prison. Disenfranchised by her sex and
aware that the 1916 Proclamation guaranteed equal rights and
equal opportunities for men and women, she must have seen the
continuing struggle for independence as a step on the road to a
brave new world. Like the rest of the rank and file who fell in and
followed orders, she probably had no idea that her uncle Joe's
election was the flashpoint for a new power struggle among the
nationalist leaders.

The idea of proposing Joe McGuinness as the Sinn Féin
candidate came from Michael Collins. After debate at home,

the suggestion was smuggled into Lewes Prison where the republican prisoners, influenced by de Valera, rejected it. Basically it came down to a judgment call that only time could prove right or wrong. Theoretically, de Valera, because of his more senior role in the Rising, was the more authoritative voice in the debate; he was also eight years older than Collins and, as a former schoolteacher, was used to being obeyed. But Collins pushed on regardless. There was no real platform to the McGuinness campaign; the posters enthusiastically hung by Brigid and her colleagues just showed the figure of a man in prison garb with the slogan: 'Put Him In To Get Him Out!' In the event, the vote was so close that it required a recount which, according to one story, was assisted by a gun to the teller's head. Had McGuinness lost, Collins' judgment would have been discredited. But he won and, besides being a huge publicity coup for Sinn Féin, his victory appeared to demonstrate that Collins' grasp of the political situation was better than de Valera's. This was the beginning of the creation – and de Valera's resentment – of the Collins legend, which would ultimately prove disastrous for them both.

In June 1917 the British announced a general amnesty and the last of the prisoners taken after the Rising were released. The men arrived to board the boat home to Dublin carrying third-class tickets provided by the authorities. But de Valera led them up the gangway into first class where they spent the voyage teaching the other passengers' children and a group of British soldiers how to sing 'The Soldiers' Song'. In my childhood this was always presented as a sort of glorious pantomime walk-down in which the Demon King dances with the Good Fairy while the Kiddies' Chorus does high kicks in the background. I wonder now just how intimidated the legitimate first-class passengers may have felt. Particularly if any of the kiddies were suffering from seasickness and Arrowroot biscuits.

When Wilf and I drive to our home in west Kerry today we travel the length of the Dingle Peninsula. To reach Dingle town you either cross the Conor Pass or skirt the foothills of the massive mountain range that divides the rest of the peninsula from its westernmost end. The road over the pass, which is the highest in Ireland, has been widened since I first crossed it as a student, but it can still be scary for nervous drivers. It rises in a series of broad curves around the contours of the mountain, and is wide enough at the outset for vehicles travelling in opposing directions to pass each other. Higher up there are passing places blasted into the rock face on your left-hand side. The low wall on your right is built of field stones. At one point a narrow torrent of water streams down the rock face, under the road and into the valley below. Miles away across the valley, down the sheer eastern face of Mount Brandon, are other silver strips of falling water and 300 metres below you are four lakes, flat as beaten metal, surrounded by open fields. Except for grazing sheep and a few grey farm buildings there is no visible evidence of human habitation. Instead you look down at the lakes through moving clouds and see cloud shadows drifting on the landscape. On the last stretch before the road reaches the summit you sidle upwards around bulging outcrops of naked rock. In winter, freezing water seeping from the mountain spreads across the road making the surface treacherous; often the pass is closed to traffic in winter when the road, if you're stupid enough to take it, is a steep sheet of ice under drifting snow. Looking down into the west you can see the wide curve of Dingle Bay and the long, steep road snaking down the far side of the mountain and into Dingle town.

The alternative, lower road around the mountain takes a longer route to Dingle. A few miles from the town is the turnoff to the village of Kinard, the birthplace of Thomas Ashe who led the insurgent troops that seized the post office and police barracks in Meath, to the north of Dublin, in 1916. Ashe, who was five years older than Michael Collins, was both an IRB member and a founder of the Volunteers and, by all accounts, a shrewd politician as well as a courageous soldier. Like de Valera, he had been a schoolmaster. In the town library is an exhibition which includes mementos presented by the Ashe family, and by de Valera who visited Dingle in 1967 for the fiftieth anniversary commemoration of Ashe's death in 1917. Ironically, had Ashe survived, he and de Valera would probably have ended up locked in combat; in Lewes Gaol he was one of only two prisoners who stood out against de Valera and supported Collins' proposal that Joe McGuinness should stand for election to Westminster. I don't know whether he had resented de Valera's assumption of authority, trusted Collins' judgment, or reckoned that the election strategy was a good idea in itself. One way or the other, as soon as he was freed under the general amnesty he threw himself into Sinn Féin's constitutional campaigning. Then, in August 1917, along with two other Kerry men who had also been involved in the 1916 Rising, he was re-arrested on a charge of sedition.

Beyond Dingle town, where the narrow peninsula tapers into the west, is the farmland where Ashe's mother's people lived between the ocean and the mountains. He was raised with a love of the Irish language and of the heritage of traditional music that is still passed on in Corca Dhuibhne today. Like the playwright Seán O'Casey, he was an enthusiastic Gaelic League member before the Rising and taught himself to play the bagpipes, then seen as both suitably Gaelic and suitably martial, although neither claim has much basis in history. One of the exhibits in Dingle Library is the uniform Ashe wore in a pipe band that he helped to establish in Dublin. I find the faded fabric under its protecting glass slightly sinister, but that is a throwback to my childhood fear of the musty Victorian bed curtains in the National Museum's doll's house. My knee-jerk objection to the fact that the uniform includes a kilt can also be traced to my upbringing.

Ashe and his companions were re-arrested under a temporary Emergency Powers Act introduced in Westminster at the outset of the First World War and increasingly used towards the end of the war to suppress the upsurge of nationalism in Ireland. He and about forty other republican activists were convicted of making

seditious speeches and sentenced to penal servitude in Dublin's
Mountjoy Prison. As soon as they got there they went on hunger
strike for recognition of their political status. It was the same
strategy that British feminist suffragists had used before the
war and Irish republicans had used in Frongoch and in English
prisons. Determined not to be blackmailed, the authorities
had developed a standard response. First, the prisoners' beds,
bedding and boots were taken away. Then, having been left to
sleep on the stone floors of their cells, they were dragged out one
by one and forcibly fed. A few hours after Ashe was taken out he
was carried back unconscious and removed to a Dublin hospital,
where he died.

Force-fed prisoners were given soup via a funnel with a
rubber tube inserted through the mouth or nostril and pushed
down to the oesophagus; one of the dangers was that the food
might enter the lungs instead of the stomach; another was
tearing and infection. The inquest on Thomas Ashe found that
he died from heart failure and congestion of the lungs caused
by subjecting him to forcible feeding in his weak condition after
hunger-striking for five or six days and lying for fifty hours on
the stone floor of his cell. There is restored newsreel footage
of Ashe's funeral on YouTube showing the massed crowds, the
horse-drawn hearse loaded with flowers, the Volunteers and
Cumann na mBan members marching in uniform, and a guard
of honour around the coffin which includes two Fianna boys not
yet in their teens. You can see the cortège arriving in Glasnevin
Cemetery, around the corner from Washerwoman's Hill, and the
volleys of shots fired over the open grave. In the last moments
of the footage the camera pulls in on Michael Collins delivering
the eulogy. The footage is silent but the words are remembered.
'*Nothing additional remains to be said. That volley which we have
just heard is the only speech which it is proper to make above the
grave of a dead Fenian.*' It was a new style of rhetoric which,
by consciously avoiding Pearse's poetic phrases, flagged a new
brand of republicanism.

I doubt if any of my family was at that funeral. Tom Stokes died in Enniscorthy within hours of Thomas Ashe's death in Dublin so I assume that my grandparents took the train to Enniscorthy, climbed the steep hill to Cathedral Street and followed a different coffin. Brigid Lyons probably walked to Glasnevin, though, a black dot in the heaving crowd of 30,000 people. During her uncle's election campaign Ashe had signed her autograph book. Presumably because she was a member of Cumann na mBan, he added a quotation from a poem by one of the women who, with Maud Gonne, had founded Inghinidhe na hÉireann: the line, 'Oh Kathleen Ní Houlihan, your way's a thorny way', invokes the time-honoured image of Ireland as an abused woman demanding sacrifice from her menfolk.

I was taught at school that the personification of Ireland in poetry arose from the banning of nationalist ballads; by composing what the thickheaded English authorities thought were love songs, the cunning Irish poets could promote the idea of independence unbeknownst. To a certain extent that is true. But the idea of the land as a woman reborn, or renewed, through sacrifice is ancient. The Celts appear to have come to Ireland from Britain, moving ahead of the expanding Roman Empire. Among them were the People of the Goddess Danú who settled in Corca Dhuibhne. Danú represents the water which animates the earth and her ritual marriage to the sun god ensures the return of fertility in springtime after the barren winter. To promote this seasonal renewal, pre-Christian Celts held communal gatherings in which the King, a shaman or a tribal leader ritually or actually sacrificed himself in an enactment of the sun god's fusion with the earth mother. Variations of the same world view appear globally and the Christian story of Christ's death and resurrection echoes the same concept without the counterbalancing female element.

In the legend of Cú Chulainn the bird on the hero's shoulder is the goddess in her third aspect, which is Death. In some stories she appears in this aspect as a withered old woman, but on the battlefield she is a 'scaldcrow' who eats the flesh of the dead. Her other two aspects, the Maiden and the Mother, complete the ancient Celtic image of life as a constant, circular flow of energy from birth to maturity to old age and death, and back again. The agitprop play *Cathleen Ni Houlihan* reworks the idea of male sacrificial fusion with a triple-aspect goddess to produce a storyline in which a young man is drawn away from his human love and responsibilities by a powerful, demanding old woman who, once his sacrifice is accepted, becomes 'a young girl with the walk of a queen'. The man's implied death becomes irrelevant in the context of a world view which assures him of rebirth.

The goddess, who is both memory and potential, reappears in later stories as a human woman who personifies Ireland. Occasionally, revealing her pagan, agrarian origins, she also turns up as a cow, epitomising both fertility and wealth. Among her names are Cathleen or Caitlín Ní Houlihan and Róisín Dubh, and, while in the romantic tradition of poetry from the eighteenth, nineteenth and early twentieth centuries she figures as weak and grief-stricken, her earliest associations are with a powerful, fertile and necessary balance of male and female sexuality.

In Lewes Prison Thomas Ashe wrote a poem. Now almost forgotten, it was probably better known in the Ireland of my parent's childhood than the works of W. B. Yeats. In its combination of the personification of Ireland as an abused woman with the Christian story of Simon of Cyrene who helped Jesus to carry his cross to Calvary, it perfectly exemplifies a defining aspect of early twentieth-century Irish nationalist sentiment: *'Let me carry your Cross for Ireland, Lord! / Let me suffer the pain and shame / I bow my head to their rage and hate, / And I take on myself the blame. / Let them do with my body whate'er they will, / My spirit I offer to You / That the faithful few who heard her call / May be spared to Róisín Dubh.'*

Given the recent scandals about sexual abuse among the clergy, Ireland's view of Roman Catholicism, even among churchgoers, is now so ambivalent that Ashe's masochistic sentiments expressed in the context of the eroticisation of Ireland as a young woman seem almost indecent. But hindsight distorts the picture. It is perfectly appropriate that the dignified 1916 memorial in Dingle town, which lists the names of local men who died in the Easter Rising and the War of Independence, is a crucifixion scene. Both the memorial and Ashe's poem represent the deep religious faith and clear-minded willingness to sacrifice their own lives for the good of posterity which inspired many of those who fought. In fact all the evidence shows that, like Ashe, de Valera and Collins, thousands of Irish men and women of their time identified their revolutionary activism with Christ's sacrifice on the cross. That is not an idea with which it is easy to empathise in an increasingly secular society. Indeed, I have never found it easy to get my head around it myself. Then again, I have no memory of cultural oppression, colonisation, famine, or of being denied the vote on the grounds of my gender, all of which were part of the shared memory of those prepared to fight in 1916 who, in most cases, were educated to equate Catholicism with Irishness.

In 1815, when Ashe was born, practically the entire Dingle peninsula was owned by an English landlord known as Lord Ventry. The word 'Ventry' is an anglicisation of Ceann Trá or Fionn Trá, the ancient Irish name for what is now a seaside village a few miles from the house where I'm typing this. The name translates either as 'The Head of the Beach' or 'The Fair Beach' and the place is the setting for one of the most famous stories of Fionn and the Fianna who, according to legend, fought a bloody battle there to repel the invading forces of the King of the World. The title Baron Ventry was created by the English Crown in 1800 for a man called Thomas Mullins who, in 1797, had already been granted the title of Baronet of Burnham. If you drive into the Gaeltacht area beyond Dingle today you pass through Burnham, where the road is lined with neat houses of dressed stone and a former forge. Designed in a very different

style from the farmhouses farther west, they were built for
estate workers who, like my grandmother's family in Galway,
served the Big House. Lord Ventry's Big House is now a school.
In Thomas Ashe's time it was the place from which the fourth
Baron Ventry wielded an authority over his Irish tenants that
was almost absolute.

My brother-in-law Seán O'Leary was born and raised in
Dingle. In the late nineteenth century his grandmother Mary
McKenna's family was living near Burnham, in a place called
Baile Mhic a' Dubhaill. Like almost every other family on the
peninsula they were tenants of Lord Ventry. The household
consisted of Mary, who was about eight, her seven siblings,
her parents and her elderly grandparents. On Christmas Eve
in 1869, Mary's entire family, including her uncle, his wife and
their children, was evicted without notice or warning. They
must have been good tenants whose rent had never fallen into
arrears because Lord Ventry didn't throw them out on the road.
Instead they were ordered out of their home and instructed
to go to a new house in a place called Baile na nGamhain. But
Baile na nGamhain was at the far side of the mountain and the
shortest way to get to it was over the Conor Pass. These days the
same journey takes about forty minutes by car. The McKenna
family crossed the pass on foot that Christmas Eve, having first
walked from Burnham to Dingle. Then they walked on to Baile
na nGamhain. They may have carried their possessions with
them on a cart, although getting a wheeled vehicle over the steep
pass in winter would have added to the danger. That part of the
story hasn't been passed down in the family. The memory of the
sudden uprooting and the freezing walk over the Conor Pass
has, though, as has the reason for their eviction. Lord Ventry,
who was a hunting man, had decided to clear the land round
Burnham of people to create a deer park. Similar stories to the
McKennas' are held in the collective consciousness all over rural
Ireland and in the years leading up to 1916 the conditions in
which they could occur were still in place.

It would be nonsense to suggest that prior to the coming of the English the native Irish aristocracy ruled the Irish poor with warm, fuzzy love. But I suppose that at least they shared a world view, cultural reference points and a sense of identity, and communicated in a language which expressed their common experience and social values. That sense of separate identity combined with the international circumstances in which Ireland's surviving activists found themselves was what fuelled the renewed struggle for Irish independence after 1916. As the First World War came to an end the power of landlords over the poor was the same in much of rural Britain as it was in Ireland and, indeed, all over Europe, and many small European nations besides Ireland had been subsumed by their expansionist neighbours. By 1917 the Russian Empire had collapsed from within and the Austro-Hungarian Empire was destabilised. In 1918 there was mutiny in the German forces and social revolution on the streets. So the growing Irish desire to claim autonomy was in step with the times.

I don't know what hopes Marion had in 1918 for the future for which she and Tom had fought and for which he had died. Maybe, in another phrase used by my Enniscorthy grandmother, she threw her hat at the lot of them, and walked away from politics altogether. Or perhaps, like many of her generation of women activists, she fought on, because to do otherwise might have seemed to invalidate Tom's death. What I do know is that, like Brigid Lyons, she went on to build a career in medicine although, unlike Brigid, who qualified as a doctor, Marion took the more acceptable route for a woman and became a nurse. Perhaps that was the option that she would have chosen but I doubt if she was given a choice.

Eva Gore-Booth died eight years after the First World War ended, having lived to see the aspirations of the Committee of Women for Permanent Peace destroyed by post-war triumphalist power-mongering. By then she had come to believe that real social change required a radical rethink of everything that sexual liberation implied. In one of her last pieces of journalism she wrote: '*There is a vista before us of a Spiritual progress which far transcends all political matters, it is the abolition of the "manly" and the "womanly". Will you not help to sweep them into the museum of antiques?*'

8
After the Ball

ONE DAY AT SOME POINT either in 1920 or 1921 my grandmother was on a crowded Dublin tram. According to my mother, she was on her way home to Washerwoman's Hill after a shopping trip to the city centre. As the tram rattled towards the north side of the city a vehicle pulled across the tracks and halted it, and seconds later the tram was surrounded by armed police. This wasn't unusual but it was frightening and everyone inside froze. Outside, passers-by quickened their steps or turned down side streets. Two policemen with rifles got onto the lower deck, where my grandmother was, and began ordering the men on board to stand up one by one. My grandmother kept her eyes down; in those years Dubliners had learnt to be as inconspicuous as possible and to avoid eye contact with the police.

The Dublin trams of the period had a gap between the padded panel against which you rested your shoulders and the seat on which you sat. As the men behind her were ordered into the aisle and searched, my grandmother was sitting with her eyes cast down and her hands clasped in her lap when, suddenly, someone behind her poked her in the bum. Being a woman with a strong sense of her own dignity, her first reaction was outrage. Bad enough that a crowd of policemen with English accents were pointing rifles at her without some total stranger seizing his chance to act like a gurrier. But she couldn't object without drawing attention to herself and, moments later, she felt the insistent hand behind her again. Then she realised what was happening. Raising her eyes, she shot a quick glance at the policemen who were hustling a young man past her towards the front of the tram. Then she slid her hand under her thigh, took the gun which the passengers at the rear of the tram had been passing forward from seat to seat and, leaning forward, poked it through the gap in the seat in front of her. The woman sitting there stiffened just as she had done. There was the same moment of outrage followed by realisation. Then, as desperate to get rid of the gun as everyone else had been, my grandmother pushed it firmly under the woman's bum and saw a hand reach down to take it and pass it on.

I don't know what they would have done when the gun reached the front of the tram. Started passing it back in the opposite direction, I suppose. Anyway, they didn't need to. The young man was hustled off the tram and into the police lorry. The other policemen broke the circle they had made around the tram and backed away with their rifles still in their hands. Then they swung themselves into the lorry and drove off. Telling the story later, my grandmother said that the idea that the gun was still on the tram had worried her, and that it crossed her mind to get off as soon as possible and to catch another tram home. But logic suggested that a tram that had just been searched was probably a safer place to be than one that hadn't. Everyone else seemed to take the same view but, as they rattled on their way again, no one discussed it. In a city full of spies and informers the safest thing of all was to keep your mouth shut.

Between 1917 and 1919 tensions had escalated in Ireland. Ashe's death on hunger strike resulted in massive recruitment to the Volunteers and Cumann na mBan. The authorities responded by banning drilling, the carrying of arms, and all cultural activities like football matches, Irish-language classes and traditional music and dancing competitions. Meanwhile it was obvious that Westminster was continuing to play political games, and that whatever Home Rule deal might appear on the table when the war in Europe was over would exclude some or all of Ulster, where the Unionists were still determined to remain part of the empire. Then, in the last year of the war, the question of conscription in Ireland came up again and the British Prime

Minister Lloyd George tried to push it through by linking it to the ongoing negotiations about Home Rule. This provoked a huge Irish backlash. An anti-conscription committee was set up, consisting of trade unionists and representatives of all shades of political opinion, and backed by the Irish Catholic bishops; rallies were held all over the country and there were widespread strikes.

In response, Lloyd George decided to crack down hard on Sinn Féin which was seen as instigating the most aggressive anti-conscription protests. So in May 1918 most of the republican leaders were scooped up in a dawn raid, accused of conspiring with Germany to instigate another rising in Ireland, and deported to prisons in England. The accusation was groundless but the move served to incapacitate the militant Irish nationalists at a time when Britain was hard pressed to deal with the war in Europe. Michael Collins, whose intelligence network was becoming increasingly efficient, had heard what was about to happen and tried to warn the others. But most of them, including de Valera, Griffith, Constance Markievicz and Kathleen Clarke, were taken in the raid. Collins himself escaped capture.

As soon as the First World War was over there was a general election. It was the first at which all men over twenty-one and propertied women over thirty had the franchise although, inevitably, not everyone who was eligible to vote was registered on the electoral roll. Seventy-three Sinn Féin candidates were elected to Westminster, including thirty-seven who were imprisoned in England at the time. Among them was Constance Markievicz who became the first woman to be elected to the British parliament. None took their seat. Instead, in accordance with the manifesto on which they had been returned, those not locked up in England assembled in Dublin in January 1919 and formed Dáil Éireann, a separate Irish parliament which ratified the 1916 Proclamation of Independence and declared the existence of an Irish Republic. But negotiations for Home Rule were still ongoing and, besides, with an international peace process about to redraw boundaries and reaffirm political alliances worldwide, no one could know what form of independent state might actually be attainable. So what the meeting meant or thought it meant when it proclaimed an Irish Republic was unclear, and what each individual who attended the meeting understood it to mean remains debatable.

Collins was elected and appointed Minister of Finance. He was to have many other roles as well, including Adjutant General, Director of Intelligence and President of the IRB, which continued to act in parallel with the other republican groups as a secret, oath-bound organisation. Shortly after the Dáil was established, the Volunteers began to become known as the Irish Republican Army and Collins subsequently became their Director of Organisation and Arms Procurement. When I was young, this force was referred to as the Old IRA, to distinguish it from the IRA that began the new struggle against partition in the 1960s. The distinction was made because in my day, in some circles at least, being a member of the Old IRA made you a hero while being a member of the IRA meant that you were a terrorist. In January 1919 it meant that you were a member of the official army of an unofficial state that was about to erupt into what is now known as the Irish War of Independence. That war, which lasted from January 1919 to July 1921, was popularly presented to my generation as a kind of *Boy's Own* adventure in which the entire country, led by Collins on a bicycle, pitted itself against the might of Britain and won. My parents, who lived through it, never spoke to me about the War of Independence when I was growing up, but years later when my mother visited me in London I discovered that her childhood memories of it remained vivid in her old age. She told me the first of them in the 1990s as we sat over cappuccino and cake in Richmond-upon-Thames, in a place called the Café Mozart.

My family is not noticeably musical. Having no cousins, we didn't do large family parties, but if we had done them they definitely wouldn't have involved singing. I don't quite know why. We didn't even go in for bawling 'Happy Birthday' around the tea table, though I do have a memory of making rabbits out of the corner of a blanket in my cot while my mother sang as she made beds in the next room. I don't know if she often sang during her housework or if I remember the occasion because it was unusual, but I do remember the songs. She interspersed snatches of 'The Croppy Boy', a Wexford ballad about 1798, with the chorus of 'After The Ball', a popular American waltz of my grandmother's youth which had turned up again in the 1930s and 1950s in films of the musical *Show Boat.*

I know only two things about the house in which my mother grew up on Washerwoman's Hill: that it had a front and a back garden, and a piano with a piano stool. A piano was a standard item of Edwardian parlour furniture and, as result, sheet music sold in huge quantities; 'After The Ball', the most popular Tin Pan Alley tune of all time, had international sales of over 5 million copies before radio and television turned most Western European families from music makers to listeners. There may have been a piano in the rooms above my Galway grandfather's Haircutting Rooms in Eyre Square as well; knowing my Galway grandmother's sense of her social position, I'd be surprised if there wasn't. The piano in the parlour on Washerwoman's Hill had a stool, which must have been either square or oblong, because there was a compartment full of sheet music under the seat. Perhaps one or both of my grandparents played it, and perhaps Cathleen, Evie and May took piano lessons. My mother never played as an adult but she retained the idea that music-making was socially desirable.

There was a piano in the house that I grew up in Dublin which came from my grandmother's house in Enniscorthy. Perhaps it once stood in the parlour of the house on Washerwoman's Hill. It was a walnut upright of the right period, decorated with carved panels of thistles and shamrocks flanking a thorny rose, and between the central panel and the outer ones were two triangular patterns of screw holes where a couple of brass candle sconces had once been attached to the case. The only reason I know that it came from Enniscorthy is because my brother remembers its arrival. I never discussed it with my mother because, in terms of our relationship, it wasn't so much a piano as an elephant in the room.

I was ten or eleven when my parents decided that I should take music lessons. Since neither of them played an instrument themselves, I imagine that my teacher was chosen for her pupils' high success rate in the Royal Irish Academy's exams. The lessons were held in her house, in a large, gloomy upstairs room dotted with several paraffin heaters, each with a saucer of water on the rucked carpet in front of it: the water was supposed to control the smell. She began by sitting me at the piano and stating that the letter C was easy to remember because it was beside the lock. I was aware that pianos had locks because I enjoyed polishing the one on our walnut upright. But I couldn't see what that had to do with music. Nor could I see why anyone would find it difficult to remember the letter C. Shortly afterwards she used a blunt pencil to scratch letters over the pleasing patterns of black marks on the first page of my music book. It had been bought specially for me and, since I was the youngest child in the family, that didn't happen often. I couldn't protest because she was in charge but I don't think I ever forgave her. And, since I never heard a piece played in its entirety before I began to learn it, or attended a concert to hear what I might aspire to, every subsequent lesson continued to baffle and frustrate me. My teacher's reputation must have been well deserved, though, because somehow I reached Grade IV in my piano exams before being allowed to give up. Each year, having spent months thumping resentfully through the syllabus, I'd take the number sixty-two bus to the Academy's Georgian premises in Westland Row, scrape a pass and gain another certificate. But the moment I walked out the beautifully proportioned door with its brass plaque, knocker and handle, every note I had just played was expunged from my memory. If you had asked me to repeat the same pieces the next day I'd have been unable to. And if you asked me to pick out 'Three Blind Mice' by ear, then or since, I'd struggle. It never occurred to me to short-circuit the whole pointless process by going on strike. Like my mother in the photographic studio fifty years earlier, I had picked up a subliminal message that when good money had been spent on what was considered desirable, good girls kept the best side out.

I did once try to break my fingers by dropping the lid of my school desk on them, but they didn't break and it hurt so much that I didn't try again. I never told my mother but the next day, faced with another music lesson, I lost my temper and accused her of torturing me. She said that if I couldn't play the piano I'd never get a man. I suspect she was dealing with a dozen other household problems when I turned on her, and that she responded automatically with a line from her own childhood. But after that there didn't seem much more to say. So, years later, sitting over cappuccinos and cake in the Café Mozart in Richmond, we weren't discussing my music lessons. We were chatting about my engagement to Wilf, an opera director then working in Covent Garden at the Royal Opera House. I had never been to an opera or a classical concert before moving to London and I asked my mother in passing if there had been much music in Dublin when she was a child. What I got in response was the first of her three childhood memories of the War of Independence.

In 1918, with the war in Europe still hanging in the balance, the last thing Lloyd George could afford to do was risk another rising in Ireland, which was why he had outlawed nationalist activity and arrested the republican leaders. But his strategy produced a knock-on effect on the Royal Irish Constabulary: police numbers began to fall. As the man at my event in Enniscorthy Library said, the police force in Ireland was made up of members of local families and everyone knew who they were. Some policemen resigned in protest against the increasingly repressive laws they had to enforce. Others left because they were intimidated by nationalist neighbours or felt shamed in front of their families. Then, in late 1919, the steady trickle of resignations became a haemorrhage. The IRA, reacting to increased repression, had begun a campaign of intimidation and violence against the police which resulted in dozens of burnt-out barracks and over fifty deaths.

Faced with a depleted police force and increased unrest in Ireland, Lloyd George approved a proposal for a new armed force to support the RIC, and advertisements were placed in British newspapers for ex-army servicemen ready to sign up for 'a rough and dangerous task'. Thousands of men had returned from the trenches to high unemployment in Britain, so there were plenty of recruits. The new force, officially called the Royal Irish Constabulary Reserve Force, arrived in Ireland in March 1920. It was followed by a second one, called the Auxiliary Division, recruited from former British army officers at the suggestion of Winston Churchill, who at the time was Secretary of State for War. Ostensibly police but effectively militia, the first force was known in Ireland as the Black and Tans, because of their parti-coloured uniforms; the second was called the Auxies. In Seán O'Casey's play *The Shadow of a Gunman*, Dubliners anticipating a police raid during the War of Independence hope it will be the Tans not the Auxies, who were known to be the more brutal. But fear of the Black and Tans, who were active more widely across the country, remains uppermost in Ireland's collective memory. I suppose that individual memories, like my mother's and those of thousands of Irish children of her generation, depended on individual experience.

I don't know if there was a copy of the music of 'After The Ball' in the piano stool in the house on Washerwoman's Hill, but I know that the mixture of sheet music it contained included *Moore's Irish Melodies,* which were standard songs of the time. Born in Dublin of a Wexford mother and a father from the Corca Dhuibhne Gaeltacht, Thomas Moore became a nineteenth-century celebrity by grafting English lyrics and sentiments

onto traditional Irish tunes. His songs, which had titles like
'She Is Far From The Land Where Her Young Hero Sleeps' and
'Let Erin Remember The Days Of Old', projected romanticised
images of Ireland into fashionable Victorian and Edwardian
drawing rooms, bringing him aristocratic friends and royal
patronage. When I was growing up, they were often dismissed
as West British, which is what de Valera's Ireland called all
aspects of Irish culture that appeared to have English influence.
So in my childhood, despite his Gaeltacht roots, which were
never mentioned, Moore's music was the antithesis of what was
perceived to be *fíor Gaelach*. In my parents' childhood, however,
its Irishness was literally terrifying.

One day when my mother was nine or ten, she found her
father on his knees in the parlour on Washerwoman's Hill
rummaging through the sheet music in the piano stool. More
than sixty years later, sitting over coffee in the Café Mozart, she
described to me how she went and sat on the floor beside him
and helped to sift out the sheet music of *Moore's Irish Melodies*
with its Edwardian steel engravings of dying heroes, broken
towers and weeping harpists. It made quite a big pile which she
divided into two stacks while her father went off and found a
box. Then they put the music into the box and buried it in the
back garden.

As a small child she hadn't needed to be told why they did
it but she could see when she told me the story that I didn't
understand. So, sitting in London, licking foam off her coffee
spoon, she explained. The night before she and her father buried
the music, a neighbour's house had been raided. The policemen
who kicked down the door may have been Auxies but my mother
called them Tans. Either the family who lived in the house had
no nationalist connections or whoever it was that the police
were looking for had escaped. Anyway, no one was arrested.
But frustrated and, according to the neighbours, half-drunk,
the Tans ransacked the house, determined to find evidence of
sedition. In the piano stool in the parlour they found volumes

of *Moore's Irish Melodies* in green and gold covers wreathed with shamrocks. So they herded the terrified family into the parlour in their nightclothes and, taking potshots at his feet with their revolvers, they forced the man of the house onto a table and made him sing the songs.

My grandparents on both sides of the family were lucky; as far as I know neither the house on Washerwoman's Hill nor the Hairdressing Rooms on Eyre Square was ever raided. But the fact remains that my parents' generation spent their pre-teen and early teenage years surrounded by escalating violence which at any moment could erupt into their homes. In Frongoch the republican leaders had recognised the folly of engaging in pitched battle with larger, better-armed forces. So what my mother referred to as the Tan War was a matter of hit and run. The IRA depended on friends, family and strangers to feed and shelter them, hide them in haystacks and attics, treat their wounds, provide them with transport, and act as spies, decoys and messengers. Effectively, and regardless of their personal politics, Ireland's entire population spent the War of Independence in the front line.

Many Tans and Auxies had been brutalised and traumatised by their experience of the First World War, and they had been recruited for what the authorities had explicitly described as a rough job of work in Ireland. It was a recipe for mayhem. Between late March 1920 and early July 1921 they responded to attacks on the police with indiscriminate reprisals on innocent civilians as well as on captured IRA men and their families. Men, women and children were shot in the streets and fields, torture and abduction were commonplace, and houses, creameries, farms, shops and businesses were deliberately burned to the ground. In response, the IRA burned and bombed houses belonging to Anglo-Irish families and to others who remained – or were perceived to remain – loyal to the Crown. As republican resistance hardened, British troops were deployed in Ireland. In the countryside the IRA was organised in flying columns of about twelve or fifteen men who struck fast and then melted into the community, which then paid the price. In some areas whole towns and villages were sacked by troops and police. On one night in December 1920, in retaliation for the ambush of an Auxiliary patrol, the centre of Cork city was burned and looted, destroying over 40 business premises, 300 residential properties, the City Hall and the Carnegie Library.

Those stories were part of my childhood cultural inheritance but we never learned about the numbers of British journalists who exposed what was going on in Ireland in the British press, or the extent to which British public opinion was outraged by what was revealed. Nor were we taught that the image of poorly armed Irish freedom fighters staunchly supported by a terrorised civilian population was a powerful weapon in a propaganda war supported by pan-pacifists as well as by republicans. But that was the case, and the fact that we were unaware of it has much to do with Éamon de Valera's determination to rewrite the story of his personal relationship with Michael Collins.

In 1919, while Collins coordinated the struggle at home, de Valera went on an eighteen-month tour of the United States, attempting to drum up Irish-American support for the republic. In fact, he seems to have alienated almost as many Irish-American groups as he impressed but, given the international climate of the time, the US press coverage of what was happening in Ireland made life doubly difficult for Lloyd George. In January 1920, following the peace conference that ended the First World War, the League of Nations was set up to prevent future wars by promoting international cooperation. It was strongly supported in Britain where the Fabians and others, including the feminists who had attended the Hague Conference in 1915, campaigned for an international council that would peacefully adjudicate all future world conflicts. The American president Woodrow Wilson supported the concept, and commissions were established in both countries to work out ways and means. Among all this idealism Britain could hardly crash over to Ireland and engage in full-scale war. But by tacitly approving a reign of terror and supplementing it with undercover intelligence operations, Lloyd George and Churchill hoped to frighten the Irish public into giving up the IRA men on the ground, and to eliminate the republican leaders.

It didn't work. Collins' intelligence network beat Lloyd George's hands down and the population continued to support the IRA. No doubt some people, like my grandmother on the tram, felt that they were involved in a terrifying game of Pass the Parcel in which they had no choice but to take part. Others, with remarkable heroism, actively risked their lives to protect men and women they didn't know and might never meet again; and as a result, in many cases, they and their families suffered brutal beatings, torture or sexual assault, and watched their homes and businesses burn. I don't know what part Marion played in the War of Independence but I know that it was fiercely fought in Wexford, and that in Enniscorthy the Tans took hostages from known nationalist families and tied them to posts at the front of their lorries. My mother said once that she'd been told that 'during the troubles' an aunt of hers brought weapons from one part of Enniscorthy to another hidden in a baby's pram. That story is such an archetype of Irish revolutionary legend that it may or may not be true. When I asked her to tell me more she said she had forgotten how she'd heard about it.

Our 1950s Dublin semi had a box on the kitchen wall in which one of a series of discs would swing if an electric bell was pressed in one of the reception rooms or the master bedroom. Although the house was newly built when we moved in, the bells were already obsolete. They belonged to a time when labour was so cheap and housework so heavy that if you could afford to live in a house at all you could probably afford to keep servants. Neither we nor anyone we knew was in that position. When I was small, Sadie, who had once worked for Maud Gonne MacBride, came in once a week to help my mother to scrub the floor and do the laundry, and I remember a gentle girl called

Joan who helped with the periodic big clean, which involved moving heavy furniture. Sometimes she used to bath me and babysit if my parents were going out. But the majority of the housework for our family of seven was done by my mother, until my sisters and I were old enough to help and Sadie's muscle was replaced by the twin-tub washing machine that had to be filled and emptied at the kitchen sink.

As well as the electric bells, the builder had installed fireplaces in the two reception rooms, and two of the four bedrooms. The idea of keeping four open fires and a kitchen stove lit, stoked and cleared was as impractical as the notion of summoning servants. So, as Nacie's bed had done in the house in Eyre Square, the cot in which I slept in my parents' bedroom till my Galway grandmother died stood against a boarded-up fireplace. In the next room, which was my grandmother's, a paraffin heater blocked the grate and a large piece of furniture beside the bed blocked access to a built-in cupboard by the chimney breast. This was because most of our furniture came from the old houses in Galway and Enniscorthy and fitted awkwardly into 1950s rooms. The living room, which we called the dining room but which was seldom used for meals except at Christmas, was heated by an open fire, laid, lit and cleared by my mother. The other reception room, which was larger and difficult to heat, was rarely used. But the piano stood in an alcove there, so I used to practice with a two-bar electric fire at my feet and the long red velvet curtains that my mother had bought from the auction at Maude Gonne's house drawn across the French doors at the end of the room, to keep out the cold.

When we moved into the house, which was bought because my grandmother was coming to live with us, my mother was pregnant with me. She hated leaving the rented home she had lived in since her marriage and dreaded living with her demanding mother-in-law, and it didn't take long for her to become Bad Mummy who was overworked and cross, as opposed to Good Granny who was fun to be with. Ensconced in bed with her meals brought up on trays, my grandmother was warm and welcoming to my siblings and she appears to have been charmed to have a baby to play with. My mother, meanwhile, was knackered and glad to have someone to take me off her hands. As a result, much of the first three years of my life was spent on my grandmother's bed with the blocked door of the built-in cupboard on my right and her restless, bony body on my left, as she drank tea, sang songs and told me stories. We enjoyed each other's company, although the cupboard in her room gave me nightmares. The possibilities of what might be in there in the darkness troubled me, and the fact that it couldn't fulfil the function it was designed for made me cross.

I don't remember where my mother and I were when she told me her second memory of the War of Independence. She stayed with me in many places in London, from the room I rented while I was a drama student, where she had the bed, I slept on the floor, and we drank tea by a gas fire, to the flats I shared with fellow actors, and the maisonette which Wilf and I bought when we were first married. I don't remember the context either: perhaps we were talking about my childhood associations with particular landmarks in Dublin, like Bewley's Café and Fusiliers' Arch. Her own childhood landmark was on the north side of the city, somewhere near the bottom of Washerwoman's Hill. When she was small she and her sisters used to be sent out for a walk each day with a maid who came in for a couple of hours in the afternoons to help in the house. One particular walk, which was their favourite, took them past a bench where a man used to sit reading a newspaper. According to my mother, he was very friendly and always had sweets in his pockets and she, Cathleen and Evie would sit on a nearby wall eating them while the man and the maid who took them for their walk chatted. She was a local girl who worked for several of the neighbours and, as she doesn't seem to have been much older than my aunt Cathleen, who was about twelve, she too may have enjoyed the toffee and humbugs on offer. Or maybe the man's gallantry attracted her.

According to my mother, he always stood up and raised his hat to them before they continued on their way.

Ireland's government at the time was administered from Dublin Castle, which began as a defensive foothold for the Norman colonists, later became the seat of the Viceroy, and by Michael Collins' time was the nerve centre of the British Intelligence service in Ireland. Its weakness was the fact that many of the people who worked there were Irish. By building up a network of espionage agents within the Castle, Collins gathered information about every aspect of police activity, from procedure to planning, to the codes used for transmitting messages to Britain and the personal relationships which could be used as pressure points. In some instances he was the only person who knew the identities of the men and women who were his most trusted agents and, having been chosen in the first instance for their discretion, many of them remained silent about their role in the War of Independence for the rest of their lives. As the war intensified the British increased the numbers of their own intelligence agents in Dublin where some, who posed as Castle informants, worked as double agents. Collins steadily identified who they were and recruited an elite group of assassins, known as The Squad, to target and shoot them. None of The Squad was older than about twenty-one or twenty-two, they worked in pairs and, like the IRA men fighting in the countryside, they struck fast and melted back into the community. Ordinary life was underpinned by a web of espionage, secrecy and bloodshed.

There was a tacit understanding between Cathleen, Evie and May and the girl who looked after them that they might all be in trouble if my grandmother knew that they talked to a stranger on their walks, so nothing was ever said when they got home. Then one day as they approached the bench near the bottom of Washerwoman's Hill there was no man sitting there. My mother remembered seeing people on the other side of the road standing in groups, talking. Suddenly the maid grabbed her by the hand

and hustled them past the bench. She wasn't quick enough to
stop the children seeing the pool of blood on the pavement. My
mother said that as soon as she saw it she knew that the man with
the sweets had been a spy. The blood itself was frightening but
the fact that she couldn't talk to my grandmother about it seems
to have been worse. But she never did. God knows how the maid
who had chatted openly to the man in broad daylight must have
felt; in those days to be an actual or perceived informer was as
dangerous as to be a spy.

My Galway grandmother died in bed in our Dublin semi,
in the room with the cupboard that couldn't be opened. Either
because we were waiting for the undertaker or to keep me
from running into her empty bedroom and asking questions,
the door to her room was then locked. No one told me what
had happened and I remember sitting on the bottom step of
the stairs trying to make sense of it. My mother would have
been horrified to know how much of the tension between her
and my grandmother I had picked up on by about the age of
four. She had resolutely kept the best side out during the years
that my grandmother lived with us and, besides, she operated
on the principle that adults always presented a unified front
before children. My Galway grandmother, however, had never
let principles get in the way of a good sulk, and I had seen how
she had demanded tea that she didn't really want, and watched
my mother climb the stairs with trays of food that was often
left uneaten. That day, as I sat at the foot of the stairs, I saw my
father coming down the hall towards me looking tired. I was
used to him looking in on my grandmother as soon as he came
in from work and, having tried and failed that morning to see
her myself, I decided to save him the trouble of going upstairs.
So I told him confidentially that my mother had locked granny
into her room and stopped feeding her. He had just lost his
dearly loved mother after years of being piggy in the middle
between her and his equally dearly loved wife so he probably
didn't feel up to discussing life, death and the complexities of

adult power struggles with a four-year-old. Anyway, he said nothing.

Both Michael Collins and Éamon de Valera had the ability to inspire intense personal loyalty in their followers. Each was accustomed to taking control of a situation by projecting immense confidence, and both were sticklers for detail, had great physical courage and, as the War of Independence continued, lived increasingly on their nerves. Collins' story reads like a cross between an *Indiana Jones* film script and the classic Irish myths in which the hero dies young at the height of his powers, having been betrayed by circumstance and forewarned by portents of his fate. The *Indiana Jones* element, which was established during the War of Independence, turned him into a legend in his own lifetime. He became the Big Fella, never betrayed by the people despite the huge price on his head, who passed through police cordons unnoticed, organised arms-smuggling routes and underground newspapers, created the hit unit that broke the power of Dublin Castle, and masterminded a national loan which funded the creation of the independent state. What the legends of that period omitted until comparatively recently was the internal power struggle that still dogged the fight for independence. But, as far as it goes, the legend of the Big Fella is very close to the truth. Dressed like the respectable post office clerk he had once been, Collins applied the strategy of hiding in full view, and travelled undetected around Dublin on his bike, coordinating the military, intelligence and propaganda elements of the war from a series of safe houses and secret offices. It was his superhuman image as much as his genius for strategy that carried the poorly armed guerrilla fighters through to 1921, when the war finally ended in a truce.

Whatever personal memories my father and Marguerite may have had of the War of Independence have been lost. I remember my father telling me that he had clear recall of the day in November 1918 when the First World War ended: his father had come into the Hairdressing Rooms in Eyre Square carrying a newspaper and called up the stairs to his wife that an armistice had been signed. If my father remembered that, which happened when he was seven, it seems unlikely that he had no memories of the Black and Tans and the Auxies in Galway two years later. The west coast of Ireland was seen by the British as a hotbed of Sinn Féin activity and Galway city was full of troops and police. While much of the violence took place in the surrounding countryside, *The Galway Express* newspaper reported 'an orgy of murder and wreckage' after one night of raids in the city, houses and businesses in Eyre Square were looted on more than one occasion, and two thirds of The Railway Hotel opposite my grandfather's Hairdressing Rooms was commandeered by the military. My father, who grew up to be a military historian, was fascinated by uniforms, flags and weaponry, even as a child. Among the papers in our house in Dublin when he died were school copybooks full of drawings of soldiers and descriptions of battles. Yet none of them depicts anything of the war that he saw at close quarters as a child.

So I am left with my mother's third memory of the Tans. After the day that the spy with the sweets was shot, Cathleen, Evie and May became acutely aware of the policemen who drove past at high speed, sitting back to back in their lorries with their rifles pointed outward. The maid, who still took them for walks in the afternoons, warned them never to look up when the lorries passed or the Tans would shoot at them. Every child in Dublin must have been given the same warning because by that stage both the police and the military were known to fire indiscriminately at civilians, and the Tans, according to my mother, increasingly drove around drunk. Then one evening in what must have been the summer of 1920 my grandparents were out and my mother, who had been playing in the front garden with a child from next door, was called indoors and told to go to bed. It was still light outside and she hadn't wanted to leave her game so, as soon as she had the opportunity, she sneaked back out again and, keeping low so she wouldn't be seen from the house, ran across the garden and wriggled through a hole in the hedge, hoping that the neighbour's child would still be playing outside. As she ran along by the hedge she heard gunshots. But there was nothing unusual in that. So, once through the hedge, she ran on through the next-door garden trying to find her friend. It was years before she discovered that the unfortunate babysitter had heard the shots just as she discovered that my mother hadn't gone to bed and, running to the front step, had seen a policeman on a lorry taking aim at what appeared to be a fugitive figure escaping in the shelter of the hedge. None of what happened next made any sense to my mother at the time. All she knew was that the door of the neighbour's house opened suddenly and an adult dragged her inside. Then, after a lot of exclaiming and hugging, she was taken up to her friend's bedroom and told she could stay the night. When she woke the next day she felt a bit apprehensive but when my grandmother came around to collect her, nobody was cross. Given what had happened, the adults in both households were probably still in shock. After the first couple of shots the Tans on the lorry must have realised that the escaping fugitive was actually a small girl; perhaps it became obvious when she moved from the shelter of the hedge to cross the lawn. Had they been drunk, or had anyone on the run been known to be in the area, they might have kept firing anyway. Instead, according to the babysitter, an officer shouted an order and the lorry drove away.

According to my mother, that incident was too much for my grandmother. By the time the truce was signed in July 1921 my grandfather had retired from his job in the post office and moved the family to Enniscorthy. Maybe the piano from Washerwoman's Hill went with them and was carried up the steep streets to the house in Cathedral Street opposite the three stones that once stood round the pump; or perhaps the piano with its carved panels of thistles and shamrocks flanking a thorny rose was already there in the house when they arrived. Later on they must have bought a gramophone because when the walnut upright arrived in our 1950s semi in Dublin it came with a miscellaneous collection of sheet music and a pile of old seventy-eights which included a tinny recording of 'After The Ball'. When my mother died in 1990 she left the piano to me. I have no idea why. We had still never spoken about my music lessons but perhaps she thought that Wilf and I might bring it to London and have children, and that they might learn to play and somehow cancel out the past. We never did have children and the piano never left Ireland. When the Dublin semi was sold after my mother's death I did a deal with a guy who took it in exchange for driving my share of my father's books to London in a clapped-out van. The house was almost empty when the van was being loaded but at the last minute my brother realised that Maud Gonne MacBride's velvet curtains were still hanging at the window of the chilly room where I used to practise my scales. We took them down and used them to pad the cardboard boxes of books and, back in London, I ripped out the old lining which was in shreds and hung them in the front room of our house. The red velvet had faded almost to grey but they still looked wonderful.

9
Silence

MY GRANDMOTHER, WHO hated family arguments, may have chosen the worst possible time to return to Enniscorthy. The truce that ended the War of Independence was about to be followed by a disastrous peace negotiation in Westminster, and the outcome was a civil war that wounded Irish family relationships so deeply that it could still hardly be spoken of in the Ireland in which I grew up. In that silence wounds festered, scar tissue distorted the body politic, and the idea that lies were safer than truth became the norm. The reasons for it, however, were more complex than my generation was taught to believe.

During de Valera's tour of the United States, the newspapers there had spun his title of President of the Dáil into President of the Republic. No one at home seems fully to have taken in the implications of the fact that he did not correct the error; perhaps he himself was unaware of them at the time. After he returned to Ireland it became evident that the peace negotiation following the truce was going to be difficult. Even before it began, Lloyd George made clear that he was not prepared to give Ireland more than Dominion status within the British Empire, and that the issue of partition had not gone away. In the circumstances Collins took the view that sending in a team of negotiators to demand a republic was a non-starter. He also warned the Dáil that the IRA was down to its last supplies of ammunition which meant that if negotiations broke down and war was resumed, the British would certainly win. But de Valera had conceived his own notion of a potential relationship between the two countries, which he called External Association, and he was convinced that it would solve everyone's problems. The trouble was that no one at home seems to have understood or accepted his concept, and there was no indication that Lloyd George would either.

The clock was ticking and the Dáil was in danger of appearing divided and indecisive, which is precisely the message you don't want to send out before beginning a negotiation. And, since they actually were undecided and divided on what could or should be achieved, no one was eager to be co-opted to the negotiating team. Collins warned that if his personal cover was blown, the intelligence network on which republican military strategy depended would collapse which, even if new sources of arms could be found, would put an end to any hope of returning to the fight. In fact Collins and de Valera each made the same argument for avoiding being present at the negotiation. Both insisted that the team sent to London would be in a stronger position if it could buy time by saying that it had to refer back to a higher – and in Collins' case, impressively shadowy – authority. And that appears to have been the problem. De Valera was determined that he, not Collins, would be seen to have the higher status: and if the negotiation should fail, he wanted Collins to be part of the team that would be blamed. Kathleen Clarke remembered him saying that, if things went wrong in London, the Dáil must have scapegoats. Ultimately he made sure that he wouldn't become a scapegoat himself by insisting that as President he was the symbol of the Irish people and should therefore hold aloof. It was a winning argument and, ironically, Collins had handed it to him on a plate by co-proposing a motion by which the Dáil ratified de Valera's title of President of the Republic. The motion had been suggested by de Valera himself; and amidst everything else that was going on, no one pointed out that the title had originally been conferred on him by a journalist who was either beefing up his copy or had simply made a mistake.

De Valera's next step was to insist that Collins be one of the negotiators. He got his way and, having got it, went on to build disunity into the team by deliberately choosing individuals who were likely to disagree. It was a strategy he used consistently throughout his political life, and in this instance he may have thought that a divided team in London would slow things down, leaving useful wriggle room for assessment at home. Or he may have been stacking the odds against Collins. Or both. One way or the other, having been manoeuvred into a position in which he was damned if he did and damned if he didn't, Collins agreed to go. The Dáil then unanimously passed a motion giving the negotiators plenipotentiary powers and de Valera followed with a side letter which appeared to limit them. In hindsight, it seems astonishing that any team would allow itself to be sent to the table on this basis. But the clock was still ticking and failure to turn up in London was unthinkable. So everyone seems to have decided that they had no choice.

When my grandparents moved from Dublin to Enniscorthy it was decided that Cathleen, Evie and May would become boarders at a nearby school; given the uncertainty of the times, it may have been felt that boarding school was the safest place for them. On my grandfather's retirement, the Lords Commissioners of His Majesty's Treasury awarded him a pension, on and from 27 August 1921. According to my mother, he retired early because God alone knew what an Irish clerk employed by the British Postal Service might be entitled to after a treaty was negotiated. He doesn't seem to have coped well with retirement or with the move from Dublin. When they arrived in Enniscorthy, he bought them all bicycles and planned family trips into the countryside. Instead his health failed soon after the move and he spent much of his time in bed.

Everyone in the Dáil was aware that Lloyd George had made it clear from the outset that the plenipotentiaries were not going to return from London with a treaty that endorsed the immediate establishment of a republic. What they did come back with, after anguished to-ing and fro-ing between London and Dublin, frenzied redrafting in committee rooms, quiet words in private drawing rooms, and much dissent among themselves, was a treaty they were all prepared to stand by and which they believed to be the best that could be got. It offered Free State status, not a republic and, while the rest of the country waited, it was debated in the Dáil. Even before the team returned from London, de Valera had expressed outrage at the result of the negotiation. The fact that he could have been there himself and influenced the outcome was brought up at the Dáil debate but lost in a welter of recrimination, justification and emotive rhetoric. One of the substantive issues in the treaty on the table was the fact that it accepted partition; however, what dominated the Dáil debate was the fact that the acceptance of Free State status involved taking of an oath of allegiance to the British Crown.

By the time I was at school the story of what happened next had been simplified into a dramatic scenario in which de Valera and his followers, incorruptibly loyal to those who had died for a republic, rose up and walked away from compromise. Actually, desperate attempts were made to come up with several different compromises and by the time the Dáil reconvened after a Christmas recess the country at large had joined in the debate. Inevitably, lacking the detail of the facts, people had begun to reduce it to personal loyalties, old prejudices and sentiment. De Valera responded with equally simplistic rhetoric. At one stage, a journalist questioned his right to make decisions for the Irish people on the ground that he was an American citizen. In response, de Valera declared that, having been reared in a labourer's cottage in Ireland, whenever he wanted to know what the Irish people wanted he had only to examine his own heart.

In January 1922 the Dáil voted to accept the treaty and de Valera immediately announced his intention to resign. This may have just been a threat intended to reopen the debate. If it was, it backfired. His resignation was accepted and he and his supporters promptly walked out, declaring that they would continue the fight for a republic. The majority of Cumann na mBan and former Citizen Army women followed him, which ultimately proved unfortunate for the rest of us. Given that Cumann na mBan had sounded warning bells about de Valera's attitude towards women during the Rising, the extent to which women supported him at this stage might seem strange. But on an emotional level they seem to have felt that loyalty to their dead comrades demanded that they stick to their guns. They may also have been swayed by the fact that many of the individuals and institutions that supported the treaty, including the Catholic Church, were traditionally conservative and anti-feminist. One of de Valera's followers was Constance Markievicz who continued to campaign as a feminist for the rest of her career. Hannah Sheehy-Skeffington, whose feminist views were far more politically and philosophically sophisticated than Markievicz's, also took the republican side. As with ordinary life, politics are a matter of endless prioritisation and reassessment and, in the end, the decisions made by individuals are dictated by personality as much as by conviction. After the walkout the remaining members of the Dáil elected Griffith as their president and reapportioned ministerial responsibilities between them. One of Collins' first tasks was to chair a committee which drafted the Free State's constitution. The committee's work was later criticised for being too heavily influenced by British law. But unlike de Valera's Constitution of the Republic, drafted fifteen years later, it included no clauses that declared the proper aspiration of women to be marriage, and our proper sphere the home. Nor did it declare, as de Valera's constitution would, that the Catholic Church held a special position within the Irish state. That came later, after yet another conflict in which Irish women took an active part that was subsequently hardly acknowledged, and, indeed, after many of the civil and religious liberties enshrined in Collins' committee's constitution had already been eroded.

I remember sitting by the fire in our Dublin semi once, with my aunt Cathleen and my mother. Cathleen was reading a newspaper and my mother and I were talking about Enniscorthy; it was shortly after my father's death in 1975 so perhaps her mind was on the past. Anyway, she produced a memory from

1922 when Ireland was plunged into the Civil War, a period I had never heard her speak of before. De Valera's walkout in January 1922 had been followed by months of political developments in which, among other things, partition became a fait accompli, Britain withdrew its forces from the Free State, an uneasy temporary pact was agreed between the pro- and anti-treaty factions, and a general election was held in Ireland. The election was not a referendum on the outcome of the peace negotiation but, since a significant majority voted for parties that supported the treaty, it was an indicator of public support for the Free State. Or of war-weariness. Or both. But regardless of the election results, skirmishes between pro- and anti-treaty supporters escalated to the point that, despite all efforts to avert it, the country descended into civil war. I don't know if the Stokes family, who had seen Marion and Tom go out to fight for a republic, supported de Valera's anti-treaty stance. If so, family tensions in Enniscorthy must have been running high because, according to my mother, my grandfather believed that the results of the general election had demonstrated the electorate's support for the treaty and that democracy must be upheld. Apparently he also had personal confidence in Michael Collins as a man who, having been trained in the post office service, could at least be relied on to keep a ledger.

In July 1922, when Cathleen, Evie and May were home for the school holidays, republican forces took Enniscorthy town. My mother remembered my grandparents dithering about whether the family should stay put or try to get out. By the time they decided that the children would be safer in the countryside most of the neighbours from whom they could hitch a lift or borrow a car had already left. Presumably the option of leaving on bicycles was considered too dangerous so Aunt Magger got in touch with a local undertaker, perhaps the friend who later gave Evie the coffin boards to build a bookcase, and he agreed to take them out of town in his horse-drawn hearse. My grandfather and Aunt Magger sat up beside the driver while my grandmother and the children sat inside. My mother remembered looking out through a glass panel and seeing Aunt Magger holding up a prayer book, and the sound of the horses' hooves as they passed the castle and crossed the bridge. It was an odd route to take out of town because the republicans and the Free Staters were firing at each other across the river from the castle to what my mother called the county lunatic asylum. Possibly other ways out were blockaded. Anyway, she said the shooting stopped when they reached the bridge and they crossed it safely.

While my mother told that story I was watching my aunt Cathleen. Her feet, in polyester damask slippers, were moving on the hearthrug and two red spots had appeared high on her cheeks below her gold-rimmed glasses. Fascinated by the *Gone With The Wind* image of the horse-drawn hearse fleeing the battle, I asked her if she had been frightened. She lowered her newspaper, met my mother's eyes briefly, and declared that she remembered none of it. Then she raised the paper again like a barrier. When I turned back to my mother she looked exactly like the round-eyed little girl she had once been, subdued by the direct glance of her elder sister. The subject was changed and I never asked Cathleen about her childhood again.

Sometime later, in London, my mother told me that they had been taken in the hearse to a house on a cliff above a little village called Ballyconnigar and left there. Cathleen was fourteen, May was just twelve and Evie was ten. I don't know if the adults they stayed with were relatives but I know that my mother and her sisters didn't get on with the other children in the house; they were laughed at for being townies and Evie got confused and upset when yellow liquid offered from a covered white enamel bucket turned out not to be lemonade at all, but pee. Their own adults had gone back to Enniscorthy for fear that empty houses there might be looted. One of the horrors of that war was that you could rely on nothing and no one. Neighbours became enemies, brothers and sisters fought on different sides, and the violence, which included atrocities that equalled those of the War of Independence, was often fuelled by emotion that bordered on madness. Having taken a stand on one side or the other, men and women who had previously been united against the British tore themselves, their families and their communities apart. Each side accused the other of betrayal, treachery and cowardice and in the mayhem old scores that had nothing to do with politics were quietly settled with arson, theft or a bullet in the back. De Valera only had minority support but the systems of law enforcement that had existed under British rule were gone and, as in all post-revolutionary states, the newly established government feared disaffection in the army and the effect of continued violence on the country's economy. So the Free State introduced increasingly draconian legislation. In the final phase of the Civil War seventy-seven republican prisoners were executed by firing parties of their former comrades; many died in the same yard in Kilmainham Gaol where the leaders of the 1916 Rising had been shot.

I don't know exactly how long Cathleen, Evie and May remained in the cottage on the cliff in Ballyconigar but they were still there more than a month after their arrival. Each day they would watch for the postman, who would wheel his bicycle up the steep cliff path. Sometimes he came no farther than the house below theirs, to which he always delivered the local newspaper, but often he pushed his bike on up the hill with a postcard from their parents in Enniscorthy. My mother didn't say so, but I imagine that Cathleen was the first to read the post; being the eldest she would have been left in charge and she must constantly have been worried about what might be happening at home. One day when they were watching for the postman they saw him deliver the newspaper to the house below and, having paused to speak to a man at the gate, continue to climb the hill. Before he reached the gate where Cathleen, Evie and May were waiting, the children from the house below rushed down the cliff path waving the newspaper, and began to dance in circles on the beach. My mother lowered her voice at this point in the story.

The neighbouring family supported de Valera, she said, and the children below on the beach were dancing a war dance because the postman had brought the news that Collins was dead.

He had been shot in the head in his own county Cork when a group of republicans ambushed the car in which he was travelling. De Valera was only a few miles away at the time and rumours persisted throughout my own childhood that it was he who had ordered Collins' death. In fact, though he seems to have been aware of what was planned, it appears that at that point in the conflict the local commander had more control over the republican troops there than he had. It also seems that de Valera and Collins were in the area at the same time because attempts were being made to bring an end to the war.

Collins was shot on the turn of a road in a place called Béal na mBláth, which in my childhood we were told means 'The Mouth of Flowers'. Local pronunciation and different spellings of the name suggest different meanings, some less poetically convenient. One way or the other, the ambush enshrined him in legend: when de Valera was old, Collins was still a laughing boy in poems and ballads, the dead hero who, had he lived, might have led us somewhere very different from where we ended up. Perhaps he would have; he had a visionary mind, an extraordinary capacity for work, charismatic presence and a ruthless ability to get things done. But at thirty-two, he was already unhealthily overweight and suffering the effects of years of living on his nerves. I remember him spoken of when I was a teenager as the lost hope of what might have been. No one mentioned that at the time of the ambush, which took place after a day of meetings in pubs, he seems to have been fairly drunk.

The ambush at Béal na mBláth carried the same whiff of Greek tragedy that Collins himself had deplored about 1916. All the elements are there: the warrior hounded by fate; unheeded warnings; fratricide; slaughter; chaos; and the lonely death of the hero that left the state bereft. There was even the required descent into madness: by August 1922 his nerves were so frayed that he grabbed his gun at the slightest suggestion of danger, yet on the day he was shot he refused offers of extra protection, insisting he was safe from attack. And in the aftermath of Collins' death, de Valera himself seems to have had some kind of nervous collapse. The day after the ambush, on a fifteen-mile journey made by foot accompanied by an escort of his men, he demanded to be left alone, spoke to no one and continually muttered to himself. At one point, close to tears, he asked himself out loud: 'now what will become of us all?' The answer was that the Civil War entered a new and even more violent phase which precipitated the executions of many of his followers and ended in his defeat. After which, following a brief period in the wilderness, he returned to politics and ultimately became head of the Free State himself.

To do so he took an oath of allegiance to the British Crown, which he loftily dismissed as 'an empty political formula', saying he had signed as he would 'an autograph'. And in a bizarre equivalent to crossing his fingers behind his back, he covered the wording of the oath before signing it, pointing out later on that he hadn't read it and that no one had read it out to him, which sounds remarkably like 'yah, boo, sucks'. So while Sinn Féin continued to oppose the Free State, de Valera's new party, Fianna Fáil, now took the line that the state offered by the terms of the treaty could be republicanised by degrees through political means. Which had been Collins' position from the outset. And in 1949, as Collins had assured the Dáil would eventually be the case, the Free State did indeed become the Republic and was largely dominated by de Valera's ideology until his death in 1975.

For those whose personal loyalties had been tested to extremes, de Valera's taking of the oath of allegiance must have been the final irony. Many were Citizen Army and Cumann na mBan women, like Marion and like Brigid Lyons, who had passed her final exams in 1922. In 1916 Brigid had tended the wounded and risked bringing crickets by throwing tea leaves on the fire. During the War of Independence, while still studying for her degree, she had carried dispatches and smuggled munitions, working closely with Michael Collins. As soon as she qualified as a doctor she became part of the Free State's Army Medical Service. And, to her horror, her first posting was as medical officer to the female republican prisoners in Kilmainham Gaol. Most of the prisoners were either her former companions or senior figures in Cumann na mBan and many went on hunger strike as soon as they arrived in their cells. Among them were Maud Gonne and her daughter Iseult. Before being released on medical grounds, Gonne spent twenty days on hunger strike while her friend Charlotte Despard staged a protest outside the prison gates, sitting day and night on a chair. Brigid passed through the gates to her work each day, tortured both by her responsibility for the health of the women inside and by the presence of 79-year-old Despard. Then, one night she was called from her bed to assess a new arrival who turned out to be Kathleen Clarke, one of her Aunt Joe's closest friends. Kilmainham was the gaol to which Clarke had been taken by the British to say goodbye to her husband and brother before their executions in 1916. All she said when Brigid was ushered into her cell was, 'we meet in strange places'. Brigid was twenty-six in 1922. She lived until 1987 and that memory still haunted her in old age.

The point of Greek tragedy is to demonstrate the extremes of which human nature is capable, and one of its functions was to create responsible citizens able to anticipate the potential impact of their own impulses and actions, not just on themselves but on the state. In Ireland the Civil War might have resulted in a form of catharsis which, if responsibly handled, could have provided a process of reassessment and reconciliation, and laid the foundation for a mature relationship between the citizens of the newly independent state and their elected representatives. Instead de Valera's Ireland became increasingly accustomed to the ideas that silence was a virtue, authoritarianism the best safeguard against chaos, and isolationism the only means of preserving both our culture and our spiritual strength. In the process, memory itself became a casualty.

The memories of the Civil War were certainly traumatic and some relationships were indeed shattered beyond repair. But not every family divided by the conflict found healing impossible; that was a myth that took hold and became fixed in the national psyche as time went on. Actually, by talking honestly or by avoiding what was contentious, many families like mine who had different views on the treaty, and in some cases were active nationalists on different sides, managed to reconcile or sidestep their differences and move forward. When my parents married in 1941 my mother's father was dead, so she was given away by her cousin Padraig Kehoe, a personal friend of de Valera's, who was involved in the founding of Fianna Fáil and became a member of the Seanad, or Senate, the government's upper house. Like Marion and Tom, Kehoe had been out in 1916, and he remained an active and vocal republican all his life. But at my parents' wedding he shared the table with my Enniscorthy grandmother whose husband had had great personal confidence in Michael Collins. My grandmother could be formidable when the occasion required, and it was a day for looking to the future so, given that she hated arguments, I doubt if anyone talked politics. The chances are, though, that Keogh, known in the family as The Senator, entertained the guests with one of the lugubrious patriotic ballads of his own composition for which he was famous. Or perhaps he stood up to recite: according to his obituary he could – and frequently did – quote long passages from the works of the great English poets from memory.

De Valera might not have had Michael Collins' particular brand of Indiana Jones charisma but he undoubtedly had charm. Like Collins, he inspired intense personal loyalty, partly because his own brand of ascetic authoritarianism was underpinned by unshakable self-confidence. But much of his backstory, if delved into too deeply, might well have tarnished his legend. His response to that problem – which has faced every revolutionary-hero-turned-head-of-state throughout history – was to do what he could to control what was written, said and remembered about the recent past. No doubt he told himself that, after years of complexity and chaos, the country needed clarity and consistency – one man and one unambivalent message for everyone to get behind and support. If he did it is understandable. But as well as providing a basis for stability, controlling and simplifying the story of what had happened served his own agenda. There were plenty of edges to be smoothed out, just one of which was the fact that it was Michael Staines, not de Valera, who was the senior surviving officer of the 1916 Rising. Staines himself never drew attention to this wrinkle in the legend – in fact, he became a loyal supporter of de Valera's – but others were well aware of it. Among them were individuals whose testimony in the Military Bureau's Witness Statement collection was deemed so contentious that it was kept from the public until 2003. — No

Even de Valera's relationship with the Catholic Church, with which his personal authority would become strongly identified, was complex. In the run-up to the Civil War the Church had strongly supported the pro-treaty Free State government and issued a statement excommunicating de Valera and his anti-treaty supporters; returning from that position to the role of senior Catholic statesman was a remarkable feat of political sleight of hand. But his political agenda co-existed alongside another that was far more personal. No one could have been more traumatised by the experience of the Civil War than he was, knowing as he did that his own actions had precipitated what turned out to be pointless slaughter. Like Pearse, he had indulged in rhetoric calculated to incite violence and, unlike Pearse, he had lived to see the full horror of the outcome. So maybe his determination to sell the rest of us a sanitised version of the truth was as much about self-hatred as it was about homogenisation or self-aggrandisement. Either way, it added to the harm that had already been caused by the Civil War.

I never heard my father speak of his own memories of that conflict. In comparison with other Irish counties, such as Cork and Kerry, the fighting in Galway was less widespread, but it was equally bitter. It ended in the execution of eleven anti-treaty republican leaders, including Liam Mellows who, seven years earlier, had come to Galway with Nora Connolly, James Connolly's daughter, to organise the Volunteers and Cumann na mBan members who rose in Easter Week. The Civil War was still raging when my aunt Marguerite, who was seven years older than my father, became a student at University College Galway (UCG), but I have no idea whether or not she was actively involved in any way, or which side she may have supported. It seems likely to have been de Valera's rather than Collins'. After the Civil War ended, my father, then a UCG student himself, was a member of the university's Republican Club and produced a hand-painted menu card for a dinner given for de Valera at the Railway Hotel in Clifden; the cover shows a tricolour and the menu on the inside is surrounded by a watercolour sketch of a tree-fringed lake with rolling hills in the distance, and a twisty design in the Celtic Art style incorporating a shield and a panoply of axes, arrows and spears. (They served de Valera five courses, including suitably Irish 'Carrageen Blanc-Mange'.) According to my mother, who heard the story long afterwards, my father and his friends cycled to the dinner in the rain and got drenched on the way. De Valera autographed the menu for him, though, so the journey and the wetting were deemed worth it.

In those years my father wrote his name in Irish in his textbooks and his copy of Dineen's Irish dictionary, which is now mine, is inscribed to him in Irish by Marguerite. Her own name, also written in Irish, appears in a copy of a book called *Rebel Irish Women*, a strongly republican work by the English socialist, feminist writer Richard Michael Fox, who was influenced by Eva Gore-Booth and George Bernard Shaw. Marguerite bought it hot off the press when it came out in 1935. A year or so after that, when he was studying in England, my father was secretary of the London Sinn Féin office. I think, however, that by 1939, when he took the job in the National Museum and became responsible for its Military History and the War of Independence collections, he had lost some of his youthful enthusiasm for de Valera. And in the course of his involvement with the Military Bureau's Witness Statement collection process, which was initiated by historians but subverted and contained by politicians on both sides of the Civil War divide, his attitude towards Ireland's political processes became a great deal warier.

I have a soft spot for Maud Gonne. Not just because her curtains turned out to be a perfect fit for the windows in my house in London, but because of a story told to me by my mother about my father's first week in his job in the National Museum. Gonne was seventy-three in the year that my father joined the museum's staff, and public perception of her possibly abusive, certainly unhappy, marriage had been changed utterly by John MacBride's elevated status as an executed hero of 1916. So while many people, like Sadie who worked for her in Roebuck House, simply called her Madam, she had taken to adding the weight of MacBride's name to her own. Although her own political career was sidelined, and she had had many overt and covert wrangles with de Valera, her status as a widow of the Rising gave her significant position in the Ireland of the times.

One morning, the phone on my father's desk in the museum rang and he picked it up. 'THIS' boomed a voice at the end of the line 'IS MAUD GONNE MACBRIDE.' Thinking that it was the girl on the switchboard messing, he replied, 'Like hell it is,' and hung up. Moments later the phone rang again and a nervous voice he recognised as the switch operator's said: 'I have Madam MacBride for you'. Upon which the original booming voice announced 'I BELIEVE THAT WE WERE ERRONEOUSLY DISCONNECTED.' My father's jaw dropped and the operator hastily removed herself from the arena, though I bet she continued to listen in. If she did, she heard nothing but a brisk enquiry about the exhibition he was working on, and a click as Madam rang off. According to my mother, he held his breath for weeks afterwards. In the event there were no repercussions, but he had good reason to be apprehensive. Unemployment was rife in de Valera's Ireland, to which my father had returned a few years earlier, after postgraduate study in Edinburgh and London, eager to secure an academic post. Opportunities for academics were few and far between so, while qualifications were necessary, patronage mattered. For the time being, in the absence of anything else, the museum job had allowed him to remain in the country, but had Maud Gonne or anyone else of her stature complained of his conduct at work he could well have been out on his ear and facing emigration. As a newly married only son with elderly parents, he had responsibilities and uncertainties hard to imagine in today's world of state-funded social security and social services. Even though the shooting wars were over, keeping your mouth shut and your head down was often still the safest course to take.

Given de Valera's personality, his aspirations for Ireland can seem weirdly romantic. Admittedly, once he came to power, he had little to work with. When the Civil War ended, the Free State had minimal industry and a pretty shattered infrastructure. Then the Great Depression which hit Europe and the USA in 1929 had a disastrous effect on Irish agricultural exports. At the same time, the British government was calling for repayment of large loans, known as land annuities, granted by Britain from the 1880s onwards to allow Irish tenant farmers to buy land from their Anglo-Irish landlords. In 1932 de Valera decided that the land annuities were covered by an exemption from other public debt which had previously been agreed with Britain, and his government stopped paying them. The result was an economic war in which each side slapped tariffs on imports from the other. But as 90 per cent of the Free State's exports consisted of agricultural products sold to the UK, the effect in Ireland was far worse than in Britain. The knock-on effect was that de Valera's government had no option but to institute a drive for self-sufficiency. And this, as it happened, fell in neatly with his personal vision of Ireland as the home of a people *'who, satisfied with frugal comfort, devoted their leisure to the things of the spirit*

– a land whose countryside would be bright with cosy homesteads, whose fields and villages would be joyous with the sounds of industry, with the romping of sturdy children, the contest of athletic youths and the laughter of happy maidens, whose firesides would be forums for the wisdom of serene old age. The home, in short, of a people living the life that God desires that men should live.' That quotation from a speech he made in 1943 epitomises the dream, but not the reality, that my parents' generation married into. With it came an absolute assumption that God desired a life in which men worked, women tended their cosy homesteads and everyone had as many sturdy children as possible, all of whom Bought Irish and embraced frugality with deep religious fervour.

The outbreak of the Second World War was the next factor to contribute to Ireland's growing isolation. In one sense it was de Valera's finest hour, although hindsight might suggest otherwise. Looking back, it seems impossible that anyone could fail to have seen the innate awfulness of Nazism or the logical conclusion of the philosophy and policies laid out in Hitler's *Mein Kampf*. But in the years between the two world wars, millions of people did fail to see, or think about, or look hard enough at, what was happening in Europe, until there came a point when it was too late. What de Valera saw, as the efforts of the League of Nations foundered on the consequences of the Treaty of Versailles, was that the independent Ireland that emerged from the fact and fallout of the First World War was unlikely to survive participation in a second one. If Ireland supported the Allies we would be exposed to German attack and, given our minimal military resources, forced to invite the British back in to protect us. If we supported Germany, which had, at least to some degree, supported us during the War of Independence, we might find ourselves colonised by new invaders: Hitler's expansionism was already evident before Britain entered the war and, if France fell, Ireland would be an obvious jumping-off point for a two-pronged German invasion of Britain. Basically, whichever way we jumped was likely to be disastrous. In 1938, having negotiated an end to the

Economic War with Britain, de Valera had regained three strategic Irish ports which the terms of the Treaty that established the Free State had left in the hands of the British. This greatly improved his odds of maintaining a neutral stance in 1939. Having served as a president of the League of Nations himself, he was in a strong position to evaluate the risks. In the end, he opted for neutrality and, by steering a skilful diplomatic course throughout the war, managed to preserve the Free State's sovereignty.

Meanwhile, as in the First World War, thousands of Irish men and women fought in the British services and became part of the war effort in Britain. I don't know when or why Marion decided to leave Ireland for London; the entry in her hand-stitched book just says that she lived at home until 1928, then nursed in Dublin, and went on to train in a London hospital. She may have become disillusioned by what had happened in Ireland or, like the steady stream of other Irish men and women suffering the consequences of the economic war, she may simply have gone to England to find work. Or it may have been for some other reason altogether. What she found there was a role in a new war, as a nurse dealing with casualties during the Blitz. I don't know what kind of injuries she may have treated during the Civil War in Ireland but I know that in her retirement she sometimes spoke about the relentless air raids she experienced in London, and the painful responsibility of deciding which of the wounded it was worth trying to save and which were too badly injured for treatment.

At home, though the lights were on, no one starved, and threats of invasion were either averted or proved groundless, people lived with uncertainty, apprehension and much the same levels of state censorship and propaganda experienced by civilians elsewhere in Europe. And while those levels of government containment and secrecy, and the legislation required to permit them, seem remarkable now, at the time they were perfectly logical. Faced with the situation abroad, ongoing political skirmishing with Britain and the need to control what was still an unstable situation at home, de Valera introduced sweeping new legislation which gave his government emergency powers to protect the security of the state. One use to which he applied them was to control the IRA.

With the start of a new war in Europe, the old theory that England's difficulty could become Ireland's opportunity had returned to haunt him. Many members of the IRA, which had also split over the treaty, had become part of the Free State army, and others who had fought for de Valera remained loyal to him after the Civil War. But a rump force which rejected both the Free State and the partition of the northern counties remained in existence. In the 1960s and 1970s it would become the nucleus of the new fight against partition, sparked by the civil rights movement in Northern Ireland. Now, although de Valera had used it to undermine the Free State government himself only a few years earlier, it had become a thorn in his side: with the outbreak of the Second World War, IRA attempts to gain German arms and support for a new militant attempt to establish an Irish Republic were a significant threat to the Free State's position of neutrality. In fact, had de Valera not had an effective state intelligence agency, and had Irish intelligence agents not had emergency powers to rely on, either the IRA or the Nazis, or both, could well have given Britain justification for re-invading Ireland.

Dan Bryan, a senior intelligence officer in the Free State army became Chief Staff Officer of the Irish Directorate of Intelligence in 1942. I remember him from the 1960s as a quiet, square man with a toothbrush moustache, who smelt strongly of pipe tobacco. He and my father, another pipe smoker, were co-founders of the Military History Society of Ireland in 1949, and were close friends. The proceedings of the Military History Society loomed large in my childhood; most of the letters and the brown paper parcels which we took to the GPO on the number eleven bus seemed to contain either the minutes of the society's meetings or my father's Indian ink illustrations of guns, swords and flags, which he drew at our dining-room table with his back to the fire. According to my mother, Dan and my father were the kind of close friends who were constantly at loggerheads, each being as determined as the other when it came to getting his own way. I was aware of none of that, nor did I know anything about Dan's work. What I remember most is the elderly black dog that travelled in the back of his car. It was left on a rug in the back seat whenever he came to visit us, and drank water from a red rubber bathing cap that was kept in the boot for the purpose.

When my father joined the staff of the National Museum of Ireland in 1939 its director was an Austrian called Adolf Mahr. Senior appointments in most of the Free State's cultural institutions were made at government level which, in practical terms, meant that they were all approved, if not actually made, by de Valera himself. After the British withdrawal from Ireland the state had turned to German expertise to develop initiatives such as a national hydroelectric scheme and scholarly Irish links with German academia had already been in place since the end of the nineteenth century. So Mahr's appointment was not surprising. He was a brilliant archaeologist who came to Dublin as the museum's Keeper of Antiquities in 1927 and was promoted by de Valera seven years later. He was also the leader of the Dublin branch of the Nazi Party and for much of his time as director of the museum his mail was intercepted and read by Dan Bryan's department, which was known as G2. The surveillance had less to do with Mahr's membership of the Nazi Party, which at the time was a perfectly legitimate organisation, than with the fact that he may also have been a spy.

It is easy to assume that Hitler's anti-Semitic agenda was paramount from the outset. But in the years between the wars, it was less evident than it later became, and the Nazi Party's appeal to the German people was more complex. The victorious powers who sat down to redraw Europe's boundaries in the aftermath of the First World War had consciously set out to humiliate Germany, which was exactly what the pacifist feminists and others who had attempted to influence the peace process had feared. One result was seething resentment among cultured Germans like Mahr, whose personal sense of identity had been outraged by the post-war carve-up: the area of Austria where he was born had become part of Italy, and the Sudetenland, where his family came from, had been ceded to Czechoslovakia. So Hitler's passionate determination to reassert Germany's national identity was as admirable to Mahr, and to many like him, as Ireland's Gaelic revivalism had been to W. B. Yeats, Eoin MacNeill and Patrick Pearse.

I doubt if the junior members of the museum's staff knew much about the director's politics. According to my mother, my father disliked him deeply, but that seems to have been because Mahr clicked his fingers at the museum porters and had no sense of humour. He was also known to favour job applicants who had worked under him on archaeological digs and, while my father would have found such work fascinating and, on one level, been delighted by the opportunity to be part of it, he resented the idea that it was required of him. However, he spent a season on a dig, got himself the job at the museum and, apparently, kept as far away from the director as possible. This must have been a great relief to my mother who was very aware of his likely reaction should anyone click their fingers at him. Anyway, before anything detrimental could happen to my father's fledgling career, Mahr's own career in the museum was cut short. In July 1939 he sailed with his family to Germany, ostensibly for a holiday. There has been speculation ever since about the circumstances in which they left, and about whether or not Mahr intended to return to his job in the museum. Whatever his intention, he never came back. Instead he spent the war working for Goebbels' state radio service, organising Nazi propaganda broadcasts in Irish. He had learnt the language in the Donegal Gaeltacht before the war, and Hitler was eager to reinforce the idea that England's difficulty could once again, with German help, become Ireland's opportunity.

I don't know if Mahr convinced his superiors in Germany that the average Irish family clustered round the wireless of an evening eager to be lectured in Irish about England's past iniquities. Perhaps he did. Or maybe Goebbels was targeting militant nationalists who might be expected to appreciate a demonstration of respect for the language; certainly, the Nazis were in touch with the IRA during the war, although G2's counter espionage agents, led by Dan Bryan, managed to contain their efforts. However, it sounds as if the broadcasts were heard by three farmers, a sheep and a series of bored intelligence agents who listened in and produced transcriptions. After the war, Mahr ended up in an Allied prison camp where he nearly died of malnutrition and the treatment he received there. On his release he was desperate to return to Ireland but Bryan advised de Valera to refuse him re-entry. Whatever had been picked up from the surveillance under which Mahr was kept while he worked at the museum, or the subsequent work of G2 counter-espionage agents, had convinced Bryan that Mahr had actively jeopardised Ireland's neutrality during the war. It is possible that the knowledge of what actually happened died with Bryan himself. He was a professional soldier but having begun his life as an intelligence agent working in cooperation with Michael Collins' Squad, his instinct for discretion was deep-rooted.

During the Second World War Bryan and his agents controlled the balancing act by which de Valera contained the constant threat of British or German invasion. By demonstrating to Churchill that the Irish government was acting appropriately, the Free State's neutral status was validated. Using postal interception, telephone tapping, telegraph supervision and constant surveillance, Nazi agents were intercepted, and German transmission from Irish soil – including from the German Embassy in Dublin – was stopped. Discreet cooperation with MI5 in London ensured that British Intelligence valued continued good relations with Ireland. Infiltration, arrests, interrogation and code-cracking contained the IRA's movements at home, in

Germany and in the USA. Yet, despite all these efforts, invasion from one side or the other seemed inevitable on more than one occasion. My mother, who shared a house with friends in Howth, where the Volunteers had landed rifles from Germany before 1916, remembered being visited by the local policeman in 1940 or 1941 with a warning that German U-boats were on their way; he told the girls to pile their mattresses against the windows and barricade themselves into a back room. The same night, or perhaps on another occasion, my father and a colleague at the museum with whom he shared digs in Dublin's Waterloo Road heard the same story and buried their money and passports in a tin box in the back garden. My mother remembered a friend in the defence forces telling her that the army had been mobilised during some diplomatic crisis to protect the border from a British invasion from Northern Ireland and then stood down when the crisis was over. Separating fact from rumour wasn't easy then because, as in every country in wartime, newspapers, publications, periodicals and news broadcasts were all censored. Technically, of course, the Free State was not at war at all but, to a public that had known little peace for twenty years, whatever had to be done to keep us out of it must have seemed fair enough. Undoubtedly, de Valera's absolute control gave him the confidence and conditions he needed to steer a hazardous, and ultimately successful, diplomatic course through the war, towards the end of which he was deflecting pressure from the US government as well as from Britain. It also allowed him to consolidate his own power base and promote his personal agendas, helped by the fact that he had founded, and his family continued to own, one of the most widely read newspapers in the country.

When my mother and her friends lived in Howth they commuted by train to their jobs in the centre of Dublin. Morning and evening, they played bridge on the train journey, and when their boyfriends visited the cottage at weekends the girls were usually seated around the kitchen table, deep in a game. Some of the visiting boyfriends gave up and learned to play bridge themselves, but my father managed to drag my mother away from the cards for long walks to the top of Howth Head. There, with the seagulls wheeling beneath them over the waves, he talked about Pre-Raphaelite art and she talked about Evelyn Waugh. At some point, at a bus stop opposite the Metropole Cinema when one of them was about to go off on a visit to Galway or Enniscorthy, they agreed not to date anyone else. Then the number ten arrived to take him to his digs in Waterloo Road. My mother remembered him swinging around the pole on the rear platform and raising his hat to her as the bus pulled away from the kerb. They married in 1941.

That year my father curated the exhibition with which the museum commemorated the twenty-fifth anniversary of the 1916 Rising. Material and advice was sourced from survivors of the period, which probably explains why Maud Gonne MacBride's peremptory call was put through to his desk. Shortly before the official opening of the exhibition, de Valera arrived with an aide-de-camp and, in Mahr's absence, was given a private viewing by the acting director with my father in attendance. There was a certain amount of tension as de Valera was ushered round the exhibits; this, after all, was a display that commemorated an episode in his own life. He was seeing flags and weapons carried in battle by his comrades, documents signed among dust and rubble, and personal objects that had once belonged to his friends. Famously reserved and taciturn, he strode on till he came to a case containing Collins' uniform. His sight was already failing so there was a pause while his aide-de-camp murmured to him discreetly. Then, so my mother's story goes, he looked wooden and moved on.

The next day my father arrived home from work in a fury. There had been a call from de Valera's office about the exhibition: it was felt that the placing of the Collins material was rather too prominent; perhaps some changes might be made. Sitting at the kitchen table in the house they had rented on the south side of the city, my father announced ominously to my mother that whoever else touched the exhibition, it wasn't going to be him. Apparently the to-ing and fro-ing continued for twenty-four hours and throughout it my mother held her breath, praying that my father would keep his head down and let his seniors do the fighting. In that instance, to the credit of an institution funded by government, history appears to have triumphed over politics. But it was a perfect example of three aspects of de Valera's character – he was happy to use his political position to lean on the state's cultural institutions, he was obsessive when it came to controlling his own legend, and, when it came to Michael Collins, his reactions bordered on the pathological. Two years earlier, on the brink of world war, as he took it upon himself to protect Ireland's sovereignty he also took time to sign a certificate that restricted the size of a memorial cross which the Collins family wanted to erect on Collins' grave in Glasnevin Cemetery. He had already specified that the only people permitted to attend the ceremony were to be a single member of the Collins family, a priest to bless the cross, and an altar boy; the cross was to be limestone, not marble, the cost of the memorial could not exceed £300, no public subscription list could be opened and no member of the press was to be informed. The inscriptions on the memorial, both in English and in Irish, had also to be approved by himself. No uncensored memory was to be carved in stone for future generations.

10
The Ceremony of Innocence

I WAS BORN INTO AN IRELAND in which national consciousness was focused almost entirely on a mythical version of the 1916 Rising and on the wrongs of our colonial past. Much of rural Ireland did indeed suffer dreadfully under Anglo-Irish control and British political and economic policies, and many nineteenth- as well as twentieth-century outrages were still preserved in living memory when I was a child. But rack-renting landlords and arbitrary evictions were not unique to Ireland. Nor was Ireland alone in aspiring to greater social justice, respect for its native culture or the removal of arbitrary boundaries imposed by horse-trading politicians. Late nineteenth- and early twentieth-century Irish nationalism had many influences, including socialism, pacifism, internationalism, feminism, trade-unionism, the pre-Christian Celtic world view, the moral philosophies of Anglican Church of Ireland rectors and Free Church Methodists, Roman Catholicism, atheism, occultism, and the theories of political economists as diverse as Karl Marx and Adam Smith. And among the men and women who struggled to conceive a new vision of Irishness in the years before and after 1916 were scholars, politicians, artists, soldiers and visionaries with humane, cultured, original minds; they were straight, gay, single, married and divorced and, while it would be nonsense to suggest that people who were born and raised over a hundred years earlier had twenty-first century sensibilities, their separate and shared aspirations offered a template for a vibrant, diverse and tolerant society. And while no revolution ever reaches its imagined potential, an ongoing debate about what they had attempted to achieve might well have resulted in a sense of national identity which embraced inclusiveness, openness and a sense of internationalism. Instead censorship, secrecy and inadequacy produced a misogynistic cult of self-sufficiency, devoid of practical economic policies and dominated by a single religious denomination.

When I was growing up I perceived Ireland's neutrality in the Second World War with one part of my brain while with another I absorbed stirring stories of Dunkirk and El Alamein filtered through the imagination of the British film industry. But the actual implications of the world war and its aftermath didn't really occur to me. It was not until I moved to England that I began to realise the extent to which our neutrality and subsequent isolation had denied us access to the processes by which the rest of the world had evaluated and moved on from what had happened during the Second World War. The propaganda machine that supported British morale during the war had increasingly focused on Churchill as an indomitable authority figure who, with a mixture of absolute authority and cigar-smoking raffishness, epitomised the slogan 'Keep Calm and Carry On'. For many British people who lived through the war, Churchill's legend never faded and their sense of a personal relationship with him, underpinned by his equally legendary wartime radio broadcasts, remained unshaken afterwards. But beneath the images of cheerful milkmen striding through rubble and heroic housewives happy to make do and mend was an exhausted electorate disillusioned by post-war austerity and longing for something different. So immediately the war was over Churchill was voted out of office and the public turned to a new Labour government. Labour's majority lessened significantly after another general election the following year and by 1951 Churchill was back in power again. But the desire for change continued to bubble through British life in the 1950s and 1960s, bringing with it huge social and cultural reassessment. In the rest of the world, just as had happened after the First World War, cultural, political and social boundaries were also redrawn and, although totalitarianism took hold behind the Iron Curtain, Western Europe's recent experience of fascism bred a healthy scepticism of authority figures. In Ireland the opposite happened. De Valera's authority, established in the late 1920s and 1930s and consolidated during the war years, increased through the 1950s and 1960s, and was significantly bolstered by the authoritarian culture of the Catholic Church.

My grandfather in Enniscorthy died in 1930. His cousin Roy was the principal of a Dublin secretarial college where my aunt Cathleen had trained when she left school. I'm not sure but I think it may have been Roy's brass buttons that my mother polished in the house on Washerwoman's Hill at some point in the First World War. Anyway, he must have been close to my grandfather because, to help my widowed grandmother, he offered to pay for my mother's secretarial training, and to find work for her in Dublin when she qualified. While she attended his college, which was in Grafton Street, she lived in the flat upstairs with Roy and his English wife, Olive. She loved it. Olive, who was chic and charming, gave bridge parties at which she served sherry and salted almonds. They went shopping together and my mother found a bottle-green wool costume which was her favourite outfit for years. It had a tailored coat and a box-pleated skirt and she wore it with a Fair Isle jumper, knitted by Olive, and a pair of two-tone brogues. My mother wasn't a knitter herself but she loved embroidery and drawn-thread work and had learned to make her own blouses at school, from ninon chiffon and what she called Nun's Veiling. Olive introduced her to the washability of rayon slips; oyster-coloured, cut on the cross, and piped in apricot or pale green, with spaghetti straps and rolled hemlines. Years later, when I was small, I remember finding an elaborately smocked frock in my mother's ragbag. She had made it for her first baby, my eldest sister, interspersing the smocking on the yoke with little embroidered flowers. But by the time I used it to dress my teddy bear she had given up fine needlework and applied herself to darning and mending. And once, on the sewing machine on which she bound the typescripts of my father's first book, she made a flag for my brothers' boy scout troop.

While I was in the process of writing this book, a retweet appeared in my Twitter feed with a photo of a letter attached to it. It has been tweeted by an Irishman called Cormac Lawler and the letter, which had three brief paragraphs, had been sent to his mother in 1967. It confirmed her appointment to the Permanent Clerical Staff of the Guardian Assurance Company in Dublin and asked her to sign and return an attached copy as acceptance of the appointment and its terms. The eight-line first paragraph, which specified her salary and referred to an enclosed copy of the company's Staff Regulations, ended with a form of words covering termination of contract. '*It may be terminated by one month's notice in writing on either side. It will also be terminated automatically by your marriage although you may apply for an appointment to the Temporary Staff from the date of your marriage.*' Cormac Lawler's tweet went viral within hours. I was one of the people who contacted him afterwards and, in an email he sent a few days later, he wrote that his mother, whose name before her marriage was Geraldine Cunniffe, had been astonished by the response that it had received. Geraldine's astonishment isn't surprising; in her working lifetime, in my own mother's, and even at the time when my sisters first entered the job market, such contracts were simply the norm.

The 'marriage bar' which required female public servants and women who worked in banking to give up their jobs when they married was enforced in Ireland in 1933. In practice, it commonly applied in the private sector as well. A month or so before I saw Cormac's tweet, when I was speaking at the Enniscorthy Library event to which Katch Kavanagh brought stories of Marion's nursing career, I asked if any of the women in the audience had resented being unable to work outside the home. Most of the women of Katch's age glanced at each other and shrugged. Then one quiet, dignified lady with a glint in her

eye smiled at me and said it was just how things were. Jobs were
hard to find anyway. Half the country seemed to be emigrating in
the 1930s, 1940s and 1950s. 'And even in the sixties', said a woman
sitting behind her, 'if there were jobs to be had, they were needed
for the men.' The older men in the room, around the same age
as she was, agreed with her. The only shocked looks were on far
younger faces. None of the young women present seemed aware
that that legislation had remained in place, and continued to be
enforced in the public sector, until Ireland entered the EU in 1973.
Or that the Employment Act, which prohibited discrimination
on the grounds of gender or marital status in almost all areas of
employment, was enacted as late as 1977.

It is extraordinary how quickly brief periods of economic
boom such as Ireland experienced during the 'Celtic Tiger'
years between 1995 and 2007 can establish new norms. More
extraordinary still is how quickly past norms are forgotten.
When I was at university, the idea that paid work was the
prerogative of married males was not confined to Ireland but it
was certainly a recognisable characteristic of Irish society; and,
since misogyny was a feature of the cultural philosophy of the
time, it is easy to believe that the marriage bar in Ireland was
an example of economic policy driven by anti-feminism. That
may to a degree have been the case. But it is not the whole story.
When the policy first emerged in Britain in the nineteenth
century it was about positive discrimination in favour of single
women who, in the absence of any form of social security, might
quietly starve to death if they couldn't find jobs. The theory was
that in a crowded marketplace with a finite number of jobs on
offer, dual-income households represented an unfair distribution
of wealth. In de Valera's Ireland, with its struggling economy and
high unemployment, the bar may have reflected an underlying
desire to restrict women's areas of influence by keeping them
economically dependent. But it was also a symptom of the
experience and memory of pre- and post-colonial levels of
poverty which have now almost been forgotten.

Somewhere in the mid-1970s, in order to save up and buy myself a bicycle, I took a summer job in a Dublin delicatessen. As soon as my father heard about it, he sat me down and told me that by taking a job that I didn't need I was choosing to take bread out of the mouth of someone who did need it. When I pointed out that I needed money to buy myself a bike, he said that it was his job to provide me with one. Somehow I was eased out of the conversation by my mother who, like her own mother, hated arguments, and who was always worried about the effect of stress on my father's health. But a few days later I took his money, used it to buy the bike, and kept the job anyway. It was an aggressive response which I knew would distress him but at the time I was so incensed that I didn't care. I wish now that I had been mature enough to talk to him instead. Perhaps we both could have learned something about assumptions and expectations. I wish too that I had understood at the time how the argument must have affected my mother. In 1941, when they married, she had given up her full-time job in the office of a shop in Grafton Street which sold silver and china. Later that year, at Christmas time, she was offered a chance to come back for a couple of weeks to help with the holiday rush. The idea of having the extra money for food and Christmas presents delighted her but my father refused to let her take the work. Having fought and lost her own battle in the 1940s, she must on some level have empathised with mine in the 1970s. But because he was ill, or because he was her husband, or maybe for both reasons, or for another one altogether, she saw it as her duty to take his side. For weeks she hardly talked to me and we never spoke of it afterwards. It wasn't until years after he died that I heard the story of the Christmas job she herself had given up.

And it wasn't until she was nearly eighty that she told me the story of her aborted career. At some point after she left Roy's secretarial school, she worked as a temp with the *Irish Independent* newspaper. The work seems to have involved little pay and much running about with teacups and included the usual embarrassing new-job moments, like the time she responded to an instruction to post a letter by walking to the GPO and buying a stamp because she didn't know the paper had a post room. But someone must have noticed her enthusiasm because when her time as a temp ended she was offered a job as a junior reporter. She was delighted, but before she could accept the offer Roy came up with a better-paid job, in the office of the shop she was working in when she first met my father. Knowing that Roy's offer of free secretarial training had been about helping her own widowed mother, my mother turned down the job at the *Independent* and took the job at the china shop, so that she could afford to send money home to Enniscorthy. But she also hung onto her dream of being a writer and, shilling by shilling, week by week, she saved up and bought herself a typewriter. This was in the late 1930s when Dublin, like London, had become home to a small population of immigrants from mainland Europe. Some were German businessmen and professionals, drawn to Ireland by the job prospects in the newly independent country's emerging economy. Others were refugees, running from the implications of Hitler's emerging power. Among them were two journalists, a German and his wife, who made friends with Roy and Olive. My mother never knew why they had had to leave their home. The implication appears to have been that the husband had written something that had got him into trouble. They arrived in Dublin with little luggage or money, and no means of support. So, although she had hardly had it long enough to make use of it herself, my mother decided to lend them her typewriter.

It had been clear for months that war was brewing in Europe. In September 1939, after Germany's invasion of Poland, Britain and France declared war on Germany and the small colony of Germans in Ireland had to decide what to do. It was possible that if they stayed put they would find themselves interned, either by the Free State or, in the event of an invasion, by the British. Mahr, the director of the museum, who had been a key figure in the colony, had already left with his family. So the remaining Germans decided to opt for repatriation. De Valera, the British Foreign Office and the German ambassador to Dublin came to a diplomatic arrangement, and a ship was provided to take them home. As soon as my mother heard what was happening she rushed around to the journalists' digs to reclaim her typewriter. By the time that she got there the ship had already sailed. Who knows if the couple on whom she had taken pity had made a conscious decision to steal her precious typewriter? When they packed it they would have had other things on their minds. The prospect of returning to a country they had already run away from must have been frightening, and by putting their names down to go they may even have signed their own death warrants. I don't know because no one in Dublin ever heard from them again.

My parents married two years later. I assume that during the engagement the shillings that my mother had once put into the typewriter fund were diverted to her trousseau. It was a wartime wedding with little fuss, and most of the few snapshots taken by their friends and family are either badly framed, slightly out of focus, or both. But it looks as if everyone spent the sunny, windless day laughing. My mother's tailored, knee-length dress was flared from the hips and had elbow-length sleeves, a high neckline, and a matching hip-length jacket. She wore it with dark shoes, a pair of dark gloves and a spray of white flowers on her shoulder. In the outdoor photos she wears a little hat with a turned-up brim at the front, her red hair curled and set to hold it at the right angle. My father has a white flower on the lapel of what looks like his good, dark suit. Cathleen is in a polka-dot dress and a pillbox hat, tipped well forward, with a veil over her nose. Marguerite has a white swagger coat with square, padded shoulders, a beret and a clutch bag. Evie appears in only one photo, sitting at the end of a bench with her head turned away from the camera. The management and staff at the china shop had clubbed together to order a silver-plated teapot and matching hot-water jug from London for my mother's wedding present. I use them now to brew my morning tea. Elegantly designed in the height of Art Deco fashion, they lived in their own drawstring bags in my childhood, and only came out for Christmas and special occasions. My mother never worked again after her marriage. She wanted to, but it was nearly twenty years before there was enough money to spend on another typewriter and, by then, mothering, cooking and housework had taken over her life.

After my father's death in the 1970s I worked for a year as a teacher, and at the end of the summer term was offered an incremental job. My mother insisted that, instead of taking it, I should follow my instincts and move to London to train as an actress. I was the only member of the family living permanently at home at the time, and at the last minute I agonised about whether or not I should go. The money I contributed to the household was not much but I feared she might miss it; and, indeed, that she might miss my company. I was also aware that by leaving Ireland I was leaving the responsibility of looking after her to my siblings. Although, to tell the truth, I'm not sure that I thought very hard about that. In the end, what swung my decision was another story from her past. It was years, she said, before she found out what had happened to the money she had sent home each week to Enniscorthy, having given up her chance of working on the newspaper. Instead of spending it on herself, my grandmother had saved it up and added it to what she called a little bequest that she left to my mother in her will. When she was dying she proudly told my mother what she had done, saying that she had put it away so she could return it with interest. It wasn't much, she said, but it was important for a woman to have some bit of money of her own. Having grown up with Aunt Magger who had worked all her life in the Co-op, and having seen the career carved out by my unmarried aunt Cathleen, she must have become worried about my mother's state of economic dependence on my father. Or perhaps she too had missed her friends and her freedom and the shop she had worked in before marrying my grandfather, back in 1907. I don't know. But I do know that her investment paid for the room that I rented when I was at drama school, and that my mother's refusal to allow history to repeat itself has given me the life I lead today.

From the late 1940s to the mid-1950s my father, who was still employed at the museum, worked as a scriptwriter and costume consultant on a number of pageants, in the tradition of the dramatic works of the Gaelic Revivalists. Precursors of the dramatic elements in the 1966 commemorations of the 1916 Rising, they were funded with government money and intended to sell Ireland to the demographic now known to marketing people as the Culturally Curious. The shows that took place in the 1950s were part of a national initiative called An Tóstal which kick-started Ireland's tourist industry. The idea for An Tóstal came from the US airline Pan Am which wanted to capitalise on post-war spending by selling holidays in Europe to Americans, and to bag a monopoly on landing rights in Dublin for their transatlantic flights to refuel. By then the Free State had quietly morphed into the Republic of Ireland and, although de Valera was still wedded to self-sufficiency, Seán Lemass, then his Minister for Industry and Commerce, was eager to modernise the economy. So the government got behind An Tóstal in a big way. I wasn't born when the first pageants took place but I remember family stories about hundreds of extras on loan from the defence forces rushing about with plywood spears while the production team argued about logistics, historical accuracy and the inevitable saffron kilts. By all accounts, the army, the budding Irish film industry, Dublin's theatre managers and my father made strange bedfellows, but apparently the results were spectacular, if occasionally dampened by rain. On the later productions in the mid-1950s he collaborated as a historical consultant with the actor/manager and playwright Micheál Mac Liammóir, and the playwright Denis Johnston who had previously worked as a war correspondent, and as a radio and television producer for the BBC.

According to my mother, Mac Liammóir, who tended to turn
up for meetings in full Leichner make-up, irritated my father by
announcing firmly at the outset that the Essence of Good Theatre
Was Imaginative Truth. Which, as it happens, was the essence of
Mac Liammóir's own persona. Born Alfred Willmore in Kensal
Green, London, he made a hit in the West End as a child actor
before coming to Ireland in the 1920s to join a touring company.
He and his lover, the English actor Hilton Edwards, met when
they played together in a show at the Athenaeum in Enniscorthy.
By the 1950s they were senior figures on the Irish cultural scene
and Edwards would soon become Head of Drama in the newly
established national television service. Homophobic Ireland's
unspoken agreement to ignore their devoted homosexual
partnership was one of the mixed messages of my teens. Perhaps
it was a case of hiding in full view and getting away with it,
or perhaps it had something to do with the fact that Alfred
Willmore, having reinvented himself as Micheál Mac Liammóir,
was a perfect example of an outsider who became More Irish
Than The Irish Themselves. He spoke Irish on all possible
occasions, declared himself to be a devout Catholic of west Cork
origin, and professed a detailed knowledge of all things Gaelic.
As he also had strong views on what constituted An Effective
Costume and attempted to overrule my father on the question of
anachronistic druids, I suspect that they never reached a perfect
meeting of minds.

As well as introducing Ireland's Tidy Towns Competition,
which still flourishes, An Tóstal provided the funding for the
Dublin Theatre Festival, and thereby sparked a series of rows
over censorship which typified the climate of the time. The first
theatre festival, in 1957, included a production of Tennessee
Williams' play *The Rose Tattoo* by Dublin's Pike Theatre
company, a choice which resulted in the director Alan Simpson's
arrest for producing a 'lewd entertainment'. The outrage at
his arrest expressed by the cultural community at home was
supported from abroad by the heavyweight Irish playwrights

Samuel Beckett and Seán O'Casey and ultimately the case against
Simpson was thrown out of court. But the following year, when
the festival scheduled works by O'Casey, Beckett and James
Joyce, the Archbishop of Dublin refused to give the programme
his blessing unless extensive changes were made to O'Casey's
script. O'Casey refused, Joyce's work was quietly dropped in
the hopes of appeasing the archbishop, and Beckett withdrew
his mime piece in protest. Over thirty years earlier, Dublin
audiences, outraged by what they saw as its lack of suitable
nationalist sentiment, had booed O'Casey's play *The Plough And
The Stars* on its first performance, at the Abbey Theatre. On that
occasion Yeats strode furiously onto the stage and accused them
of cultural chauvinism. But now Yeats was dead and nothing
much had changed.

The influence of the Archbishop of Dublin, John Charles
McQuaid, dominated artistic decision-making in the Ireland in
which I grew up. In 1966 he took exception to a Nativity scene in
a church that had been built in Dublin airport two years earlier,
designed by an Irish architect who had studied under Frank
Lloyd Wright. The stylised figures chosen to reflect the modernity
of the architecture were pronounced offensive, and a statement
issued by the archbishop's office declared that the presence of
the Nativity scene contravened canon law. It was immediately
replaced by a Victorian notion of a medieval idea of what the
aftermath of a virgin birth in a stable in Bethlehem would have
looked like in the first century. In reporting the incident to the
Dáil, the Minister for Public Works announced that 'monuments
commemorating the past must resemble the past'.

Whenever I describe the levels of cultural censorship I
grew up with, Wilf reminds me that when he was in his teens
a licence from the Lord Chamberlain's office was required for
virtually every theatrical production in Britain, and that the
obscenity trial brought against Penguin Books for publishing
D. H. Lawrence's novel *Lady Chatterley's Lover* took place there
as late as 1960. He is right, of course, and I'm not suggesting that,

even in the late 1970s when I first arrived there, Britain was free
from misogyny, conservatism, narrow-mindedness or racism. It
wasn't. Nor is it now. But the Britain that Wilf grew up in became
increasingly liberal in the years after the Second World War,
while the Republic of Ireland's cultural and spiritual experience
was permeated by arid authoritarianism as long as de Valera was
alive. Both he and McQuaid died in the 1970s and I remember
my generation of university students living in expectation of
what would happen when they were gone, although much of our
speculation focused on the myth that if either of them died in
early summer, the obsequies were likely to be so elaborate that
our exams would have to be postponed.

The year after my parents married, the Irish writer Eric Cross
published a non-fiction book about a west Cork tailor called
Timothy Buckley and his wife Anastasia, both of whom were
fluent Irish speakers. Cross, an incomer to the locality, had been
friends with the elderly couple for several years, joining other
neighbours by the fireside while the tailor, sitting on an old butter
box which he called 'Cornucopia', smoked his pipe, told stories
and philosophised with robust interjections from his wife. The
book, called *The Tailor and Ansty,* reflects the life of a community
rooted in the same tradition of storytelling that informs Peig
Sayers' Blasket Island memoir. One central difference between
the two works is that Cross's book presents both an unsanitised
version of rural Ireland and a beautifully observed portrait of a
woman who saw human sexual relationships as simultaneously
fascinating and hilarious.

When *The Tailor and Ansty* was published in 1942 it was
banned by the Irish Censorship of Publications Board, which
had been established in 1929. In a Seanad debate about the
Board's criteria, which raged over four days, Timothy Buckley
was described as 'sex-obsessed' and as an example of 'the sores of
moral leprosy' that could undermine Christianity. When the ban
was upheld by the government, local priests went to the Buckleys'
home in west Cork, forced the old man to his knees and made

him burn his copy of Cross's book in his own fireplace. Some local people, whipped up by a sermon given in the parish church, ostracised the Buckleys, whose cottage had been a gathering place in which the area's wealth of traditional songs and stories had been preserved and passed on for future generations. Yet in the same year an official of the Irish Folklore Commission, established by de Valera's government and operated under the Department of Education, carefully collected, classified and preserved a number of Timothy Buckley's stories, noting his importance as a traditional storyteller. Eric Cross's book was still banned in Ireland in the 1960s.

Given that I was born into a Catholic family in Ireland in the mid-1950s, I was remarkably lucky where religion was concerned. Although I was raised a churchgoer, the barbaric elements of Irish Catholicism passed me by; I don't know if that was by accident or by my parents' deliberate design. In my school Religious Knowledge classes were taught by lay teachers who set us questions and answers to learn by heart from a book known as *The Catechism*. I imagine that there must have been some explanation and discussion of the dogma they contained but if there was I have no memory of it. The text we were required to learn was precise, rhythmic and dynamic and, having inherited my Galway grandmother's sense of drama, I was happy to get up and repeat it on demand. The book was illustrated with line drawings of scenes from the New Testament and you could add a luminous, oily effect to the halos if you used a yellow crayon – the trick was to apply it very thickly and remove the excess with a fingernail. This produced tiny golden petals of colour which were pleasing in themselves. Later on, we also learned large chunks of St Luke's Gospel by heart. Pupils were expected to provide their own schoolbooks, many of which were second-hand. My worn copies of St Luke and of *As You Like it* had arrived in boxes on some train sometime, from Galway or Enniscorthy: the Shakespeare's leather cover had been replaced by cardboard but the gilt-edged pages were soft as silk and smelled wonderful.

In fact, the majority of my childhood religious experience involved beautiful smells, books and artifacts, and beautiful music and buildings. My school was in a slightly scruffy Georgian terrace with two classrooms on each floor, the loo and stationery cupboard on the first landing, and a flat-roofed, pebble-dashed drill hall at the end of the garden. Each year we went on a week-long retreat to a convent owned by an order of contemplative nuns, walking there and back from school in a crocodile, and spending our days in beeswaxed corridors and sparsely furnished, beautifully proportioned rooms. There was a chapel, smelling of incense and dimly lit by a red lamp hanging before the altar, in which a litany of invocations and responses was murmured day and night by nuns on balconies hidden by fretted screens. The language of the litanies and the theatricality of the settings delighted me, and the food, served on long refectory tables to gospel readings from a lectern, was delicious. Its seasoning may have had something to do with the fact that the order was originally Belgian. Admittedly, it all went a bit wrong in my final year at school, when the reader at the lectern was replaced by a huge reel-to-reel tape recorder playing evangelistic sermons, reedily voiced in a strong Australian accent. But, along with the Rathmines & Rathgar Musical Society's productions of Rodgers and Hammerstein, and Visconti's *Death In Venice* and Zeffirelli's *Romeo and Juliet,* which were shown in a Dublin cinema in the late 1960s and early 1970s, religion was my introduction to theatre, music and art.

Yet behind the beauty there was a terrible lack of balance in the institution of the Church itself which resulted in decades of institutionalised brutality meted out to Ireland's most vulnerable citizens, including children and pregnant women. The assumption that women were second-class citizens was written into the constitution of 1937. So was the assumption that the Catholic Church held a special place within the state. The combination proved disastrous. Early drafts of the constitution actually endorsed a more central role for Church authority, but even the final text was presented to the Vatican for review and comment, and to Archbishop McQuaid for input on religious, educational, family and social welfare issues. There was no public debate on, or discussion of, the final document. Instead it was brought to the electorate in a plebiscite as a single question, 'Do you approve of the Draft Constitution which is the subject of this plebiscite?' The only option was to say yes or no. I have no idea which way any of my family voted. At the time, the country was still deeply unstable politically, socially and economically, which may have been a factor in the majority of the electorate's decision to cling to what stability had recently been achieved, and to keep on keeping on.

In the Seanad debate which considered issues of censorship in 1942, Ansty Buckley, who had been reared in the native Irish tradition of earthy humour and robust sexuality, was described as 'a moron'. This linking of female sexuality with mental deficiency, and of mental deficiency and illness with moral depravity, was one of the darkest features of de Valera's Ireland, and its effects are still felt today. I was writing for BBC television in London when the department I was working for commissioned a one-off drama called *Sinners* from the British writer Lizzie Mickery and I first became aware of the scandal of Ireland's Magdalene Laundries. Set in the 1960s, *Sinners* tells the story of an unmarried Irish girl who becomes pregnant and is sent by her family to an institution run by Catholic nuns. Confined there against her will, she is subjected to physical and mental humiliation and put to work in a laundry staffed by women and girls considered by their families, the Church or the state to have loose morals. Those who are pregnant give birth in agonising conditions attended by nuns who believe that pain is their due punishment for the sin of having become pregnant outside wedlock. Afterwards, the babies are forcibly taken away for adoption and the women are returned to a life of slave labour.

In *Sinners*, the principal character manages eventually to escape. In reality, many women who were confined in Magdalene

Laundries lived and died there abandoned by their families, and are buried in unmarked graves. The first of these institutions, then referred to as Magdalene Asylums, was called after Mary Magdalene, the prostitute in the New Testament who repented and was forgiven. It was founded in London in the eighteenth century to provide shelter and work for 'penitent prostitutes' who otherwise might have no way of staying off the streets. Magdalene asylums funded and run by philanthropic social reformers spread throughout the rest of Britain and abroad. The first to be opened in Ireland was founded in Dublin in 1765 by an Anglo-Irish Protestant philanthropist called Lady Arabella Denny. At the outset, although the administration of the asylums had a strong religious basis, women entered and could leave them voluntarily. But later the asylums came under the control of the Catholic Church and were converted into commercial laundries where inmates were confined against their will and used as an unpaid workforce. By the mid-twentieth century they were known as Magdalene Homes and the growing belief that female sexuality was inherently sinful had made them centres of brutality and criminality on what was literally an industrial scale.

When I saw *Sinners* in a preview theatre in London in 2002 I was unaware that its storyline exposed but the tip of an iceberg. In Dublin in 1993 a mass grave containing 155 corpses had been found in the grounds of a former convent and given rise to an extensive police investigation. But the truth of what had been happening in our midst had yet to become public. It was television, the success of a mainstream film called *The Magdalene Sisters* which premiered at The Venice Film Festival, and an increasing number of books by, and interviews with, former inmates of Magdalene Laundries, that caused Ireland to demand answers. What emerged was almost incredible. An estimated 30,000 women and girls had been confined against their will in Irish Magdalene Homes, the last of which closed in 1996, and it turned out that almost any one of us could have found herself among them. In de Valera's Ireland even the suspicion that a woman might be in danger of having sex outside marriage was good enough reason for her family or the clergy to have her 'sent to the nuns'. In some cases, orphans were confined in Magdalene Homes on the grounds that their lack of family placed them in moral danger. In the 1950s and 1960s the belief that engaging in what was deemed to be inappropriate sexual behaviour was a symptom of hereditary mental illness resulted in girls who had been born out of wedlock being locked up in their early teens. And for decades, because of the deep cult of secrecy that surrounded them and the fact that there was no court of appeal for those who were incarcerated, Magdalene Homes were used to conceal evidence of rape and sexual abuse by the clergy, and by inmates' family members and employers. Women who attempted to protest or escape could be registered as insane and removed to a secure mental facility. Those who did escape were hunted down by the Gardaí.

Incidences of physical and sexual abuse in other Irish institutions such as the equally brutal Industrial Schools and Reformatories, many of which were also run by religious orders, were systematically covered up by the authorities. And in state- and Church-controlled hospitals surgeons routinely cut through the pelvises of women in labour, ignoring a legal requirement to gain their patients' consent. This procedure, called symphysiotomy, was a dangerous alternative to caesarean section and was said only to have been used in circumstances when an anaesthetist was not available and intervention in labour was necessary. But symphysiotomies were also frequently performed during pregnancy, and many Irish women were told by medical professionals that the procedure must take place because repeated childbirth was inadvisable after a caesarean and family planning was sinful. Many of the women who underwent symphysiotomies are crippled, incontinent and still suffer physical pain and mental trauma today. Many testify that for decades they had no idea what had been done to them. Shortly before my own mother died we talked about childbirth and pregnancy. She told me that she had loved having babies but feared and disliked her obstetrician, who she described as an arrogant man who regularly induced births to fit his work around his annual fishing trip. Despite the fact that money was short, my siblings and I were born in a private nursing home. I never asked my mother why she made that decision and I don't know if it saved her from symphysiotomy, but I know now that her obstetrician, a devout Catholic, was a strong advocate of the procedure. I shudder to think what might have happened to her, and what did happen to hundreds of her generation, in the wards of Ireland's state-run hospitals.

I remember the May altars of my Dublin childhood, smothered in flowers and decked in starched linen. At school we had one on the mantelpiece in each of the classrooms. In winter the rooms were heated by open fires but by May Day the fireplaces were concealed by vases of white blossoms. Creating the altar involved washing the thin layer of winter ash from the statue of the Virgin Mary, positioning her in the centre of the mantelpiece, and removing the litter of copybooks, old biros and ends of chalk that tended to gather at her feet. For the rest of the month she held the central place on the altar, surrounded by flowers and flanked by the statues of Christ with his exposed and bleeding heart and St Anthony on whom we relied absolutely in my childhood to find and return anything that we might have lost. One year I was one of four girls elected to carry the statue of the Virgin in a May procession. She was swathed in lace and anchored in some discreet way to a small table, and we grasped a leg apiece as the whole school bounced smugly across the road chanting hymns and holding up the traffic. 'MOHther of Christ, STAR of the Seeeea, Pra-ay FOR the WAH- hon- d'rer, PRAY for mee …' At the nearest church, in our shiny-bottomed gym frocks, knee socks and Clarks' sandals, we stood among flowers with our First Holy Communion veils over our hair while an altar boy held a gilded vessel from which the priest showered us with holy water, after which we chanted our way back across the road in time for lunch. *'VIRgin most PURE, Star of the SEEEEA, Pray for the SIH-Hin -ner, PRAY for mee ...'*

Nearly fifty years later, I am amazed to see little girls dressed and veiled in virginal white still lining up on their First Holy Communion day on the steps of their local church. The veils now glitter with a lot more fairy dust, but photographers from local newspapers still urge them to join their hands as if in prayer, and to cast up their eyes. Beside them, as marginalised in terms of attention as the groom whose tie has been chosen to match the colour of his bride's bridesmaids' dresses, are their little male classmates, smugly holy in dark suits. When those photographs become part of some future family album, what memories will attach to them and how alien will they seem?

In a statement in 2014 about a home for unmarried mothers and their children run by the Bon Secours nuns in Tuam, County Galway, between 1925 and 1961, a spokesman for the archdiocese said: 'we can't really judge the past from our point of view'. He was speaking about yet another scandal which continues to unfold as I write. It had been revealed that, over the years, hundreds of babies born in the home who had subsequently died were buried there in unmarked mass graves. Mothers who had given birth there had been refused access to their living children and denied information about the fate of those who died. It is easy to dismiss the archdiocesan statement as a despicable attempt to justify a culture of abuse. But the truth is that we cannot judge the past from our own point of view if our own point of view is uninformed. Nor can we understand or learn from it. To do that – and we have a responsibility to do that – we must study what happened in its context. Otherwise we simply add more layers to the lies and misinformation that we need to strip away. There is little difference between the old myth that portrayed Ireland as an island of saints and scholars and the new myth which portrays our parents and grandparents as hypocritical, priest-ridden snivellers who knew what was happening and failed to act to prevent it. Each myth is as dangerous as the other because neither expresses the whole truth and both are rooted in complacency. I don't know if the whole truth about anything can ever really be revealed. But I do know that to achieve any kind of justice for those abused victims and survivors, we must sweep away all lies, question all sound-bite assumptions that masquerade as history, and engage in something far more dynamic than blame. Of course people knew about the Magdalene Laundries, the Mother and Baby Homes, the criminal medical practices, and the Reformatories and Industrial Schools. And, just as there were different levels of active cruelty or criminality, there were different levels of knowledge. The task of understanding those different levels and what each meant in terms of responsibility and culpability begs so many questions that it is hard to find a starting point. Maybe when a society has been poleaxed by communal shame and blame, the best way forward is for its members to seek individual starting points of their own.

I knew about the Magdalene Laundries. There were two near my home in Dublin in the 1950s and 1960s and I remember seeing women and girls standing about the grounds in lumpy overalls, and being told that they were in trouble and were being looked after by the nuns. I was told that by my mother and I believe that she believed it to be true. I know that when she was desperately seeking interim home care for my ageing grandmother, who had been unwell, she went to the nuns in Enniscorthy for advice, and a quiet friendly girl was sent round each day to help granny with the housework and the shopping. She was paid by the hour and, looking back now, I wonder if she ever saw a penny of her wages. But I suspect that if my mother thought that the money was taken by the nuns she might well have said that, since the convent was feeding and clothing girls, finding them work and giving them shelter, then that was fair enough. She lived at a time when jobs were prized and food, clothes and shelter were not easy to come by. She had had no negative experience of nuns herself, she had five children at home, a husband whose work took him to the other side of the country, and no way of making arrangements for her ageing mother except by physically getting on a train and travelling from Dublin to Enniscorthy. Life in Ireland was like that then. People were grateful to turn to the Church for help in practical as well as spiritual matters, largely because they had few other safety nets. We need to understand why that was so. Otherwise we are in danger of wallowing in generalised recriminations until a point comes when we tire of the story and sweep it back under the carpet.

Irrespective of denomination, or even belief in a god, human beings have a built-in requirement for communal rites of passage and for somewhere to enact them. We need places to present our newborn children to the community, celebrate their coming of age, demonstrate our commitment to partners, seek consolation and healing in grief and illness, and to dispose of our dead with ceremony and reverence. In Ireland, across centuries, the Catholic Church as an institution has worked to ensure that churches have become the only accepted places in which to carry out these rites. Its subsequent corruption of these places by association is high on the list of its crimes against those it purports to serve, not least because many Irish people now attend churches in a state of ambivalence and suppressed anger which injects an unhealthy subtext into ceremonies that are vital to communal and individual lives.

There is hardly a family in Ireland without relatives in religious orders, and many of those relatives are now old. People instinctively feel that old age requires respect and that criticism of a priest implies criticism of those members of families and communities who, by continuing to be practising Catholics, appear to endorse his authority and right to be respected. I have no relatives in religious orders, I'm no longer a Catholic, and I spend much of my time out of the country so perhaps it is easy for me to say this, but I believe that we must challenge Church control in secular matters such as education and healthcare, regardless of the respect we may feel we owe to individuals, communities or the aged. Still, it's complicated. Maybe part of the answer lies in the fact that church buildings were largely financed by collections from the communities in which they stand. Perhaps, instead of walking out of churches, we should crowd into them whenever we feel we want to, and begin a process of reclaiming them. But in order for wounds in any society to be healed all the stories must be told: the troubled, complicated unthought-through ones as well as those that make horrific tabloid headlines. And among them we need to hear the difficult, hard-to-tell stories of those priests, nuns and brothers whose arrogance and cruelty had roots in their own fear, ignorance, stupidity, or sense of being trapped and overwhelmed by circumstances they couldn't control.

Rural poverty in de Valera's Ireland was extreme and its urban slums were notorious. TB and polio were rife. The infant-mortality rate was high. The country's infrastructure was underdeveloped and underfunded. Both education and medicine were underpinned by Church schools and hospitals. And ever since Henry VIII had announced that the power of the English monarchy trumped that of the Church of Rome, faith in Catholicism had been a powerful symbol of native Irishness. This was the climate in which the Catholic Church gained what we now know to be a deeply unhealthy influence on the state. It was a climate in which Irish society's perception of both the Church and its functions in society were not what they are today. Throughout the nineteenth and early twentieth centuries religious foundations provided healthcare, education, and therefore opportunities for advancement, for thousands of men and women who would otherwise have lived and died in poverty. The support of the Church of Rome and of individual members of its religious orders had made a huge difference in the fight for independence. In the early years of the country's independence, religious societies provided financial and social services which the state couldn't afford. The sense of shame and social stigma associated with what the Church declared to be immoral could destroy job and marriage prospects, not just for those accused but for their families, many of whom saw the option of sending family members to the nuns as the only available form of damage limitation. None of this justifies the arrogance, cruelty, ignorance and perversion of Christian values which led to the horrors of places like the Magdalene Laundries. But nor does their ghastliness cancel out facts. If the majority of the people in de Valera's Ireland had an exaggerated regard for the Church, at least some of that regard was rooted in a justifiable sense that the religious orders had supported them, culturally, practically and spiritually, across centuries of colonial abuse and neglect. There was much to admire about the work and influence of individual Irish priests and nuns and, indeed, about de Valera's constitution of 1937. But the constitution's clauses relating to women combined with its copper-fastening of the authority of the Church to that of the state produced a recipe for disaster.

The flag raised over the Enniscorthy Athenaeum by Una, Gretta and Marion in 1916 was a tricolour and in de Valera's constitution of 1937 it was the tricolour that was declared to be the Republic's national flag. But flags of several different colours and designs had flown over the rebel strongholds. There was much controversy in the Military History Society in my childhood when one member who was a 1916 veteran repeatedly insisted, despite photographic evidence, that a particular flag had not flown on one corner of the GPO because he had looked out from a particular window and seen that it wasn't there. I remember the arguments because my father was writing a history of Irish flags at the time, working in the trains on his journeys between Dublin and Galway, under the lilac tree in our back garden, and sitting at the dining-room table with his back to the fire. In those years the dining-room table was covered with sketches, statements and photos and I remember dire warnings about what would happen if I touched them. Among them was correspondence with Seán O'Casey, then living in England and resolutely refusing to allow his work to be produced in Ireland. In one letter the playwright's memory, filtered through time and his own imagination, played him false. According to what he told my father, and wrote in his autobiography, O'Casey, who was secretary of the Citizen Army before the Rising, remembered the Citizen Army flag, which depicted the Labour movement's symbol of the plough and the stars, as having a blue ground. But the Citizen army flag flown in 1916 has a green ground, not a blue one. In 1954, trying to reconcile memory with fact, O'Casey suggested that a second flag might have been sneaked in at the last moment by Connolly, who, he said, was always more inclined to nationalism than socialism and, therefore, liked the colour green. Then, to substantiate his theory, he remembered that on Palm Sunday in 1916 Connolly had hoisted a green flag over the Citizen Army headquarters at Liberty Hall. In a footnote in his book, my father points out with an exclamation mark that O'Casey had stated in 1919 that the flag hoisted over Liberty Hall on Palm Sunday was a tricolour. 'Memory', concludes the footnote, 'is as fickle as a changeful dream.'

My father's history of Irish flags was published after his death. It was seen through the press by my mother, to whom he had dedicated it, as he dedicated all his books, and was edited by a former colleague of his in the museum whom my mother thanks in a note which she adds over her own name under my father's preface. I am fond of the book's footnotes because I can hear my father's voice in them, offering asides in which he permitted himself the italics and exclamation marks that never appear in his texts. In one note he acknowledges his great debt to O'Casey and 'many pleasant meetings with other Citizen Army veterans in the National Museum of Ireland'. In particular, he recalls the statement of one veteran who was asked what he remembered about a 1916 flag that the museum was investigating in 1954. The old man looked at it for a moment and dismissed it. 'That faded old thing couldn't be our flag', he said, '*our* flag was *beautiful*.'

11
The Pikeman and The Heart Stone

AFTER WILF AND I WERE MARRIED, one of his father's family gave us a gift of two character Toby jugs. They depicted Winston Churchill and Field Marshal Montgomery, by then enshrined in British legend as heroes of the Second World War. The circumstances of the presentation weren't formal; as far as I can remember, Churchill, with his bowler hat and cigar, and Monty, with his smartly cocked army beret, emerged wrapped in tea towels from a shoebox. But, although they were given with a typically British lack of fuss, they were Royal Doulton china, designed in 1946, and consciously intended to provide us with heirlooms. It was a generous gift, handed down with love, which we accepted gratefully. It would have been idiotic for me to have pointed out that it was Churchill who developed the strategy which sent the Auxies and the Tans to Ireland or that Montgomery had declared that, as a brigade major serving in Ireland, it didn't bother him a bit how many houses his men burned to the ground in west Cork. For a while we used the jugs as vases. They sat on a kitchen shelf in the sunlight with sprigs of rosemary stuffed into Monty's beret and grey-green sage blooming in Churchill's bowler. Then, during some orgy of packing between one flat or house and another, they disappeared back into their shoebox and we moved on.

Today I looked again at Marion's memorial card. Printed above a quotation from the liturgy of the Mass, the text reads 'In Loving Memory of Marion B. Stokes, Enniscorthy, Co. Wexford, who died on the 1st January, 1983 Aged 87 Years'. Her face in the faded colour photo still gives nothing away, and the glare from her 1970s spectacles makes it hard to see her eyes. But this time, concentrating on the background, I recognised where the photo was taken. Upright, enigmatic and looking straight into the camera, Marion sits on a sofa which once belonged to my grandmother. When my brother built the new house in the orchard of the old family house in Enniscorthy, he reupholstered the sofa, two chairs and a footstool in the blue fabric that is visible behind Marion's shoulders on her memorial card. So the photo was taken in the room where I sat myself after the event at Enniscorthy Castle, when I clicked idly on a search engine and found the reference to Marion that led me to write this book.

The house in the orchard was built for my aunt Cathleen, who moved into it when she retired. Both she and Marion, each in her own time, chose to end their lives in Enniscorthy. I don't know why, having fought for an independent Ireland, Marion got on a boat and went off to work in London. But I wonder if it was an inherited sense of belonging that eventually brought her home. Strong personal identification with place is not unusual in rural communities and can still be found in many parts of the world today; but in much of Europe it was a casualty of the mass movement to towns and cities that occurred during the Industrial Revolution. The majority of Ireland, however, was untouched by nineteenth-century industrialisation and, growing up in Enniscorthy over a hundred years ago, Marion would have shared a sense of communal memory rooted in place that was as intense and detailed as that of my neighbours in Corca Dhuibhne today. Maybe in the end it was the steep streets, the castle and the cathedral, the bulk of Vinegar Hill above the town, and the three stones that guarded the pump on the green across the road that drew her home.

Cathleen's return to Enniscorthy feels stranger, but then Cathleen had enigmatic qualities of her own. She never lost the formidable stare captured in the studio photo taken with my mother and Evie in her childhood, and she grew up to be both fiercely independent and deeply reserved. In her retirement she was delighted by her grand-nieces and -nephews, welcoming

visitors with Mi-Wadi orange juice, sherry, biscuits served
from my grandmother's cut-glass biscuit barrel, and plates of
melting ice cream. Cathleen always wanted to hear news of the
family but was never forthcoming about her own life. Even her
retirement took us all by surprise, and I remember my mother's
astonishment at her announcement that she wanted my brother,
who had just qualified as an architect, to build her a house in
the Enniscorthy orchard. She was the most cosmopolitan
career woman I knew in my childhood, a Francophile, and an
inveterate traveller whose work as the personal assistant to the
head of Ireland's national airline gave her a freedom that she
guarded jealously into old age. As a child I was impressed by the
glamour of her little flat in Dublin which overlooked St Stephen's
Green and always seemed dusty and chaotic, as if she never
wasted much time there. Her meals tended to consist of cheese
and crackers and a bowl of soup or a glass of wine, she dressed
in the height of fashion, and her crowded bookcases were full
of map books and the latest novels. Sometime in the late 1950s
she joined us on an Irish seaside holiday wearing a sleeveless
piqué shirt with a turned-up collar, and a calf-length circular
skirt cinched at the waist by a broad buckled belt. I remember
being delighted by the crisp, white fabric of the skirt which was
printed with a repeated motif of cocktail glasses, cigarettes in
long holders and little Parisian café tables, sketched in black and
backed by vivid splodges of green, yellow and red.

Nearly twenty years later, when I was at university, Cathleen
gave me a short beaver jacket with huge turned-back cuffs, which
she had bought in London in her own youth. I remember her
flashing me a grin when I pedalled off on my bike, wearing her
1930s style over a crushed-velvet maxi dress, with Guatemalan
toe socks under my platform clogs. Later still, when my mother
was dead and Cathleen was in her late eighties, Wilf and I invited
her to London for a weekend. She arrived with a single piece of
cabin baggage from which emerged underwear, lipstick, a pair of
slim, black slacks which she teamed with ballet flats and a jade

silk shirt for the opera, a fine wool jumper which she wore with the slacks, a trench coat and low-heeled ankle boots for walks by the river, and a large scarf which became a stole by night. In her Enniscorthy retirement she lived alone, apparently content with her friends, her books and the local French and Gramophone societies. She walked down the hill to Mass in the cathedral each day, pottered around the garden in old clothes, using a large, silver serving spoon as a trowel, and regularly took the train up to Dublin to catch the latest films. I have no idea why she never married. Perhaps she didn't want to. Perhaps she never found a man to suit her. Or perhaps she turned her formidable gaze on the options available to her as a woman in post-revolutionary Ireland and made her choices accordingly.

By joining in the struggle for Ireland's independence, Marion must have imagined that the women of my mother's generation would live in a very different world from the one that they ultimately inherited. I wish I knew what she thought, and what she and her companions said to each other, when they saw what became of their dreams. From the time I first went to London in the late 1970s to a week or so before her own death in 1990, my mother and I wrote each other letters; always once and sometimes twice a week and occasionally – since international phone calls were prohibitively expensive at the time – more than once on the same day. I am sure that she wrote to me about Marion's death in 1983, and described her funeral in a letter. But I have no memory of it, and I have yet to visit Marion's grave. Perhaps it was in 1983 that my mother and I walked by the Thames, when I remembered Marion's bottle of Mercurochrome and her instructions for using egg yolks as a hair conditioner, and my mother remembered how she hadn't liked to talk about the past. Like hundreds of other Irishwomen who took part in the struggle for Ireland's independence, Marion was buried without reference to her part in the 1916 Rising. Maybe that was exactly what she would have wanted. She, too, never married. I don't know why.

The first significant attempts to claw back some of the equality that had been lost to Irishwomen after 1916 began in 1965 when, after much campaigning, widows became entitled to a share in their husband's estate even if the husband had died intestate. In 1970 a Deserted Wife's allowance was established. Then in 1971, when I was at university, the Irish Women's Liberation (IWL) movement was founded in Dublin by a small group of women, most of whom were journalists. They produced a manifesto, called *Chains or Change*, which listed the 'civil wrongs of Irishwomen' and, being media-savvy, opened the debate on television and in a series of publicity stunts calculated to get attention. I remember the euphoria of my peers when a female senator, Mary Robinson, later to become the first female president of Ireland, tried to introduce a bill on liberalising the law on contraception into the Seanad that year, and our fury when, because it wasn't allowed a reading, it couldn't be discussed. Then came more euphoria – and outrage – when a group of banner-waving IWL activists crossed the border between the republic and Northern Ireland by train and came back carrying armfuls of illegal contraceptives. Those were the days of bad-ass journalists, feminists and civil-rights campaigners like Nell McCafferty, Mary Kenny and Nuala O'Faolain. They were the days when Irishwomen were still constrained by the marriage bar and denied equal pay and the right to sit on a jury; and when a married Irishwoman had no right to see her husband's tax forms, put her children on her passport, or even to undergo certain gynaecological procedures, without her husband's permission.

The year I left drama school my mother and her best friend from school, Minnie, came to London. I was living in an Ealing flat full of out-of-work actors and actresses who dodged in and out with disaster stories about auditions and requests for loans of each other's make-up, money and clothes. My mother and Minnie, who had once shared a flat themselves, entered into all our traumas with enthusiasm, bought a large box of teabags for the kitchen, and slipped a £5 note under my pillow when they left. While they were with us, Minnie bonded with my flatmate Arthur Bostrom, who had yet to get his first break in television, and for years afterwards the notes that came with her Christmas cards always ended with the anxious request to be told if he'd got himself a pantomime. My mother's letters repeatedly enquired after my friends from drama school, our jobs and our auditions, while gently nudging me away from acting and towards writing, which she always wanted to see me pursue. In the same way she had encouraged my father during his years at the museum to spend his evenings sitting at the dining-room table building up the body of published work which established his academic career. Looking back now on that fund of energy and enthusiasm, I am wrenched by the sense of a whole generation of female lives lived out through others' experience.

I wish I had kept the hundreds of letters that my mother sent me; nearly twenty years' worth of family news, stories about the grandchildren she adored, descriptions of people she met, and analyses of the books she read and the plays she occasionally went to. But in moving from flat to flat and from job to job I travelled light, like Cathleen, and now I have only two of my mother's letters, written in biro in a round hand with interpolated comments and asides between the lines and crammed into the margins. Almost every letter she sent me was folded around newspaper cuttings which she thought might interest me or help me with my work, but it was years before I realised how much she valued her own sense of involvement in it. The morning after my wedding she wrote me a letter on two sheets of scrap paper, which she headed 'Friday, 9.15am'. *'When I came downstairs for my breakfast I was weighed down by the thought "you can't expect many more letters from Felicity", so when the postman rattled at the gate I knew without any doubt that it was my Income Tax bill. However, I was overjoyed to find two letters from you, and all about your work and plans. You see I have followed your work so closely over the years, it was simply a continuance of my work and life with Daddy. The effort and desire of all of us for Continuity.*

I expect that is why family Christian names occur through generations. I hope you will continue to write to me: I don't want to hear about Wilf locking you in the broom cupboard because you had not his supper ready, but I should like to hear about his work also.' The second of the two letters that remain to me had arrived a few months earlier, a day or two after I telephoned her to tell her of my engagement. She wrote it on blue notepaper, sitting up in bed at 6.30 a.m. on 1 May 1986, and signed it in the margin 'Love from The Mistress of Novices'. It begins with a description of the sun on her face, the maple tree outside her window and the fact that there is 'no sound of traffic to disturb the songs of the birds'. It ends with a shrewd summing-up of my character and an admonishment to strive in times of stress for 'balance, reason, logic and tolerance'. Looking back now, over twenty years later, lack of balance seems to me to have been the greatest curse of the Ireland I grew up in, closely followed by lack of reasoned, logical debate informed by tolerance.

I wonder too just how trapped the men of my father's generation must have felt in a country which cast them as the sole breadwinners, offered them so few chances of employment, and demanded such levels of social, moral and intellectual conformity if they were to keep their jobs. Long after he died, my mother told me that one day in the early years of their marriage my father came home late from work. She had made Scotch eggs for tea from a recipe in a magazine, laid the table with one of the cloths she had embroidered for her trousseau, and then sat around for hours worrying that he might have fallen under a bus. When he eventually arrived home he told her that he had walked for miles from the museum towards the mouth of the Liffey, watching ships setting out to sea and longing to sail away leaving everything behind. I was outraged to hear it, imagining my mother stuck at home with her housework and her women's magazines while he fantasised about leaving her. But she just smiled when I said so, and apparently her only response at the time was to serve his Scotch eggs in a marked manner. I don't believe that either of them would ever have left the other, but it is a fact that, if he had got on a ship and sailed away, Irish law at the time permitted him to go as he pleased and to resume all his marital and parental rights if he chose to return, having left her with no financial support in the interim. Whereas, if she had left him, she would have forfeited all her marital rights, including that of access to the marital home and to their children.

It is important to remember now how courageous some of the stances taken by my father and his fellow academics were in the climate of the Ireland in which they worked. Even as early as the 1920s, when W. B. Yeats was a senator, smugness and self-satisfaction had begun to characterise Irish nationalism, and the realities of the country's underfunded education system were regularly brushed aside with references to Ireland's medieval scholarly heritage or to nineteenth-century Irish peasants conversing in Classical Greek. Yeats' Seanad speeches repeatedly drew attention to insanitary classrooms, poor teaching, badly produced books and the resultant high levels of illiteracy among the new state's electorate. At one stage, in a wry reference to his own role in building up the nation's pre-1916 sense of cultural self-esteem, he pointed out the danger of post-revolutionary states believing their own pre-revolutionary propaganda. But that seems to have been regarded by most of his fellow senators as bad form. Later on, complaints from my father and many of his academic colleagues about the standards applied to the teaching of history in the republic's schools produced the same effect: comparisons with international standards were seen as attacks on Irishness and, as with the Military Bureau Witness Statements, attempts to disentangle history from hagiography were suppressed. Even my father's calls for better book design and illustration in school textbooks were considered disloyal, and his opposition to the policy of restricting university faculty positions in Galway to Irish-speaking academics was cited, covertly and overtly, as evidence of a lack of patriotism. On a more frightening level, his repeated attempts to gain recognition for Irishmen who had served in the British army, and for members of the Royal Irish Constabulary, resulted in anonymous threats, which, according to my mother, he simply ignored.

The trips that my mother made to London, and the holidays she and I took together, were the experiences that she and my father would have shared had he lived longer. His death in 1977 shattered her plans for a retirement in which they could regain the easy companionship they had had in the years before his work took him from home for extended periods and his illness had begun to dominate their life together. A few years after I was born, he was diagnosed with diabetes, having been unwell for extended periods. His case was complex and medication then was far more aggressive and less sophisticated than it is now, so for the rest of his life his condition was a constant source of anxiety, complicated by the fact that he refused to allow anyone outside the family to know of it. According to my mother, he also decided that his ill health should be concealed from me altogether, in case it overshadowed my youth. As a result I grew up with the unspoken knowledge that something dreadful might happen to him at any moment, with no idea why, or what it might be. Considering the extent of my mother's own levels of childhood awareness, I have always been astonished that she went along with his decision with regard to me; but, perverse though it may seem today, his concern about the outside world's reaction to his state of health was sound common sense. In the Ireland in which he was the sole breadwinner for a wife and five children, physical illness carried a stigma almost comparable to that which still surrounds mental illness in Ireland today. Spiralling out from a fear of tuberculosis so deeply rooted that simply to admit to its presence in your family left you open to social ostracism was a pervasive sense that all illness implied inherited weakness. In my parents' lifetime that perception, combined with fierce levels of competition for work, produced a climate in which, in matters of health as in many others, it was best to keep the best side out.

Although my father's sister Marguerite had far more paper qualifications than my mother's sister Cathleen, she never built a career. My mother told me that Marguerite tried more than once to gain an academic position but, despite her PhD and her Arts and Law degrees, it never happened. The implication was that there was nothing available in Galway, where she worked as a teacher in the vocational school, and that, being female, it was expected she would continue to live at home and look after her parents. In the event, Marguerite died in 1946, aged thirty-seven. She had had a car which she left to my father but he sold it because he thought it would be too expensive to run. We had no car in Dublin when I was growing up but, for a term or two at university, regardless of the fact that they didn't fit me, I wore Marguerite's motoring gauntlets. She must have had very small hands because the fingers were half the length of mine and the flared leather cuffs began halfway down my palm, just at the joint of my thumb. I don't know what she died of: when I asked my eldest brother he said that it wasn't spoken of so he had always assumed it was tuberculosis. It was after Marguerite's death that her widowed mother, my fearsome Galway granny, moved resentfully into the spare bedroom in our Dublin semi where she delighted me with stories and tormented my mother with tea trays. Years later, a family friend told me that Marguerite had wept loudly during my parents' wedding. When I heard that story I assumed that it must have been the Galway drama-queen gene emerging at an inappropriate moment. Now I wonder if Marguerite was facing the fact that her brother's decision not just to work but to marry in Dublin had put the tin lid on her own hopes of flying the coop and making her own career.

At the opposite side of Dublin's St Stephen's Green from Fusiliers' Arch, or Traitors' Gate, is a memorial of yet another war. When I was a child, whenever my father and I would enter the Green from the Leeson Street side, we would stop and consider it. In the centre of a round pool bounded by a low parapet are three robed female figures, one behind the other, grouped on a rock. The tallest stands at the rear looking over the shoulder of the second, who stands behind a third figure, seated in front of the others. They are the Norns of Scandinavian and Germanic mythology, who correspond to the Fates of the Greek and Roman tradition; three sisters who spin, measure and cut the destined lifespans of humankind. Like the statue of the doomed Cú Chulainn in the GPO, the attraction of the Norns was that their narrative was three-dimensional. Viewed head on, it wasn't evident that the bronze thread unwinding from the skein held in the tallest figure's hand snaked over the shoulder and through the fingers of the central figure to the seated one in front. You had to walk all around the pool to see that it was the delicate thread that carried the weight of the story. And unless you stood on the left-hand side of the seated figure you would never see the shears lying half concealed in the bronze drapery in her lap.

Walking around their circular pool in St Stephen's Green, I first discovered the idea that, in the northern hemisphere, moving with or in opposition to the perceived trajectory of the sun across the horizon was once thought to have powerful significance. I remember my father teaching me the word 'widdershins' and telling me that, in European folklore, charms and spells spoken when moving clockwise or anticlockwise around a fixed point were held to be particularly potent. It was one of my earliest introductions to the links between mythology and folklore, and between religion and art.

The darkness of the pool and the brooding presence of the impassive Norns delighted me. The figures represent Present, Past and Future personified as the Maiden, the Mother and the Crone. The monument, which was a gift to the Irish people in recognition of humanitarian aid given to German children after the Second World War, was my first awareness of the idea of the female life cycle as an image of the mystery of Life and Death. From the rear you could see the upturned sole of a foot, rendered with far less definition than Cú Chulainn's: it was blurred and heavy as if the figure was as much a part of the earth as the rock that she stood on. That lack of definition and the mask-like faces of the figures, sculpted by Josef Wackerle, offer a world view which expresses the supernatural in terms of abstract concepts and characteristics, rather than personality. In an Ireland in which Catholicism represented eternity as a sort of civil service department in which those with the right contacts could be badgered, pressured or cajoled into putting in a good word for the rest of us, the idea that these figures would respond to no prayer, bribe or force was oddly liberating. So was the thought that power over life and death was a female attribute. The Catholic Ireland of my childhood and teens adored the idea of the Virgin Mary as the power behind the throne of heaven whose worth was measured by the extent to which she could influence her son's – and, by extension, his father's – behaviour. In such a culture, the idea that the hand that rocks the cradle rules the world can far too easily become a justification for female disenfranchisement.

In the end, my father died aged only sixty-four, after a car crash. He lived to see his children, whom he had worked tirelessly to educate, become a teacher, an artist and designer, an architect, and a creative and enterprising businessman. Six months or so before he died I got the university degree that he was concerned I might fail to achieve. Looking back, I am full of admiration for the pragmatism he brought to our education. He was fierce in his defence of the autonomy of Ireland's universities. But, having studied under and worked with educators like Eoin MacNeill, Liam Ó Bríain, who was a veteran of the 1916 Rising and University College Galway's Professor of Romance languages, and Margaret Heavey, who became the university's Professor of Ancient Classics a year before my father himself became Professor of Modern History there, he took their view that the business of an academic was first to inspire enthusiasm for knowledge and then to teach disciplined methods of study. Other than that, he believed, education was a lifelong process which individuals should be left to get on with themselves. And although I know now that he fought to improve the standards of the history books we were given at school, he chose never to undermine my schoolteachers' authority by pointing out that much of the history I learned in school was skewed, censored or plain nonsense. I wish I had had the chance to talk to him about that choice and why he made it. For years I resented and was confused by it. But on balance I think it was a good one: although it added to the mixed messages that dogged my youth, it also stimulated an investigative and analytical approach to information which has been invaluable in my own work. And it has made me endlessly fascinated by irony. Among the many things I discovered after his death is the fact that Josef Wackerle, who created the Norns in St Stephen's Green, was exempted from conscription to the army of the Third Reich because he was one of Adolf Hitler's favourite artists. Had that not been so, his statue of the Norns who spin the destiny of each human being might never have been sculpted.

My mother survived my father by fifteen years. After her death I found a newspaper cutting sellotaped behind a print of a Pre-Raphaelite painting of a bowl of primroses which he had framed himself with passe-partout tape and given her as a wedding present. The cutting, which dated from just after his death, was a quotation from the Quaker writer William Penn: 'and life is eternal, and love is immortal, and death is only an horizon, and an horizon is nothing, save the limit of our sight.' One day, in the hospital where she would shortly die after an operation for cancer, I asked how she was and, troubled by the nurses' efforts to make her sip water to avoid dehydration, she said she was a seagull with a broken wing on the turn of the path on Howth Head, pecked at by all the birds around him. A day or so later she turned to me urgently before receiving a top-up of what I assume was morphine, and said that they were keeping her drugged but she wanted to tell me something. She had never been afraid of death, she said, because she wanted to see my father again, but she had thought that dying would be difficult. But, she said, it wasn't: it was easy.

Cathleen died in 1998, the last of the three little girls who had been taken for walks down Washerwoman's Hill and played in the Botanic Gardens. Always a law unto herself, she left a will saying that she wanted to be cremated, a procedure which for most of her life had been banned by the Catholic Church. So her body was brought back to Dublin, to the crematorium in Glasnevin Cemetery, and her ashes returned to Enniscorthy for burial. The funeral Mass was held on a chilly, misty day in Enniscorthy cathedral. As we gathered afterwards by the hearse, I found myself beside an elderly woman who remarked that Cathleen was a very private woman but very well respected. I nodded. Then the woman put her hand on my arm and drew me a few yards away from the hearse, onto the lawn that surrounds the cathedral, which itself is surrounded by railings. 'Do you know about the heart stone?' she asked. For a moment I must have looked blank. Then I looked down and saw a weathered, oblong slab at our feet, with a heart-shaped stone lying flat at the head of it. It is clearly a grave but, having no headstone, it had been almost invisible until we walked up to it. In the background, I could hear car doors slamming as people prepared to join the funeral cortège to the new, sprawling graveyard on the outskirts of town. I crouched down, feeling the heels of my shoes sinking into the damp earth under the grass. The name carved on the heart-shaped stone was Stokes. When I stood up again the woman took my arm and told me a story. 'It was a young man and his wife,' she said. 'This was their home. That was their hearth stone.' She pointed to the stone heart at our feet. 'It was their hearth, the heart of their house.' Her hand tightened on my arm and she lowered her voice, eager to make her point. 'The houses were knocked when they built the cathedral. The family had to move out, they had no choice. But, whatever happened to her in life, she said, when she died she'd be buried here. This was their hearth and she said they'd lie under it.' I came away from

Cathleen's funeral intending to find out more about that story but, as happens in life, I never did. Whoever she was, the woman who was buried with her husband under the heart stone must have been removed from her home sometime between 1843, when work on the cathedral began, and 1860 when, although its spire had yet to be completed, the building was dedicated. I don't know how she managed to insist on a gravesite directly outside the imposing cathedral door but her story suggests that Marion Stokes came from a long line of determined women.

The 1798 Rebellion continues to dominate Enniscorthy's sense of its insurgent past. The town boasts the national 1798 Rebellion Centre where visitors are offered a state-of-the-art 4D Battle of Vinegar Hill Experience. If you turn left out of Enniscorthy Cathedral's gates and walk down the hill through the market square you pass an older memorial to 1798, sculpted by Oliver Sheppard, the man who made the Cú Chulainn statue that de Valera wanted installed in the GPO in Dublin to commemorate the 1916 Rising. My mother and I used to stop by the memorial in the market square in the 1960s, to catch our breath on the steep climb from the train station up to my grandmother's house. Marion and her comrades passed it on Thursday of Easter Week in 1916, as they marched down through the market square to take the town for the republic. It is a powerful image of Enniscorthy's enduring collective memory. But it carries mixed messages of its own.

Like Sheppard's Cú Chulainn in the GPO, the statue in Enniscorthy's market square is a fascinating example of art as propaganda. Cast in bronze and raised on a stone plinth, it depicts a young man holding a pike as the staff of a flag which furls behind him linking his figure to that of a priest, who points the way to Vinegar Hill. In the pikeman's other hand is a sword but his breeches and his open-necked shirt with rolled-up sleeves suggest that he is a farmer, not a soldier. Rosary beads hang from the priest's greatcoat pocket and his figure is larger and more dynamic than the youth's, emphasising his authority. It is a work about the rational principles of the eighteenth-century enlightenment produced by an artist whose sensibilities were shaped by the Romanticism of the Gaelic Revivalists, and paid for by the efforts of a committee that saw nothing immoral about rewriting history to suit the agenda of the Church.

Around the time of the centenary of the 1798 Rebellion, local committees in both Enniscorthy and Wexford town commissioned Sheppard to produce memorial statues of pikemen. The statue in Wexford, which is equally impressive, shows a single figure. Both projects were funded largely by public subscription, and much of the money was raised in America. This was because the idea of erecting the centenary memorials originated from the IRB, which had strong connections with Irish emigrant communities in the US. It was also because many Irish Americans at the time retained living memories of the blight that, over successive years in the mid-nineteenth century, had destroyed the potato crops that were the staple food of Ireland's tenant farmers. When the British government failed to respond effectively to the famine conditions that followed the crop failure, an estimated 1 million people in rural Ireland died of starvation and disease. A farther million or more fled the country, taking with them a deep hatred for Britain. Their increasing prosperity and presence in US politics in the half-century that followed gave them significant political influence, and they were generous in sending money home. But their visceral response to the Famine, handed down to their children and grandchildren, would often oversimplify their responses to the complexities of the Irish politics in which they continued to be involved.

Sheppard's statues in Enniscorthy and Wexford town offered subscribers both at home and abroad an opportunity to link their varying individual and collective grievances to a single iconic event, regardless of historical accuracy. Irish emigrants in America and elsewhere responded to the image of Irish tenant farmers rising up against tyrannous English landlords, which was certainly central to the egalitarian principles that underlay the rebellion. Redmond's Parliamentary Party associated the struggle for Home Rule, then inching its way towards the statute book in Westminster, with the legend of the rebels' stand at Vinegar Hill. In doing so, it ignored the fact that the radical revolutionaries of 1798, who were ready to die for a republic, would probably have dismissed Home Rule as mere pussyfooting. Meanwhile, the committees that commissioned Sheppard's statues, which were dominated by Catholic priests, presented the 1798 Rebellion as a gallant fight against alien religious repression. In fact the rebels, who were inspired both by the egalitarian and the secularist ideas of the French Revolution, were roundly condemned by the Church of their time for rejecting religion itself.

But life is complicated. We have no way of knowing if each of the individuals who fought in 1798 was or was not a secularist, or how varied their republican aspirations may have been. What we do know is that the figure that stands beside the Enniscorthy pikeman is a depiction of Father Murphy, a Catholic priest who was, indeed, one of the leaders of the rebellion, and who fought at Vinegar Hill. We also know that Father Murphy was initially opposed to violence and found himself swept into the action without necessarily endorsing the principles that inspired it. The nuances have been lost. In the end, like the outrage of the Famine nearly fifty years later, what endured in shared memory was the outrage of Father Murphy's death. When he was eventually run to earth by the victorious British yeomen in a farmyard, he was sentenced to death, stripped, flogged, hanged and decapitated. His corpse was then burnt in a tar barrel, and his head was impaled on a spike. The idea was to discourage further sedition. The action produced exactly the opposite result.

All post-colonial states preserve collective memories of their perceived and actual oppression by the invader. In a healthy society they fade with the passage of time, and the morphing of fact into legend is fairly harmless. In Ireland, three specific factors intervened to influence that process. It was affected by a deliberate suppression and distortion of shared memory that took place during an extended period of cultural and economic isolation. The authority and legitimacy of the republic continued to be challenged by those who saw partition as a sell-out. And a large diaspora with roots that go back for several generations has preserved, and projects onto the present, simplified, outmoded images of the past. At conscious and unconscious levels which were seldom acknowledged, the combination of these factors resulted in a sense of Irish identity in the republic which, until comparatively recently, was rooted both in a rejection of state authority, which the collective memory identifies with alien oppression, and in the acceptance of the authority of the Catholic Church, which is identified with the pre-colonial, native Gaelic culture. Towards the beginning of the twenty-first century, confidence generated by the boom years of the Celtic Tiger produced a new climate in which it appeared that the country had moved on. But the subsequent economic crash, the humiliation of international bailout and the disillusionment generated by the collapse of the moral authority of the Church in the wake of continuing revelations of abuse have revealed that the perceived change was only skin-deep. Lacking an accepted source of moral authority and thrown back into the familiar role of the victim, Ireland's current sense of its relationship with its elected representatives is widely characterised by cynicism, resentment and irresponsibility, qualities that are rooted not just in centuries of colonialism but in the lack of open, informed analysis in the early years of the independent state. The way forward is to engage in that analysis now, with balance, reason, logic and tolerance.

Last year an elderly woman came up to me at a book signing and told me that she had never known her mother, who had died in childbirth. 'I saw you were going to be here today and I told my daughter I'm going to meet that woman. My daughter thought I was mad but I said I don't care. I said I'm going in there.' She spoke as if approaching an author in a bookshop were the equivalent of entering a minefield. 'I never got my stories the way I should. I had nothing to tell my daughter.' At that point the manager of the bookshop appeared with a pot of tea. It was a midweek afternoon and people weren't exactly beating the doors down looking for my signature. He took in the situation with a glance, produced a second mug and a chair, and for the next ten minutes the woman sat with tears in her eyes, telling me about her lack of memories. After her mother died her father had married again. 'She was a nice enough woman; I wouldn't say a word against her. And he was a good man. But, the way it was, I could never ask him a thing about my own mother. And look at me now without even a photograph.' Her hands were shaking on the mug. It was obvious that she had felt bereft of her mother's companionship in her own life but what bothered her most was the fact that she had nothing to hand on.

Two years ago I sat in the Charles Dickens Museum café in London talking about this book with my agent over lemon drizzle cake. I worried then that by imposing a structure on ideas yet to be explored I might leap from conception to conclusion without passing through discovery in between. I knew that, for a creative artist, the act of creation is a complex one which requires at its outset a structure clear enough to communicate, firm enough to act as a template, and supple enough to be bent without breaking. What I hadn't realised was that, by mapping a specific absence of memory onto a larger picture, I would discover that the politicians, soldiers and strategists involved in the 1916 Rising and the War of Independence, the negotiators who struggled with the terms of the treaty, and the diehards who fought in the Civil War, had engaged in a similar creative process. They imagined a desired end result, set about achieving it, and then uncovered the unforeseen layers of practical, emotional and intellectual complexity that constantly ripple between what is imagined and what can be achieved. Most of the 1916 leaders died before they could pass on what they learnt. But all of them seem to have believed that it was up to the generations who came after them to continue to engage in what they saw as an ongoing process. The silence and stagnation that had become woven into the fabric of the society I grew up in were the antithesis of what Marion Stokes and her companions aspired to.

The *Who Do You Think You Are?* phenomenon epitomised by the BBC television series was first brought to my attention by the emotional response provoked by particular postings on *The House on an Irish Hillside*'s Facebook page. That book, which focuses on one house, considers the rich treasury of collective memory that is stored in the oral history of Corca Dhuibhne. It offers artefacts and anecdotes as starting points for the themes I wanted to explore and, as a result, adapted easily to promotion on social networking platforms designed to encourage interactive commentary about images. Overwhelmingly, the photographs that prompted readers to share their own family stories produced the greatest response, and some of the most powerful comments, many of which came in emails and Facebook private messages, expressed regrets about broken threads of communication and lack of continuity: '... *all I know is that the house was at a crossroads*'; '... *all I know is that she loved dancing*'; '*I'll never know where they came from, all I can do is honour their courage*'; '... *my grandparents wouldn't talk about the old country*'; '*I think my grandmother suffered in Russia ...*'; '*my mother never spoke of it*'; '... *I'll never know what their fate was*'; '*I kind of feel bereft.*'

12
The Patient Goddess

ONE OF THE DEFINITIVE IMAGES of the Civil War in Ireland is the huge explosion of paper that was hurled into the air above the Four Courts in Dublin on 30 June 1922 in a column of smoke and dust that was black as ink. After de Valera and his followers swept out of the Dáil, anti-treaty forces barricaded themselves into the Four Courts in Dublin and turned the Public Record Office there into a munitions store. Following a standoff of several weeks, the building was shelled and then stormed by Free State government forces, and the retreating garrison blew up the munitions store. Among the papers that drifted over Dublin like a snowstorm that day were wills, proved testamentary records, and two centuries of export and trade records. The Irish Censuses of 1821, 1831, 1841 and 1851 were almost entirely destroyed in the explosion and the ensuing fire. So were more than half of the Anglican Church of Ireland registers deposited in the Public Record Office following the disestablishment of the state Church in 1869, all pre-1900 documents from the legal courts and many local government records. That vandalism was still spoken of in hushed voices when I was a child, though the extent of the loss involved can be overstated. Baptism, marriage and burial records for Catholics, Presbyterians and Methodists were not housed at the Public Record Office. Among the records that survived the fire and the explosion were the 1901 and 1911 Irish census returns, civil registration records, a large number of Church of Ireland parish registers, and other material dating back as far as the early seventeenth century. Griffith's Valuation, which contains land and property records for the middle of the nineteenth century, also survived and is often the starting

point for Irish emigrants' research into their roots. But for hours
Dublin was showered by fragments of printed white paper and
curled feathers of charred, blackened manuscript, which drifted
down the quays on the wind and were carried towards the sea.

Weeks earlier, during the Dáil debate on the treaty, Collins
had crossed the floor and offered his hand to de Valera, saying
that, whatever else happened, civil war must be avoided. De
Valera was about to take his hand when Mary MacSwiney, a
founder member of Cumann na mBan, intervened. MacSwiney
is one of the women whose fervent republicanism is celebrated
in *Rebel Irish Women*, the book that my aunt Marguerite bought
hot off the press in 1935. Terence MacSwiney, Mary's brother,
had been Sinn Féin Lord Mayor of Cork during the War of
Independence. He was accused of sedition, arrested and, after
seventy-four days on hunger strike, starved to death in a British
prison. His sister, watching him sink steadily towards a coma,
protested at his prison gates herself, rallied international protest
from America, France, Germany, Australia and South America,
and appealed for intervention from the Pope. When his coffin
was carried back to Ireland, the British authorities, fearing
further demonstration, physically removed it from the family's
custody and diverted it from Dublin to Cork. The effect on his
sister was devastating.

MacSwiney, who was elected to the Dáil on a Sinn Féin ticket
after her brother's death, had wanted to be included in the team
that negotiated the treaty, but de Valera is said to have judged
her to be too extreme in her hatred of Britain to be useful. Yet
in the charged atmosphere of the Dáil debate, during which
many people were in tears, de Valera allowed her intervention to
stop him taking Michael Collins' hand. MacSwiney's passionate
denouncement of compromise fuelled much of the hysterical
anti-treaty rhetoric which characterised that debate. Men and
women alike screamed abuse at each other across the chamber
and MacSwiney's position, expressed in a three-hour speech,
consciously echoed that of Pearse before 1916. 'This matter has

THE PATIENT GODDESS 235

been put to us as the Treaty or war. I say now if it were war, I would take it gladly and gleefully, not flippantly, but gladly, because I realise that there are evils worse than war, and no physical victory can compensate for a spiritual surrender.' Other female members of the Dáil became equally shrill. In one speech Constance Markievicz insisted that Michael Collins had secret plans to marry into the British royal family and rule over Ireland himself.

Looking back now, MacSwiney's glad and gleeful acceptance of civil war seems obscene. So does the fact that when the Civil War was over Ireland continued to harp on about British atrocities without acknowledging and reflecting on its own. In County Kerry, in 1923, nine men were taken from Tralee to Ballyseedy crossroads and tied, back to back, to a landmine, which was detonated. The mutilated survivors were then machine-gunned. This was not an isolated incident. Within days, five other men were deliberately blown up in Killarney and four in Cahersiveen, and others elsewhere in the country were physically abused and shot in cold blood without trial. As the war escalated the atrocities increased, perpetrated not by alien oppressors but by neighbour upon neighbour. Afterwards, both sides in that war presented themselves as victims of circumstances over which, like characters in a Greek tragedy, they had no control. The role of the victim leaves no room for questions of responsibility.

The idea that women are natural peacemakers is as daft as the notion that women who enjoy and are amused by their own and others' sexuality are mentally deficient. The imposition of gender stereotypes, either in politics or in religion, is a recipe for dangerous imbalance. Eva Gore-Booth, whose own politics and sense of spirituality ultimately fused, was aware of that when she suggested that the idea of 'manly' and 'womanly' should be swept into 'the museum of antiques'. But for that to happen in Ireland the constitutional clauses dealing with the position of women in society will have to be swept away first. Along with lingering homophobia, cultural chauvinism, and the neurotic belief that

the conventional two-parent, heterosexual marriage is the only
acceptable model for a stable society, those clauses represent a
vision of Irishness which belongs to a dysfunctional past.

I paused when working on these last few pages of this book,
wandered around the room with a cup of coffee, came back to my
computer and idly opened my Twitter feed. A series of tweets sent
from a mobile phone at the annual Sheehy Skeffington School
in Dublin drifted steadily upwards before my eyes. The School,
which is a one-day event, considers human rights issues in Ireland
and abroad. The tweets came from a woman who organises a
similar annual school, called after Countess Markievicz, which
considers issues of gender inequality in Ireland. The work of
such organisations provides a powerful counterbalance to irresponsibility and apathy, and a platform for reasoned debate in the
present based on an honest analysis of the past.

> **Lucy Keaveney**
> @Luighseach • Apr 18
> At the Sheehy Skeffington school. About to watch video of
> Micheline Sheehy-Skeffington. Inherited protest gene from
> grandparents.

I put my coffee cup on the desk and sat down again in front
of the screen. The scientist Dr Micheline Sheehy-Skeffington,
granddaughter of Hanna and Frank, recently protested against
what she perceived as institutionalised gender inequality in the
Galway university where my aunt Marguerite and my father
studied in the 1920s and 1930s and where my father was a
professor of history through the 1960s and 1970s. Sheehy-
Skeffington, then a member of the university staff, took the
matter to tribunal in 2014 and her case against her former
employer of thirty-four years was upheld.

> **Lucy Keaveney**
> @Luighseach • Apr 18
> #sheehyskeffington Micheline hopes that her case will
> inspire others to challenge inequalities in work place.

It is fascinating that the college from which Brigid Lyons had bunked off lectures to join the Four Courts garrison in 1916 had, nearly 100 years later, become a focus for debate on employment rights for women.

> **#sheehyskeffington** Inspired by activities and principles of her grandparents. Both lost their jobs bec of their beliefs.

It was both strange and heartening to approach the end of this book with the evidence of change literally passing before my eyes. I watched the tweets moving up the screen as Dr Sheehy-Skeffington's video address was followed by a live response from Dr Margaret Ward, a feminist historian from Belfast whose 1997 biography of Hanna Sheehy-Skeffington has fuelled the honest appraisal of Marion Stokes' generation that was denied to my own generation of Irishwomen as we grew up.

> **Lucy Keaveney**
> @Luighseach • Apr 18
> **#sheehyskeffington** Mgt says Hanna was inspirational. Met husband Frank in university & they kept both surnames in interest of equality.
> **#sheehyskeffington** Both Hanna and Frank left religion behind. At end of her life Hanna said she was an unrepentant pagan.

To the pagan Celts, and to indigenous peoples worldwide who retain an animist world view, the earth was and is perceived as a woman. In Ireland, long before native Irishness was identified with Catholicism or Ireland itself was personified as Róisín Dubh or Caitlín Ní Houlihán, the ancient Celtic goddess Danú personified both the Earth itself and the water which animates it. In this world view the goddess encompasses and expresses all that was, is, and all that may be. She is both memory and potential and in the absence of memory the potential for the future health and balance of individuals, families, communities, nations and the Earth itself is dangerously compromised. To the pagan Celts the marriage of Danú, the earth mother, and Lugh, the sun god, represented the interdependence of the natural world. It was also an expression of a dynamic world view in which apparently opposite forces are actually complementary and, by interaction, produce a more powerful whole. We know little or nothing about the religious practices of the ancient Celts, but extrapolation from the inherited beliefs of 21st-century indigenous peoples, such as the Kogi of Colombia and the aboriginal peoples of Canada, American, Scandinavia and Australia, suggests that they saw art, religion and science as fundamentally interconnected.

But we do know quite a lot about the pagan Celts in Ireland, passed down to us in the native oral tradition. Their stories and poems, preserved in the Irish language, show that they loved the moments of balance between one possibility and another. They crackle with energy. A stag's head turns in the forest as a twig snaps under a hunter's foot. A boat hangs poised on the crest of a wave. You share the terror of a scream in darkness. You feel the heart-stopping moment when iron crunches into bone. Our ancestors' intense awareness of nature is locked into their poems, like insects suspended in amber. Their lives were shaped by the rhythmic cycle of the seasons, seed-time and harvest-time, birth, death and rebirth. I love their humanity, vitality and the breadth of their imagination. They loved sex – straight, gay and bi – huge, noisy parties, grotesque humour, mind-blowing fantasy and complex, curling patterns made in images and words. And alongside their fascination with the detail of the natural world lives an awareness of the dynamism of emptiness and the fertile potential of space.

One function of art is to present and rework stereotypes, and offer imaginative alternative angles from which they might be perceived. If you climb the stairs to the top floor of Enniscorthy Castle today you find an exhibition celebrating the work of the Irish furniture designer, architect and modernist Eileen Gray.

In the oddly domestic interior of the medieval castle, which was built in 1205 and remained a private dwelling until 1951, the replicas of her 1920s chrome and tubular steel furniture and her iconic Bibendum chair look perfectly at home and strangely out of place. Gray was born in 1878. Her Anglo-Irish father was an artist and her early life was spent between London, Paris and the family home just outside Enniscorthy. She was a pioneer of the twentieth-century Modern Movement in design and architecture and her work, now celebrated as one of Ireland's cultural claims to fame, would have been anathema to the cultural censors of de Valera's Ireland. So would the fact that Eileen Gray was openly and cheerfully bisexual.

Before the Second World War, Gray and her Romanian lover, the architect and writer Jean Badovici, designed and lived together in a house in the South of France. The couple split up shortly afterwards and in the late 1930s, the house was visited by the architect Le Corbusier, with whom Gray had previously worked in Paris. Gray had left the house by the time of the visit and, with Badovici's permission, Le Corbusier, who was an artist as well as a hugely influential modernist architect, painted large colourful murals on the walls. To Gray, this was an outrage. She had conceived the interior of the house, which had floor-to-ceiling windows and a spiral stairway, as an open space with plain white walls, within which the inhabitants would be constantly aware of the relationships between their physical, emotional and intellectual interior and exterior worlds.

When I first read Yeats' poem 'Sailing to Byzantium' at school, his invocation to the sages standing in God's holy fire, as in the gold mosaic of a wall, conjured up an image of Tenniel's wood engraving of slithy toves in the copy of Lewis Carroll's *Through The Looking Glass* that my father once read aloud to me by the fire in our Dublin semi. Yeats' sages 'perne in a gyre'. Carroll's toves, which in Tenniel's illustration are some class of a badger with corkscrew noses, revolve on their back legs. Like all poets and politicians, Carrol and Yeats use words as Humpty

Dumpty does in *Through The Looking Glass*, to mean what they want them to mean. The word 'perne' is Old English, or medieval French, or Scots Gaidhlig, or comes from somewhere else. It means a weaver's bobbin or a saltwater mussel or luminosity. Or something else. 'Gyre' means a spinning motion, a ring or a hawk. Or all three. The nature of a work of art is that its meaning is never constant, because the business of art is to reflect the experience of life. Awareness depends on angles of view and on memory, and both can play us false. Like shards tumbling in a kaleidoscope, images of who we are, and what that means to us, constantly change.

When a kaleidoscope is turned, light falls through moving shards. The image of Ireland shifts from a silken cow to the spectre of death, to a woman with the walk of a queen. Yeats castigates a Dublin audience from the stage of the Abbey Theatre for rejecting a pacifist drama by Seán O'Casey. A child's hands polish a soldier's brass buttons at a kitchen table and an actor sits on a barstool with his head in a paper bag. Elderly women at the end of the Dingle Peninsula dance jigs in the aisle of a church. Voices echo back from painted walls and high plate-glass windows. Birds wheel over battlefields, their feathers drifting like charred parchment over broken bodies and bones. The Internet pulses with energy, casting out threads of aspiration, vituperation and creativity, wisdom, hatred and love. In 2014, on the stage of Dublin's Abbey Theatre, in his persona as the drag queen Panti Bliss, a gay rights activist from County Mayo protests about homophobia and the audience stands to applaud. Within hours the eloquent cry for tolerance goes viral on YouTube, with Russian, Chinese, English, Hebrew, Polish, French, Irish, Turkish, Portuguese, Spanish, Japanese, Greek, German, Dutch, Italian, Serbian and Slovakian subtitles. That protest was made after the performance of a play about the 1913 Lock-Out. Spiralling out from contemporary Ireland's increasingly articulate concerns about freedom of expression and gender inequality, it is as powerful a call for individual

involvement in the definition of Irishness as anything expressed
on the Irish stage by Gregory or Yeats.

And then, when I was back in London again, a few weeks
after the Sheehy Skeffington School, came a turning point in
the history of the Irish State. Up to that point, although civil
partnership between same-sex couples had been legal since
2010, it was not possible for two women or two men to enter into
marriage on the same basis as a heterosexual couple. On 22 May
2015 the Irish electorate voted on a proposal to amend Article
41 of the constitution to include the statement 'Marriage may
be contracted in accordance with law by two persons without
distinction as to their sex.' If a majority voted to accept the
amendment to the constitution, legislation to permit same-sex
marriage would follow, so a Yes vote in the referendum would
make Ireland the first country in the world to approve equal
marriage rights for all its citizens by popular vote.

The debate in the run-up to the referendum was remarkable
on the one hand for its restraint and on the other for its vitriol,
and much of it took place online. Under Irish electoral law,
which is amongst the most restrictive in Europe, emigrants
retain their right to vote for a period of eighteen months,
provided they plan to return home within that time frame. But
even eligible emigrants cannot avail of the postal vote which
is available to students in Ireland living away from home,
prisoners, members of the police force based overseas and
people whose line of work prevents them from voting at their
local polling station. So for Irish men and women domiciled
abroad who had no right to vote, and for those who simply
couldn't make it home to take part in a process which refused
them a postal vote, the Internet, and Twitter in particular,
provided a forum for involvement and debate. On the day of
the referendum it even provided the hashtag *#BeMyYes* which
was used by thousands of Irish women and men overseas who
desperately wanted to vote for equality. If we couldn't cast a
vote ourselves at least we could urge others to participate in

the referendum. For many, this issue became a touchstone by which Irishness would be defined.

Those who opposed the constitutional amendment also saw it as something that touched on Irish identity. In the weeks leading up to the referendum the specific issue on which the vote was to be taken was repeatedly obscured by campaigners who feared or believed, among other things, that same-sex marriage would undermine public morality, in some way 'promote' homosexuality or, by redefining what was perceived to be the traditional Irish family unit, strike at the heart of Irishness itself. Despite reassurance from constitutional lawyers, some 'No' campaigners insisted that changing the constitution to give all Irish citizens an equal right to marry implied an acceptance of surrogate parenthood. Some took the view that children have a natural right to a father and a mother and believed it appropriate for that view to be enshrined in the constitution. Many such individuals and organisations were supported by views expressed by the Roman Catholic hierarchy. Others were motivated by strongly held beliefs which had no religious basis. Among the clergy and religious orders were many individuals who privately and publicly supported the amendment and voted for it on the day, a course which cannot have been easy.

One feature of the marriage referendum that fascinated me was how it was characterised by story-sharing. As the polling day approached, many men and women who had previously lived hidden lives broke their silence about being gay. Young and old, in public and in private life, they chose to share their stories and, in doing so, risked the consequences of a life-changing step that couldn't be reversed. No one should underestimate the courage of those who made that decision as the debate continued online, in print, on TV and radio, on doorsteps and in homes throughout the country.

In the event, 1.2 million Irish people voted for equality. It was confirmed just before 7 p.m. on 23 May, although the result had been clear early in the count. The Yes vote prevailed by 62 to 38 per cent. Perhaps because the issue transcended party politics, there was a large 60.5 per cent turnout. Throughout the previous day airports and ferry ports were jammed as thousands of Irish women and men arrived home from abroad to join in the democratic process. The yard at Dublin Castle, which was opened to the public for the count, was crowded with voters and campaigners who gathered to witness the result. Even though the outcome was already evident, the announcement was greeted first with a breathless silence and then with a huge outburst of emotion. And then, spontaneously, the crowd in the Castle yard began to sing the national anthem. I watched it online, trying to analyse my response to the fact that the song sung by Tom Stokes 100 years ago for Pearse and The O'Rahilly in the Barley Field in Enniscorthy was being used by the voters at Dublin Castle to celebrate this new commitment to an Ireland characterised by equality. In the weeks before the referendum, 'Yes' campaigners had repeatedly Tweeted images of the text of the 1916 Proclamation, quoting its statement that the Irish Republic 'guarantees religious and civil liberty, equal rights and equal opportunities to all its citizens'. Each time I hit retweet I wondered what Marion, Tom, my grandparents, my aunts, and my parents would have thought. I don't know how any of them might have felt about the idea of same sex marriage but I hope they would have endorsed the principle of equality which the amendment upholds.

But the mixed messages continue. Only a few weeks after the Marriage Referendum, Amnesty International published a report stating that the human rights of women and girls in Ireland are violated on a daily basis because of a constitution that treats them like childbearing vessels. There are many more steps to be taken before the guarantees in the 1916 Proclamation of the Republic are fulfilled. But the outcome of the Marriage Referendum feels like a step in the right direction because it is a rejection of the suggestion that silence is preferable to openness, and an affirmation of the idea that each individual member of society should be equal under the law. Most heartening of all is its fundamental assertion that where matters of civil rights are concerned distinctions of sex are immaterial. So perhaps it is right that it should precede the task of removing the elements of the constitution which continue to deny Irishwomen the equality and freedom for which Marion and her companions were ready to fight and die.

For the ancient Celts water was an image of life. Their oldest image of the universe is a triple spiral which expresses a flow of energy constantly balanced between fluidity and what is contained. Wherever they went they carved it in stone. Their perception of the place of humanity within the universe is expressed in the concept of the triple-aspect goddess who, as the Maiden, the Mother and the Crone, presents the cycle of female fertility as an image of energy and renewal. Through the union of the goddess with the sun god, promoting the health of the land, the image of balance is completed. And, from the poems and stories the Celts made in the Irish language it seems that their world view was informed by a sense of continuity in which past, present and future lives co-exist, and can affect each other, within the dynamic whole. This is all just imagery, but without memory and imagination how can we tell ourselves who we are?

As I type these words, in my mind's eye I am climbing the turret stair in Enniscorthy castle. The steps are cold, and the only light comes in through narrow windows. With one hand I am touching the curved stone wall beside me. With the other I'm clutching the tail of Marion's tweed skirt. Her feet in their sensible shoes move from one step to the next, feeling for the hollows in the stone steps worn down by the feet of generations. Outside, people move up and down through the steep streets, going about their lives as they have always done. And across the road from my grandmother's house, somewhere beneath clipped grass and municipal planting, is a well of water that once was guarded by three faceless stones.